La Clase Mágica

*Imagining Optimal Possibilities
in a Bilingual Community of Learners*

La Clase Mágica

Imagining Optimal Possibilities in a Bilingual Community of Learners

Olga A. Vásquez
University of California, San Diego

2003
LAWRENCE ERLBAUM ASSOCIATES, PUBLISHERS
Mahwah, New Jersey   London

The camera ready copy for this work was prepared by the author.

Lawrence Erlbaum Associates, Inc., Publishers
10 Industrial Avenue
Mahwah, New Jersey 07430

Cover photograph by Lourdes Duran.

Library of Congress Cataloging-in-Publication Data

Vásquez, Olga A.
   La clase mágica : imagining optimal possibilities in a bilingual community
   of learners / Olga A. Vásquez.
      p. cm.
   Includes bibliographical references and indexes.
   ISBN 0-8058-4023-0 (cloth: alk. paper)
   ISBN 0-8058-4024-9 (pbk.: alk.paper)
      1. Minorities–Education–United States. 2. Education, Bilingual–United
   States. I.Title.

   LC3731.V37 2002
   370.117'0973–dc21

                                                                    2002067162

Printed in the United States of America
10 9 8 7 6 5 4 3 2 1

Esta obra la dédico a Yolanda, Lourdes, y los chiquitines de La Clas e Mágica
[I dedicate this work to Yolanda, Lourdes and the kiddies of La Clase Mágica]

Whose vision I hope to have captured in word and deed.
[Cuya visión espero haber captado en palabra y hobra]

CONTENTS

Preface

This volume tells a story of the many sides and many levels of an educational activity that developed and grew beyond everyone's expectations. It gives a blow-by-blow account of the early transformations of a project that began as an educational activity and slowly but deliberately turned into a social action project whose aim was to serve those with little access to educational resources and low economic and political means. It is a multivocal account detailing research in action and action in practice for effectively serving Spanish–English bilingual speakers from a Mexican origin community as well as for effectively serving the diversity that increasingly characterizes American society. Although more can and will be said about the state-of-affairs at the time and the subsequent developments after 1996 (e.g., the national and international recognition of the project, the college-going patterns of its long-term participants, and the transplantation of the project to new cultural communities), this book focuses specifically on the intensity, extensions, and exhilaration of the early foundational work. In many ways, it chronicles the intellectual journey my fellow participants and I took between 1989 and 1996.

The book also attempts to capture the social and intellectual developments and the promises of an ongoing after-school project called *La Clase Mágica* [The Magical Class]. It speaks out from the "zones of contact" between the university and a language minority community about new ways to extend and intersect theory and practice in many areas of the educational enterprise. It defines contact not only in the physical sense of face-to-face interaction but also as symbolic interaction between languages, cultures, histories, and epistemologies. Thus, I speak of optimal possibilities situated in those middle grounds or, more technically speaking, those borders between Spanish and English, Mexican and Mainstream culture, minority and majority designations, and between school and community contexts where contact is made and new arrangements can be imagined. Inquiry into optimal possibilities takes us back and forth from abstraction to reality and back again, often through the ploy of a fantasy world known as the Fifth Dimension and the common wisdom of the people who purportedly are at the margins of knowledge. Not infrequently, the account uses the musings of participants to take us from the scientific to the everyday to make real and concrete the theoretical conceptualizations that box in human behavior. In so doing, it defines the theories, methods, and philosophies for linking multiple disciplines, institutions, and participant groups into a concerted effort that has the potential to reframe the educational opportunities of underserved populations.

In place of definitive conclusions and detailed prescriptions, *La Clase Mágica* offers researchers, practitioners, and policymakers much-needed guidance, insight, and perhaps, inspiration for rethinking educational goals and objectives. Both the work represented within and the writing itself take risks that push the limits of scientific knowledge to touch on the fantastic and the quotidian, both arenas held in suspect by academics but nonetheless critical to the work done on-the ground and in the head. The account offers a close look into the intricacies and the fundamental principles for building and sustaining effective learning environments and institutional relations that are necessary for enhancing the learning potential of learners of all ages. In the process, it also suggests ways in which community members and institutional agents can take an active and integral role in creating learning opportunities that serve both constituencies. By extension, educators and policymakers, too, will find useful the systems approach for pursuing parent and community involvement in the educational enterprise.

I anticipate that this volume will also find an enthusiastic reception by research teams; implementation efforts that are already in place or developing after-school projects based on the Fifth Dimension/*La Clase Mágica* model should benefit. As independent efforts, or as part of the University of California UCLinks consortium that was organized as a postaffirmative action strategy for assuring diversity at the university, these new initiatives will find useful the descriptions, reflections, and findings I lay out here. Although each new project will set its own agenda and develop independently according to the local conditions, there are many recognizable and avoidable pitfalls in establishing cross-system relations as well as culturally and effective curriculum that addresses diversity in the educational setting and in the society at large. For those projects doing specifically minority-oriented work, I am confident that the rationale for and the context within which this work was accomplished will resonate with their resolve to make a difference in the educational experience of their target population. There is much to share in principle and experience that other minority-oriented projects could consider. I know this from feedback after presenting parts of this volume to teams of established projects. On hearing about *La Clase Mágica*, the staff, as well as the parents, come to understand the greater goals of their own project and the impact their individual participation has on development of both the project and their children. Many of these new projects will face the same institutional obstacles, ask the same questions about theories, practice, research, and teaching, and seek to achieve optimal possibilities for their institutions and their participants that are addressed throughout this book. My hopes are to help these new initiatives build on earlier research and serve as catalysts for developing new insights to the existent body of knowledge in the same way that the *La Clase Mágica* added to the foundations of the Fifth Dimension. At the very least, I hope the insights I share within would help new projects avoid the many pitfalls that invariably lay ahead.

ACKNOWLEDGMENTS

Acknowledging all those individuals and units who contributed to this manuscript is as impossible a task as it was to capture the complexity and multidimensionality of the work that it represents. No amount of accounting can acknowledge the origin of so many bits and pieces of wisdom and advocacy that fueled the development of the project and the subsequent writing of the manuscript. There are many to thank and many to honor, however, space constraints make it impossible to name everyone involved. Thus, I name just a few with hopes that many others who contributed can see themselves in those chosen for recognition. One individual, however, is singular in his contributions to the development of the project, the manuscript, and my own development as a scholar. That individual is Michael Cole whose influence on my scholarship dates back to my first quarter at Stanford University where I read *Psychology of Literacy*, which subsequently changed the focus of my graduate work to literacy. It would be the first of many times that I would experience a rush of exhilaration, bewilderment, and engagement, all at the same time; a state I would later call "being in the zone"—the sensation of expanding one's understanding and development that happens most of the time when one is working with Mike.

It goes without saying that this project and manuscript would not have come to fruition without the love and energy of the chiquitines [the little ones] and their families. Both young and old taught us to learn, to stretch our imagination, to share. and more importantly, to experience the true meaning of "commitment to the community." The smiles and hugs of Ralph, Maria, Lisa, Reyna, Jonathon, Cesar, Javier, Nancy. Selene. Jason, Juan, Azusena, Nancy, Angel, los Carter, los Toth, los Rubalcaba, los Nuñez, and oh so many others repeatedly warmed my heart and took away any and all heavy burdens I bore at the time. St. Leo's Mission opened its doors to us and I am very thankful for their welcome. But, it was the Mexicano community of Eden Gardens who opened their arms and their hearts and worked closely with the research team to make the project serve the needs and talents of Spanish–English bilinguals. Father Bud, Lourdes Duran, Deacon Graff, Ann Silver, Maria Nieves, Monseignor Percell, Victor Tostado, los señores Gomez, Chavarin, Castañon, and la señora Orozco y la señora Aristondo found time and space to help *La Clase Mágica* adapt and flourish.

Forging ideas, strategies, and extensions into the conceptual, organizational, and theoretical framework of *La Clase Mágica* was accomplished collaboratively across numerous age groups, academic quarters, institutional contexts, and multiple intellectual venues of the sponsoring unit, the Laboratory of Comparative Human Cognition (LCHC). This is particularly true of the often-invisible yet stalwart contributions that LCHC's long list of collaborators made to the foundation of *La Clase Mágica*. The cutting-edge work of such individuals as Estevan Díaz, Luis Moll, Lonnie Anderson, Bud Mehan, Robert Rueda, and Ray McDermott situated diversity front and center in the educational context and their ideas were recycled over and over again and given new meanings and new contexts in the form of *La Clase Mágica*. Margie Gallego, director of *La Clase Mágica*—Midwest and later member of the lab not only helped propel the adaptation of *La Clase Mágica* but also served as my intellectual partner whose wit and brilliance never ceased to amaze me. Peggy Bengel, Lisa Scaltrito, Karen Fiegener, Tony Scott, Amy Olt, Scott Woodbridge, as well as Vanessa Gack and Yrgo Engeström, all members of the LCHC "family" gave me the opportunity to do my thing within a warm and optimal learning environment.

There were other sources of support at the university that were essential and constant to the development of the project: the undergraduate course and the research team, both composed of talented and committed young adults. Every academic quarter—in the course or in special mentorship arrangements—the undergraduates and I fine-tuned the language, theories, and strategies that came to embody *La Clase Mágica*. Many stayed on for another quarter or formed part of the research staff. Tim Andre, Consuelo Baez, Mark Chavez, Erin O'Dwyer, David Frank, Vicky Garcia, Celia Gonzalez, Tabitha Hart, Cristina Marquez, Steve Melton, Natalie Rice, Leylan Piceno, Dina Hernandez, Elaine Camuso, Alicia Villabobos, Jackie Bustos left an indelible mark on the participants and/or the material make-up of the project. Trisha Henry, Yolanda Venegas, Bertha Jotar Palenzuela, Cathy Sheppard, and Joy Yang, at one time or another gave the fledgling project definition and a driving force. Although few and far between, graduate students such as Lisa Tripp, Honorine Nocon, and Marc Camras crystallized aspects of the project into theoretical formulations or other forms of representations. Lisa Tripp, a seasoned ethnographer, produced a widely distributed video, *"La Clase Mágica,"* that captured the theoretical and ideological essence of the project.

Like the child participants and their families, the support of the Andrew Mellon Foundation was essential to the life of this project. It funded and guided our collaborative, "The Distributive Literacy Consortium" for six years with wisdom and bounty. I suspect that this manuscript cannot do justice to the impact this private foundation has had and will have on minority individuals and future generations of Americans. I salute the members of the "Mellon Patch," as our consortium was affectionately called, for their genius, their openness, and their friendship. The Latino Eligibility Task Force, headed by Gene Garcia, Richard Figueroa, and Aida Hurtado were not only a source of inspiration for their commitment and their brilliance, they were also a source guidance in defining the sociopolitical aspect of this work. Another important unit that valued the goals and objectives of *La Clase Mágica* and offered the funding to write it up was the Center for Chicano Studies at the University of California, Santa Barbara. I am particularly thankful to the Center director, Denise Segura, who guarded the time I needed in isolation but who also concocted social events so that I would not lose myself in my abstraction. The fellowship also gave me the opportunity to share my work with Richard Durán who on many occasions illuminated my way through the puzzling complexity of the work. I am also thankful to the members of the Department of Communication at UCSD who often did not understand my articulations from "the zone" or my absence from department life but nevertheless gave me a vote of confidence on an early draft of this manuscript.

Finally, I want to acknowledge those members of my social support whom I am inclined to call in a moment of quandary and need and they invariably take the time to hear me out or lend a helping hand: Ricardo Stanton-Salazar. Lisa Catanzarite, Angela Valenzuela. Cindy Pease-Alvarez, Maria Alaníz, Virginia Escalante, and Tony Rosas. I am especially grateful to Alicia Arrizon and Gina Ong for holding my hand in the last stretch of this work as I dealt with the death of my father and the pressures of tenure. Rosalina Calderón, Cathy Mooney, and Kelly Kramer are especially appreciated for their time and expertise in the production process of this manuscript.

Introduction

The new millennium ushered in an enormous task of redefining educational policy in terms of new social realities of American society at the end of the 20th century. The political climate of the 1990s was often marked with offensive and exclusionary discourse regarding curriculum content, language of instruction, admissions policies, and public entitlements. The contestation settled squarely on which knowledge base, language, or identity would define the imminent future, pitting public institutions, ethnic groups, and religious organizations against one other in a bitter struggle for the rights to definition. Minority voices, once absent or impotent when present, increasingly clamored for the right to participate in the decision-making processes over the distribution of material resources and the shaping of the intellectual landscape. Their modest political might, relatively weak economic strength, and absence in positions of power, however, weakened their ability to contribute to a new vision for how social institutions should serve non-White constituencies that speak languages other than English. The increasing diversity in the society, however, heralds a need for change and responsive action.

Advocates of change argued that the existing educational curricula were inadequate for preparing students to meet the complexities of new advances in technology and the exigencies of an increasingly multicultural global society (Cummins & Sayers, 1995; Moll & González, 1995; Philips, 1993; Vásquez, 1993, 1994, 1996). Rather than limit the learner to one knowledge base, one history, and one language, they proposed reworking the content and medium of instruction to incorporate the rich and varied experiences of diverse learners. They advocated for drawing skills and knowledge from a multitude of sources beyond the classroom walls and the expertise of the teacher, a strategy that contrasted with the conventional practice of validating knowledge and expertise associated only with mainstream educational structures and its personnel (Nocon, 1997). They called for an education that prepares learners to participate successfully, not only in the realm of mainstream institutional culture, but also in the multiple communities in which they are members (Vásquez & Durán, 2000.

Behind these arguments lays an even more radical alternative that has been theorized by critical scholars, but has yet to be fully articulated. It is a call for systemic change based on the principles of participatory democracy. Some scholars (Luke, 1999; Sleeter, 1991; Sleeter & McLaren, 1995), for

1

example, proposed new perspectives, discourses, and social relations which, if instituted, could potentially reverberate throughout the entire system. Others suggested new ways of conceiving and achieving competence and power (Cummins & Sayers, 1995; Vásquez & Durán, 2000). This book weaves these ideals of diversity into practice. It theorizes what can be if access to educational resources and institutional support is made possible. It imagines new possibilities at every level of educational practice. Through a system of collaborative relations that brings together three cultural systems, institutional contexts, and multiple intergenerational groupings to serve a Spanish–English bilingual community these imaginings are articulated and achieved. It builds on research and practice aimed at understanding and interrupting processes and products produced by educational inequities. At its core, it embraces a multiplicity of cultural and linguistic perspectives as well as a multiplicity of intellectual tools. It reorganizes power relations and patterns of access in favor of dynamic relations of exchange in which resources and power are redistributed according to mutual accord and need, forging a unique form of social action that shows great promise of systemic change.

Making diversity the central organizing principle of action and thought is not an optimist's illusion of a possible distant future. Rather, it is very much grounded in the social, technical, and economic developments in an increasingly global world. Intense intercultural contact in both real and virtual time is rapidly becoming a large part of everyday life in American society. New communication technologies, globalization, and massive migrations bring people together at such rapid pace that distances, time, and the "unknown" disappear in a blink of an eye. With the turn of a knob or the tap of a key, individuals come in contact, directly and immediately, with the social and political conditions of others in faraway places. Local conditions and experiences lose their peculiarity and become intimately related to broader understandings of how the world works. To understand the complexities and ably transact these multiplicities will require a multidimensional citizen who is able to transcend personal, social, spatial, and temporal dimensions to identify with and have allegiances and responsibilities to both local and global communities (Cogan & Derricot, 1998).

Successful participants in today's world are necessarily successful border crossers. They immediately and skillfully distinguish and act upon different ways of thinking, doing, and talking as called for by changing contexts. Their competencies extend beyond knowledge and language of the dominant group to those that enable them to negotiate norms and expectations of a variety of distinct cultural domains (Vásquez, Pease-Alvarez, & Shannon,1994). They are able to thrive in cultural systems situated along the wide spectrum of the monocultural–multicultural continuum. Thus, whether they find themselves in the monocultural context of the home or mainstream institution or in the multicultural contexts made possible by technology or the massive migration of people, these individuals can fulfill their needs and desires effectively and felicitously. They are versed on multiple knowledge sources, speak a variety of languages, and intimately negotiate a diversity of norms and expectations. A society that does not educate its citizens for such prospects, not only limits their ability to transact communities outside its borders but. more egregiously. limits their ability to participate fully in its own realm.

Relevant educational activities that prepare individuals for life in the global village draw on knowledge sources from the local community as well as from the world at large. This interconnectedness between the local and the global can only be nourished in an inclusive form of teaching and learning based on the realities of a multicultural, multilingual society (Moll, 1992). In their work on intercultural electronic networks, Cummins and Sayers (1995), proposed a cross-system, cross-cultural educational approach they called "collaborative critical inquiry" used to achieve a multicultural, multifaceted curriculum and instruction. Rather than holding teachers and students to one context, one form of knowledge, or one understanding, the computer-mediated educational activities transcend conventional notions of what is to be taught and learned, and who should be the principal actor in such an activity. Teachers coordinate and facilitate learning within and across institutions, cultures, and languages to help their students seek, interpret, and integrate new knowledge as they engage in posing and solving problems. Knowledge is co-constructed and extends beyond the limits of the physical contexts and expertise of the educators. These learning environments set in motion a new approach to education that has powerful social implications for redefining teaching and learning.

This kind of education, however, is not the norm throughout the country. Rather. the educational system, charged with preparing citizens for the demands of society, is operating from a perspective that at best, fits the realities of the previous century (Vásquez, 1999). Not only are its frameworks and methods inadequate for the demands of an information-based society, it is failing large segments of the society. Adequately educating ethnic minorities, and in particular, Latinos, for example, continues to be an illusive goal for practitioners, researchers, and policymakers. Many causes have been explored ranging in scope from the microanalyses of language and culture to more macro-investigations of institutional structures. Yet, minority underachievement in K–12 and their underrepresentation in higher education remain prevalent throughout the country.

MULTISYSTEM PARTNERSHIPS: AN ALTERNATIVE VISION

The implications for underpreparing large segments of the population are costly in economic as well as in intellectual terms. In 1988, Hayes-Bautista and collaborators laid out the long-term effects of such social policy. These scholars reasoned that undereducating Latinos, a young and growing segment of the population, and relegating them to low-skill wage jobs, would seriously effect the viability of both the retirement system and the nation's ability to maintain its international leadership in commerce, science, and humanitarianism. While their sheer numbers—a quarter of the labor force—positioned them as the "burden of support" for an aging Anglo population, their socioeconomic standing jettisoned their ability to contribute substantially to retirement coiffeurs or to enter into the high technology sector, the key to the future of economic growth (Hayes-Bautista, Schink, & Chapa, 1988).

In spite of these bleak predictions, national and state policies continue to be shaped by a singularity of vision and complete lack of foresight. In California such policies have flourished and been the impetus for legislative action in other states. Initiatives to dismantle affirmative action (Proposition 209), eliminate resources for noncitizens (Proposition 187), and abolish Bilingual Education (227), for example, reinforce an ill-conceived notion of what it means to be "American" and to benefit from its social and economic reserves. These initiatives designate sectors of the society as illegitimate constituencies, unworthy of equitable access to resources. At the same time, they falsely presume a society of "equal opportunity and justice for all." The reality, however, is that these initiatives privilege those who are White, English speaking, and well-versed in Western culture. In particular, they single out Spanish-speaking individuals who come from south of the U.S. border in search of the "American dream." Along with the accompanying English-only movement, these initiatives represent a social investment in unilinear, monocultural approaches to social action.

The social realities of American society and the complexity brought about by advances in information technology, however, expose the inadequacies of unilinear and unidimensional approaches for addressing the growing diversity in society. For example, the Black Eligibility Task Force, a 3 year study commissioned by the University of California, concluded that multidimensional social problems such as minority underrepresentation in higher education require multidimensional social action. Observing that African American underrepresentation in higher education was "complex" and "multifaceted," this action committee stated unequivocally that "Uni-dimensional, unilateral approaches by single institutions are unavoidably inadequate" (University of California Black Eligibility Task Force, 1992, p. 1). To bring about immediate and dramatic increase in the numbers of African-Americans at the university, the Task Force strongly recommended a comprehensive effort that linked key institutions in concerted social action. Although not calling explicitly for systemic change, the committee did recommend that African-American eligibility be considered an institutional problem at the core of the university's mission. If enacted, such a policy could, however, radically change the way the university approached minority underrepresentation.

The Black Eligibility Task Force called for a multisystem approach to social action, one that systematically linked the university, community, and business sector in partnership. What it did not address, however, was the inability of previous multisystem efforts to bring about substantive change. For the past 20 years, if not more, multisystem partnerships have become increasingly popular, creating what some scholars call "the partnership movement" (Wilbur & Lambert, 1991). Yet, the persistence of minority underrepresentation in higher education and the resoundingly high dropout rate in the public school system raises the question of how effective these efforts have been in serving minority communities. It also raises a more critical question of who has to bear the burden of change, the institutions or the underserved minority populations?

A close examination of past efforts strongly suggests that approaches based on the epistemological, cultural, and linguistic norms of the sponsoring institutions do little to disrupt the status quo. That is, putting the burden of change on minority communities is unsuccessful in reducing the large-scale failure among these populations. Fundamental change in the way that education is conceptualized and implemented comes about only through what Auletta and Jones (1990) called, "reconstituting the inner circle" in numbers and philosophical foundation. In other words, change must be reciprocally situated within a bidirectional system of relations in which both sides not only come to understand each other but adjust their goals and objectives in accordance with the ongoing collaboration. This means that minorities are represented not only symbolically but also materially in the aims and content of the new education. And, as the Black Eligibility Task Force foresaw, these new efforts must be necessarily multisystem, multidimension, and multipurpose. Ultimately, they must generate new institutions that are open to new possibilities at the same time that they build on the knowledge base and identities of local and global communities.

Although new kinds of multisystem collaboration are possible, and there are numerous effective examples around the globe, they do require careful articulation and observance of their vision and their underlying principles.[1] Exhilaration produced by novelty often carries the new efforts through the initial periods of uncertainty and false starts but ultimately, building a solid foundation requires tremendous labor, time commitment, and attention on the part of select individuals. Otherwise, these new institutions will be drawn to convention by the constant tug of tradition and complacency common in entrenched bureaucracies and unenlightened political action. Individuals, who hold a greater vision of how education and society could work, must firmly guide these new institutions away from the seduction of convention. They must guide them through the perilous lure of fame, holding them true to the principles for which they were recognized in the first place. The lack of attention to these concerns inevitably results in one more failed attempt to bring about social change with the structures and ideas of yesteryear. And, like many other failed experiments, the new system becomes one more way in which to assimilate an errant minority group. It achieves what other well-intended efforts have accomplished: Prepare learners to negotiate neither the cultural contexts of their homes nor those of mainstream institutions.

In effect, what must be created is a functional system that is constituted by a "complexity of structure but also by the flexibility of the roles played by the constituents" (Griffin & Cole, 1984, p. 49). The levels and components of such a system must work in symmetry to bring about substantive and sustainable change in the way we do education and social service—and in particular, in the way that minorities are integrated into the educational enterprise. The goals of the project, those of the leading figures, and those for whom the efforts were galvanized in the first place, must be aligned and coordinated across levels and participant groups. And, thus, when one of its many parts becomes inoperative, the rest of the system assumes its labor without major a disruption to its aims and outcomes.

Such multidimensional functional systems are increasingly achieving varying degrees of success in generating new institutions that are grounded in a multiplicity of form and action. This is particularly true at the local community level where unprecedented multisystem collaboration is fast becoming a preferred choice of action for addressing a variety of social concerns plaguing public institutions across the country. An interesting example comes from my own previous employer, a high school district in San Jose, California, where I served as a research specialist in Special Education at one of the area high schools. Located in a poverty zone drained of resources by both white flight and middle income flight, the San Jose school district redefined school violence as a community problem and thereby was able to seek the assistance of relevant public institutions in combating a growing problem in the schools (Gibeau, 1997). Representatives from the police department, city, and county governments joined district personnel in developing typologies of what constitutes school violence and proper strategies to address it. In redefining safety at school as the responsibility of the community-at-large, rather than the exclusive domain of the school, administrators were able to secure a larger funding base and a long-term plan for dealing with school violence and related issues. The plan also prompted systematic retraining of key personnel whose job descriptions were redefined to include interacting with representatives from a diverse group of public institutions. Although the membership, content, and goals of the new initiative differed dramatically from those of its constituent parts, it nevertheless functioned as a unit—forming in essence a new institution.

The intercultural, global learning networks proposed by Cummins and Sayers (1995) more loosely exemplify this same kind of system—specifically those that transcend time and space to address the challenges of the new world realities.[2] These global learning networks facilitate access to intellectual and cultural resources "crucial for success in the multicultural national and global societies they will help form" (p. 12). They link public school students in both elementary and secondary schools to distant systems and regions through telecommunication technology. They provide students with access to knowledge and resources found outside their classrooms and create new learning environments in which teaching and learning become an open process of collaboration and critical inquiry. Students and teachers come to understand and accept differences in language and culture by learning not only about world events but also by actively taking part in them through raising funds, writing letters of support, and disseminating information.

La Clase Mágica (The Magical Class), the focus of this manuscript, is a form of multisystem collaboration that functions as a new institution with the aim of social change. It is a community-based, multilevel, multisystem experiment in locating a disenfranchised community at the center of the decision-making process with university researchers. While the university personnel propose a theory-based approach to learning and development, leading members of the community assume active roles in the development of curricular materials and interactional routines. These resources form key elements in providing the comprehensible input that Krashen (1988) believes second language learners need in order to achieve a greater understanding and acquisition of new concepts. They also are the basis from which the university personnel can understand and apply Vygotsky's (1978) sociohistorical theory to research and practice.

LA CLASE MÁGICA: A NEW COMMUNITY INSTITUTION

Organizationally, *La Clase Mágica* is an innovation of the Fifth Dimension, an after-school educational activity linking university and community institutions in a partnership that funnels resources to local children at a community-based computer club (see Fig. I.1). Designed to promote elementary school-aged children's literacy and cognitive development, the Fifth Dimension simultaneously mixes play and education to motivate the children's on-task behavior by creating a fantasy world instantiated through a system of artifacts in a real-life setting. The combination of fantasy and skill-building activities give life to a culture of collaborative learning in which learners direct their own development scaffold by adults, more knowledgeable peers, and a magical electronic entity known as the Wizard (Nicolopoulou & Cole, 1993). *La Clase*

Mágica, on the other hand, expands the Fifth Dimension's conceptual and organizational structure vertically and horizontally to include three extra age groups—early childhood, adolescence, and adulthood and expands outward to involve families and community. It targets an ethnolinguistic population and aims at rectifying the group's educational underachievement in K—12 and its underrepresentation in higher education. Furthermore, *La Clase Mágica* integrally aligns and coordinates the activities and curriculum of several age groups, effectively creating a pipeline of individuals equipped to meet the cultural and academic expectations of higher education (Moll, Anderson, & Díaz, 1985). Thus, in practice, *La Clase Mágica* is an emergent and context-sensitive form of social action that pushes the limits of our understandings for creating and sustaining social institutions that serve a diverse society.

At the community level, *La Clase Mágica*, is an after-school computer club where bilingual children from the surrounding Mexicano community meet three times a week to play computer games in collaboration with undergraduate students from UCSD. Throughout any given day, one can find learners engaged in culturally and developmentally designed activities for ages ranging from early childhood to adulthood. Undergraduate students enrolled in a practicum course at the university work closely with the learners to move them through a series of prearranged computer and telecommunication activities. The students and the system of artifacts (e.g., maze, task cards, and constitution) prompt children to imagine themselves in a journey through a bilingual–bicultural fantasy world ruled by a magical being known as *El Maga*.[3]

In this book, I use *La Clase Mágica* to lay out a vision for achieving a multicultural and multilingual future. Basically, it exemplifies one solution to the critique of the system posed by critical theorists who argue that the individual and institutions can achieve their optimal potential given adequate access to material and intellectual resources. Although in many respects, I am still describing the ideal with only the bare essentials in place, my hopes are to imagine optimal possibilities that lay out a direction for future research and practice. Alongside the ideal, I also tell the story of what it takes to bring about social change with the many tensions, contradictions, and failures that come with breaking new ground. Social change is long-term, deliberate, recursive, exhilarating, yet oftentimes, painful. So it has been with *La Clase Mágica*. Adapting it from a learning activity to a social action project has been labor extensive and time consuming. But, it has taken hold. The ripple effect it has had on the ability of individuals and institutions to reach new heights in their social and intellectual development becomes increasingly visible with the passing of time.

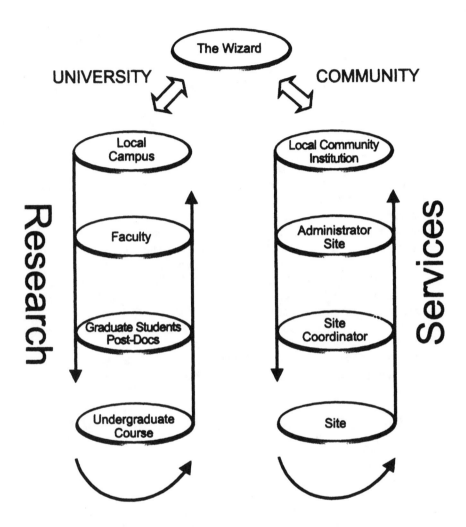

Figure I.1 Fifth dimension organizational structure.

This book focuses only on the period from the Fall Quarter of 1989 to the Spring Quarter of 1996. For the most part, this is a period of profound change and philosophical discovery during which I directed the research initiative in collaboration with community representatives. The organizational structure, the goals and objectives, and the pedagogy of the parent project were examined and adapted during this time to suit the educational needs of Spanish–English bilingual learners and their families— transforming the focus of the project from a educational activity to a social action project. It was also during this time that the fledgling project developed a separate identity, a separate language, and a separate culture from its predecessor. This period of growth and development gave light to a growing envisionment of what the university and community partnership could and should accomplish in terms of providing equitable and culturally relevant educational resources for a greater range of learners. In essence, it was the gestation period for developing the kind of social institutions that show great promise for adequately serving an increasingly diverse and highly technological society of the 21st century.

Although, *La Clase Mágica* continues to evolve after this initial period, the greater changes thereafter take part in the community side of the partnership. The end of the 1996 academic year, as I removed myself physically to write the manuscript, marked the beginning of the eventuality that both sides of the partnership had been preparing for from the time I had walked into the mission grounds (i.e. the take over of the project by the community). Our sustainability plan and our pedagogical philosophy anticipated this turnover and for several years the university staff and I had periodically held in-service training for the parents as we gradually pulled back. However, it was not until 1998 that the management of the project was handed over to Mrs. Durán, our site coordinator who acquired the title of "Meta-coordinator." While my university staff and I continued to conduct our research at *La Clase Mágica* after this time, our role in the decision-making processes associated with the operations of the site turned to that of consultants rather than managers.

MULTIPLE PERSPECTIVES OF AN INNOVATION: THE CONTENTS

In making *La Clase Mágica* the focus of this book, I emphasize not only its success as an educational activity, but also its role as a design experiment in which we study our own innovations and our (my) own learning development (Brown, 1992). *La Clase Mágica* provides an exceptionally rich context for studying the intersection of the micro–macro processes involved in creating social institutions. Institutions, I may add, that truly reflect a new conception of diversity that embraces innovation at the same time that it reflects a paradigm of multiple perspectives of both insiders and outsiders (Greenfield & Cocking, 1994). Because the on-site activities and the institutional relations are designed to be flexible and responsive, perhaps the most consistent quality of *La Clase Mágica* is its continually changing nature. This dynamism means that the kind of descriptive analysis that I undertake here is necessarily open-ended and will not do full justice to the evolving, experimental character of the program, especially the role of the ongoing relations of exchange that lie at the heart of the program.

Involving various institutions (UCSD, St. Leo's Mission, Head Start, LCHC, and the Mexicano family) and focusing on multiple participant groups and their specific educational resources and needs, makes *La Clase Mágica* a multisystem, multidimensional initiative. Implementing and documenting its development was a daunting undertaking. Its multifacetedness became both its strength and its weakness. On the one hand, keeping track of its broad-based approach aimed at making a difference in the essential educational experiences and cultural exchanges was no easy task given the resources. On the other, hand capturing its essence and its impact on participants became an extraordinary feat. First, every participant and every context were in perpetual change as developmental goals were achieved and new ones were formulated. Second, attempts at adequately representing its many facets often led to such disruption of the narrative that, ultimately, all that could be captured was what Stuhr and colleagues (1995) called a "partial truth." *La Clase Mágica*'s multidimensionality, however, was only part of the difficulty in writing this book. The centrality of my role in creating and studying the project, not to mention its fantasy aspect, the mediation of a magical being and the involvement in a virtual community of scholars, presented enormous difficulties in writing a lucent tale.

Not easily discouraged and welcoming the challenge, I try to portray this complexity and multidimensionality, hopefully successfully, in every aspect of the story I tell about *La Clase Mágica*.

La Clase Mágica represents the possibility of creating and studying a model system of relations (i.e., a functional system) that aims at funneling educational resources and institutional support to a minority population. Although some of its aspects have not achieved full development and some are still in the domain of possibility, the model allows us to entertain the possibility of what we could accomplish if we were able to fully coordinate the goals and activities of disparate cultural systems. And, in particular, it provides us with a vision of what it could be like to intervene in children's schooling difficulties as early as preschool. From my perspective and experience over these last 7 years, it grants us the possibility of providing a quality education, unique research opportunities, and exceptional learning experiences for individuals across a wide range of ages, experiences, and backgrounds. Imagining these possibilities has led me to repeatedly emphasize the points of contact between the three cultural systems (the university, community, and family) throughout the text. As relevant contexts for student achievement, these points of contact allow us to envision the possibilities for immediate and meaningful social action when they are closely aligned and coordinated through interrelated research themes and pedagogic aims (Moll et al., 1985). When further articulated with a distributive network of scholars conducting similar work in distant places with distinct populations, the possibilities become even greater. The lessons we learn at each of these points of contact can have great implications for understanding and enhancing the educational experiences of minority populations in other parts of the country, or the world.

At ground level, the book relates the unique partnership that was forged between the University of California, San Diego (UCSD) and a small Catholic mission located about 8 miles north of the campus (and about 35 miles north of the California–Mexico border). It was a partnership to support an after-school educational activity designed to optimize the learning potential of bilingual elementary school children of Mexican descent. By linking the cultural systems of academia and a *Mexicano* community, *La Clase Mágica* became a coordinating mechanism within and across institutions at the same time that it merged multiple histories, goals, and perspectives. It became the means by which the university and the community collaborated to provide quality undergraduate education, unique research opportunities, and exceptional learning experiences for individuals across a wide range of ages, experiences, and backgrounds. Importantly, it became the focal point for attending to critical social and educational issues that challenge the greater society.

Each chapter examines different facets of an ever-changing research initiative, providing a fresh look at issues such as access, equity, and diversity that continue to be hotly debated in current social, political, and academic arenas. Cultural relevance, collaboration, and development are common threads that run through chapter-length discussions on institutional relations, methodology, language use, and a community of learners. These chapters provide perspectives on aspects of the project that are in continual change and transformation but are held momentarily for analysis. Weaving them together captures a fuller account of the project but not quite the "true" or "complete" description of its basic nature or the magnitude of its impact. The steady flow of change prevents a neat and packaged description, and in its stead gives form to the rippling effects it has on participants, contexts, and methodologies within a multicultural reality. As such, it lays out how it could be possible to conduct community studies, educational reform, and social action at the dawn of a new century. Importantly, for those of us who work for the University of California, it provides different visions of possibilities for doing research, practice, and service, the threefold mission of the university.

Chapter 1, "Reconceptualizing Educational Activities Into Social Action," introduces the organizational structure, the basic principles, and the locality of *La Clase Mágica*. It lays out the prominent objectives and questions that lead to reconceptualizing an educational activity to optimize rather than structure or limit children's learning potential. The basic premise of what it means to receive access to such education is best exemplified by a young man's reflections on a presentation given by child participants of *La Clase Mágica* in one of his undergraduate courses. The chapter opens with an excerpt from his fieldnotes expressing the discomfort and anomie he experiences throughout his university career in contrast to the confidence and mastery he sees the children display as they talk about *La Clase Mágica*.

The following two chapters examine the process of change in the project through a macrolevel perspective: the curricula and organizational structure. Chapter 2, "A New Identity and New Possibilities: An Introduction of the Fifth Dimension," recounts the complex process of and the rationale for shaping the material and intellectual environment of *La Clase Mágica*. It tracks *La Clase Mágica*'s cultural and linguistic changes as it unfolds from the theoretical and organizational structure of the Fifth Dimension. The chapter answers two guiding questions that led the adaptation process: Given the existing resources and capabilities of the parent project, what does it take to create an ideal learning environment for bilingual, bicultural children? And furthermore, how does a game-driven activity convert a culturally relevant approach to social action? In answering these questions I lay out the principles for shaping a culturally relevant approach to learning and development. Two characteristics of *La Clase Mágica*'s curricular framework are highlighted: (1) its ongoing process of innovation, reflection, and transformation and, (2) its reach beyond the celebratory, surface incorporation of the learners' language and culture to integral inclusion of these background resources into the very fabric of the philosophy and organizational structure of the project.

Chapter 3, "A System of Relations for Acting Locally, Thinking Globally and Planning Long Term," sketches the social and historical trajectories that converge in the making of *La Clase Mágica*. The system of relations between the university and community institutions characterized as points of contact are described and aligned together to metaphorically represent the educational system. Each point, correlating to educational benchmarks (i.e., preschool, elementary school, junior and senior high school as well as adult education) provides an opportunity for the bidirectional flow of cultural knowledge between two disparate and often hostile cultural systems, making real the possibility of greater understanding, integration, and equitable distribution of resources among and between each other. The chapter also provides a reconceptualization of the notion of "eligibility" to participate in higher education. Eligibility (or lack of it) occurs through social and cultural practices between and among members of an academic community. Success in college or at the university, we are discovering, is related to the incoming students' competence in negotiating the norms and expectations rather than to their specific skill levels in discrete subject areas. Many students frequently have had little or no contact with the world of higher education before they arrive on campus as freshmen. Often times, participation in outreach programs at the end of the high-school career does not provide them the depth of understanding they need in order to negotiate a cultural system with a distinct language, knowledge base and norms of behavior. In deliberately interconnecting various levels of the educational system, *La Clase Mágica* establishes a pipeline of precollege students whose prior experiences (now) include consistent interactions with college students and faculty, and possibly campus visits, as well. These "qualified students" are capable of excelling in the intellectual environments of the university, home, and community (Moll et al., 1985). The chapter closes with an addendum to the university's commitment to promote a steady flow of qualified minority students through the auspices of UCLinks.

Chapter 4, "A System of Artifacts for a Methodology In Action" presents the reader with a deeper understanding of the complexity and multidimensionality of the acculturation process and the system of artifacts that support it. It presents the tools used to weave and study a pedagogy-in-action based on the languages and cultures Mexican-origin learners use as a function of daily life. I use the metaphor of a "journey through the maze" to illustrate the socializing force behind the system of artifacts which concretize a fantasy world for the participants and frames their behavior and interactions with one another. This metaphor is not arbitrary. It represents a core concept used to capture children's imagination of a fantasy world that is represented by a 20-room maze. In the real world of the site, the maze organizes the learners' self-directed movement through a prearranged series of activities. As children move through the games and activities making decisions, solving problems, setting goals, and negotiating their path with adults and/or their electronic pal, *El Maga*, they simultaneously imagine themselves journeying through the fantasy world of the Fifth Dimension. Here, I invoke a pedagogical strategy I call, "collapsing the paradox," to provide the reader with a vicarious experience of the children's thinking and doing as they move step by step, problem by problem, choice by choice, through the many rooms of the maze. Although limited by the technology of print, my hopes are to give the reader some sense of the spontaneity and unpredictability of the interactions that characterizes the children's journey through the maze.

Chapter 5, "Language and Identity in a Bilingual Learning Environment," looks at the mediating the role that language choice has in the construction of social and personal identities in educational activity. From this perspective, *La Clase Mágica* is seen as facilitating a broad range of individual identities that coexist with a strong support for a group identity—that of *Mexicano*. These multiple identities are nourished by the free access participants have to both their home and second language. Language data from a variety of sources such as ethnographic fieldnotes; video and audio transcriptions and electronic communication illustrates the ways in which bilingualism is a resource for achieving ones' own optimal learning potential. It also demonstrates its efficacy for supporting the learners' successful crossing of the many learning domains that make up their daily life as members of a language minority group. A case study of two long-term participants of *La Clase Mágica* accents the dominance of English in language choice and language loyalty, in spite of our tremendous effort to cultivate bilingualism. Through these case studies and other relevant data, I draw strong connections between the freedom to choose either language at-will and the development of a positive and competent sense of self.

Chapter 6, "The Politics of Participation: Navigating Cultural Borders," depicts *La Clase Mágica* from the perspective of its many participants. It portrays a community of learners "all playing active but often asymmetrical roles in sociocultural activity" (Rogoff, 1994, p. 209). To capture the multiple roles and the multiple voices of joint activity, the chapter combines objective and subjective accounts of the intellectual growth experienced by six different levels of participants: the electronic entity, children, parents, undergraduate students, research staff, and project director. The discussion draws on a variety of data sources to lay out a general pattern of development for each group and uses these developmental profiles as an introduction to brief self-reports by selected members of each participant group.

Chapter 7, "The Risk of Challenge," depicts *La Clase Mágica* as an intercultural body that makes innovation and diversity its goals. It calls on researchers, practitioners, and policymakers to takes risks and see beyond the true and proven and construct an education of the future. It implores us to envision how *La Clase Mágica* and its successors in the UC Links project can enhance the University of California's ability to carry out its mission of research, teaching, and service alongside its new mission: diversity.

NOTES

[1]For example, for almost a decade, at the international level, the former Soviet Union has been developing a Conflict Monitoring Network (Foot, 1996). The Network links disparate and often hostile systems based on a multiperspective of what constitutes conflict and adequate system of collaboration in one of the most volatile regions of the world. Through an elaborate system of telecommunication, the Network coordinates and consolidates electronically submitted reports from ethnic scholars, thus creating an effective early warning system regarding levels of tension among and between specific ethnic groups. Although the coming years will more adequately define the nature and effectiveness of this system of relations (Foot, 1999) as a means for preserving peace, the Network promises to affect international policy not only in its ability to maintain peace but also in its ability to bring together multinational, multidisciplinary, and multicultural collaboration in effective social action.

[2]See Foot (1999).

[3]El Maga is a neologism composed of both feminine and masculine forms of the word Wizard in Spanish. The strategy is used to avoid assigning gender to an authority figure which the electronic entity called the Wizard in the Fifth Dimension was originally designed.

1

Reconceptualizing Educational Activities Into Social Action

Reflections. Their poise was the most remarkable thing to me, considering the context they were in and my own experiences as a Latino in the educational system. These kids had walked onto this university campus and stood in front of this class and seemed comfortable and in control. The strange thing to me was their level of confidence, for this was not an environment in which these kids had grown up. This has been, and for the most part still is, a White (Anglo) institution. The university has historically been inhospitable to persons of color. I myself have to constantly re-situate myself to maintain some type of comfortable position within the university. However, they seemed oblivious to this fact. Could it be because it was late when they arrived? I mean the campus was quiet in comparison to midday business. They did not have the opportunity to see all the everyday students—the ones who are different in appearance, culture, and social status. But, again, they did come face-to-face with a microcosm of UCSD. The ComHip122 class was a good sampling of the homogeneity of the racial composition at UCSD. Nonetheless, they appeared unintimidated, uninhibited, and free to express themselves—the things that an institution like this constantly attempts to take away from a person, particularly those of color. I excused their posturing as an act of innocence, a brave naiveté. Give them time, I thought. Perhaps I felt a sense of envy. They had a head start, an ethical pragmatic educational program. They are building confidence, obtaining skills, and receiving access to education—something many (most) of us never had the opportunity to experience. And now they sat in front of this class with more confidence than I would have had up there or, for that matter, any of my White classmates would have had. Being in a UCSD classroom—in an institutionalized educational environment—seemed natural to them—and indeed it should be. However, that's not how I felt at that age. [MC/11/23/93]

It is reasonable to expect for someone to acquire a sense of belonging and comfort within 4 years of entering a new cultural system. However, for the Latino student whose "Reflection" segment of a longer fieldnote I cite above, this was not the case. MC, like many other minority students, still did not feel at home at the university after 4 years of active participation. Furthermore, he found it remarkable that bilingual children from a nearby *Mexicano* community should feel so at ease in front of a university class of 60 students while he repeatedly and deliberately felt the need to "re-situate" himself within the cultural norms of a "White (Anglo) institution." The "institutionalized educational environment" and the "predominantly White" members of the class generated discomfort for him. The seven children in front of him, on the other hand, demonstrated a comfort that had escaped him even though they had not "grown up" in such an environment nor had they ever visited a college campus before. He searched deeply for an answer to this paradox and rationalized that perhaps it was the children's "brave naiveté" about the homogenizing power of the institution—a process he understood well and strongly resisted.

How had this role reversal taken place when MC had spent years participating in both minority-oriented activities and those related to the broader university culture? What prior personal experiences had made the difference for the children? Or, what type of program could shape such strong sense of confidence to help them feel "unintimidated, uninhibited, and free to express themselves" in such an unfamiliar context? What was the "headstart" or that "something many (most) of us never have the opportunity to experience?" Although not stating it outright, MC suggested it was an after-school educational activity called *La Clase Mágica* that made the difference for these children. Data collected for this book overwhelmingly supports this claim: The early association with institutional agents at *La Clase Mágica* facilitates entré to and alliance with the academic culture of the university. Through a carefully crafted set of activities and social interactions, *La Clase Mágica* affords minority learners the opportunity to access and make theirs the cultural and social capital needed to successfully meet the exigencies of both the community and the educational systems. Educational resources and institutional support for "building confidence, obtaining skills, and receiving access to education" are made available through numerous theoretically informed interactional opportunities with institutional representatives, an electronic entity called *El Maga*, and a socializing system of artifacts.

Thus, participation in *La Clase Mágica* had had a slow but profound effect on the socioemotional make-up of the participants. The children's confidence had been carefully crafted in their numerous theoretically informed interactions with the undergraduate students, giving them a powerful advantage over the peripheral participation that MC had maintained at UCSD up to that point. Although he had been at UCSD for 4 years and had been involved in some of the minority-oriented programs on campus such as MeCha (*Movimiento estudiantil Chicano de Aztlan*) and Latino Lawyers Association, the ease with which the children managed the situation was still beyond MC's reach. As Tinto (1987) concurred, MC did not feel at home at the university because along the way he had not acquired and made his own the competencies necessary to negotiate the social and cultural essentialities of academic life. His journey to the university had been strewn with disillusionment and periods of absence from an educational system that offered few optimal learning opportunities. The active and meaningful participation in the cultural activities of *La Clase Mágica* on the other hand, had made it possible for the children to acquired the social and cultural capital privileged in institutions of higher education (Stanton-Salazar, Vásquez, & Mehan, 1995).

Social action had taken place. The children had acquired the language and cultural knowledge to be on equal par with high-status members of the institution. They had transferred what had been lived as part of an engineered environment to an unfamiliar context (Stanton-Salazar et al., 1995). They felt at home at the university. So much so that at the end of their presentation, a 10-year-old boy looked straight at the students, pointed in the manner of the Uncle Sam on the Army poster and loudly announced, "WE NEED YOU!" The order of things had been disrupted. Instead of feeling different, out of sync, or acquiescent, language minority learners had assumed a position of leadership within a prestigious institution. They had achieved "expert participation" in a system that although spatially removed from their everyday lives formed an integral part of the social and intellectual activities of *La Clase Mágica*.

This snippet of evidence illustrates the promise that *La Clase Mágica* holds for bringing about change in the educational experience of Latinos who have one of the most persistently high rate of failure in the public school system. Their historically poor representation in the membership and intellectual content of institutions of higher education make it almost impossible for others to follow in a similar path. Although there are many explanations for this state of affairs, several are worthy of mention: Demographically, Latinos tend to be first generation, come from low income background and speak a language other than English in the home (Hurtado, Figueroa, & Garcia, 1996). They often have little access to the social and cultural capital that would facilitate their ascendance to institutions of higher learning (Margolis & Romero, 1998; Stanton-Salazar, 1997). They also frequently arrive somewhat distrustful of, if not, alienated from institutional agents and the schooling system itself (Tinto, 1987; Valenzuela, 1999). Furthermore, the university's entrenched monoculturalism often makes it difficult for them to find a protective niche from where to negotiate an uninviting system (Tinto, 1987).

Change is possible, however. And, although there are many angles from which to examine the actualization of this possibility, I have chosen aspects of individual and institutional development as the starting point. The most suited concept for observing development in both of these realms is Vygotsky's notion of the zone of proximal development, a frame that offers past, present, and future perspectives on the developmental process whether it is at the individual or institutional level. We gain several insights from using this frame to examine the effects of *La Clase Mágica*. First, by focusing our attention on the material and intellectual resources needed for accomplishing optimal performance, we focus on a present past and a future present (Vygotsky, 1978). Interpreted in the context of *La Clase Mágica*, past history—or background experiences—is integral to the project of the present whose aim is to achieve the future in the present through resources strategically provided by more expert participants. Whether we examine individual or institution development, this perspective situates the researcher or practicioner's gaze in the in-between two stages of development—the past or actual level of development and the future development, the conceptual space called the zone of proximal development.

Using this perspective on individual development of bilingual learners reveals the multiplicity of resources available to them and the possible links that can be made between old and new knowledge. Importantly, this perspectives locates the assistance of the more expert peer, in many cases the assistance from the undergraduate student, at a critical juncture in the learner's developmental process, in the border between what the learner knows in the moment and that which he or she will know, as Vygotsky points out, in the future. Thus, the role of the expert can be scrutinized for its strategic positioning, a position subordinate to the needs, goals, and interests of the learner rather than a didactic one leading the learner toward a priori goals and objectives. It is a view of much dynamism, multiplicity, and in many ways, much ambiguity.

The same can be said of the view that the zone of proximal development affords us when we examine the structure and properties of the institution we are trying to create. The dynamism, multiplicity, and ambiguity of individual development are replicated in *La Clase Mágica* as an institution-in-the-making. Constituted in collaboration with three cultural systems—the university, the community, and the family—and three institutional contexts—the Laboratory of Comparative Cognition (LCHC), a three-quarter course, and an after-school program with four activities—*La Clase Mágica* affords multiple resources and multiple possibilities for building a multicultural project. The reasons for and the processes by which institutional relations are organized as well as the probable outcomes come under full view from this perspective. Change can be tracked in the form and content of cross-system collaboration, its system of artifacts, and its influences on its constituent partners. The expected transformation in the case of the institution is innovation rather than a replication of the parent project. On the other hand, the transformation of the individual from this perspective achieves a level of development and identity greater than the sum of the multiple cultures from which he or she draws.

    In what follows, I sketch out the most influential concepts for understanding the institutional structures, the cultural contexts and the individual achievements that constitute everyday life of *La Clase Mágica*. I begin with the most current and most insightful explanations of the formidable challenges a multicultural project faces in adequately educating diverse populations: the institutional structures that reinforce the social and cultural capital of the dominant group and deny access to or devalue those who differ from these norms. Then I argue that education is a cultural system with its own particular norms and expectations, and thus, we must re-define eligibility to higher education as a social practice acquired through early and sustained access to institutional agents. I follow with a discussion of the ways in which language and culture organize what learners learn and how extending the frameworks of these aspects of human existence gives us new understandings of the complexities and potentialities of diverse learners. I conclude with weaving these new frames of individual and institutional development in diverse contexts together to create new vistas and new expectations for education as social action.

AN UNEASY PRESENCE: LATINO REPRESENTATION IN HIGHER EDUCATION

Bourdieu (1977) and his American counterparts (Lamont & Lareau, 1988; Mehan, 1992a, 1992b; Swartz, 1977) offered one of the most provocative explanations for the dramatic underrepresentation of minorities in higher education. Although initially designed to explain the social reproduction of inequality in France, Bourdieu's theory adds significantly to our understanding of the hidden mechanisms of institutional exclusion in the U.S. context. According to Bourdieu, educational institutions are organized to reward students who display cultural knowledge and skills consistent with those of the dominant class. Viewed as capital, these cultural and social attributes favor individuals from the dominant classes, aiding them in gaining access to resources, privileges, and promotions. Michelle Fine (1991), for example, illustrated how a constellation of administrative and ideological practices and beliefs—what she called "institutional fetishes"—unintentionally lead to the expulsion and exclusion of low-status students. Of particular relevance to these processes are the unquestioned adherence to notions of universal access to public education, the "good intentions" of educational professionals, and the distinctions that exist between the public and private spheres for some populations. As Fine (1991) aptly concluded, these factors lead institutions to "construct and legitimate a set of beliefs about equal opportunity, the inevitability of failure, and the immutability of home problems that undermine academic achievement" (p. 184). As a result, educational resources and institutional support is not equally distributed to individuals whose background experiences differ from the mainstream English-language template. In other words, it is the background experiences of these groups of students that impede their entrance and success in higher education.

Mehan (1992a, 1992b) more closely examined the processes by which differential treatment is conferred upon those children who deploy cultural and linguistic resources inconsistent with the dominant classes. Elaborate selection processes, including referral, educational testing, and placement decisions, often sanctioned by law or normative practices, areused to allocate materialand educational resources and opportunities. Linguistic minority children and educationally handicapped children are sorted into low educational tracks, where they receive a fragmented, watered-down version of the standard curriculum. That is, different knowledge is made available to these children based on their presumed ability (Oakes, Gamoran, & Page. 1992). Tragically. their learning trajectory is deflected away from challenging and demanding cognitive tasks, making it extremely difficult for them to keep up with the mandatory grade-level objectives set for their peers. Thus begins a series of failures to achieve educational benchmarks that jeopardize their chances to complete a public school education, a course that seriously handicaps their eligibility to higher education. Without the opportunities to acquire the social and academic skills that would gain them access to further educational resources and institutional support, these students opt out of the system in distressingly high numbers. Or. if they manage to make it to higher education, these students, much like MC above, lack the proper socialization to the cultural norms to feel at home at the university.

The structural separation between linguistic minority children and native speakers of the dominant language. as well as the social distance between the two communities, plays out dramatically in institutions of higher learning where minorities are severely underrepresented. Minority students in general and Latinos, in particular, are socially and economically differentiated in institutions of higher learning. This is the case in every institution in the country with the exception of the 103 Historically Black Colleges and other institutions in the Southwest where Latinos are in the majority.[1]   The latter, nevertheless, report a slightly lower rate of increase in the enrollment of minorities over the last two decades. Because so few linguistic minority students attend institutions of higher learning, university personnel outside of these minority-centered institutions, have little opportunity to assess the needs and interests of these students and thus often fail to develop programs that are both rigorous and meaningful. Although increasingly noted as a loss to the university (e.g., the Hopwood case in Texas) this loss pales in comparison to that of the students and their communities. Unable to acquire the proper culture capital to enter, let alone succeed, in postsecondary institutions, students find that higher education is an illusive future option. If by sheer tenacity they manage to enroll, they experience great difficulty in gaining access to the extensive system of rewards that these institutions have to offer.

Part of the university's inability to actively recruit underrepresented students stems from its limited success in retaining the minority students it has admitted in the past. The early departure of minority students from 4-year institutions can be traced to the narrow definition of eligibility, the lack of formal and informal support networks available to minority students, and the lack of systematic mechanisms to mediate familiarity with the cultural norms and social practices of academia. Many of the minority students I mentored through the federally funded Roland McNair Program and the Faculty Mentor Program at the University of California, San Diego (UCSD), for example, repeatedly lamented the relatively few places on campus where they can feel at home. Invariably many expressed distress over having to be the "minority" authority on social issues in many of their classes.

Individuals who come from backgrounds without access to the social and cultural capital privileged in academia, must either acquire it in school or through their own personal ingenuity (Stanton-Salazar, 1990). However, students often face structural arrangements and underpreparation of teachers that present formidable obstacles (California Basic Education Data Systems [CBEDS], 2000). As scholars like Oakes, Fine, and Mehan have pointed out, unfounded and unexamined beliefs as well as institutional practices often obstruct the flow of capital to low-status students. Moll and Diaz (1987) provided an ingenious example of how the unexamined assumptions about the abilities of minority children affect the instruction in and the dispersal of intellectual resources by well-intended teachers. Had it not been for the Spanish language arts teacher who was able to appreciate and martial the cultural, linguistic, and intellectual capabilities of these children, they would have joined thousands of other Spanish–English bilingual children who receive less than a quality education.

Acquiring institutional know-how is a long-term process. In order to negotiate the intellectual and cultural practices of the academy, minority individuals must have access to members of resource-rich networks—a prospect generally not available to these students (Stanton-Salazar, 1997; Stanton-Salazar et. al., 1995). In specific, the acquisition of such knowledge can be facilitated by well placed institutional agents who are stable and invested in minority individuals. Regrettably, few opportunities exist to establish the kinds of sustained relationships that make this flow of knowledge possible. Furthermore, programs that make knowledge explicit are often rare and late in these students public school training (Mehan, Villanueva, Hubbard, & Lintz, 1996; LES Report

4). Heath and McLaughlin (1993) suggested that minority youths can acquire valuable social skills for negotiating mainstream society by participating in community-based activities. However, little is known about the value of these activities for generating the social and cultural capital that can be traded in for educational rewards at school. Generally, minority students are ill prepared to effectively transact the cultural norms and expectations set by the university and therefore are at risk from the moment they reach its doorstep.

   La Clase Mágica's broad-base approach attempts to circumvent this apparent institutional malaise. It does so by organizing a system of material and intellectual artifacts (Holland & Cole, 1995) and a system of relations across cultural groups that have previously had little if any history of cross-system collaboration (Vásquez, 1996). By creating an unprecedented partnership with relevant social institutions, *La Clase Mágica* forms a complex and multilevel functional system aimed at facilitating the transmission and acquisition of social and cultural capital (see Stanton-Salazar, Vásquez, & Mehan, (1996) for further discussion on relevant social and cultural capital). Capital flows to and from three cultural systems, three institutional contexts, and seven points of contact (see Fig. 1.1) yielding knowledge and skills to all its constituent parts.

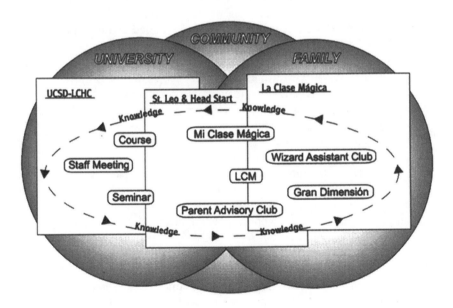

Figure 1.1. The flow of knowledge.

Capital. then. is redistributed to segments of the system that are at once connected but disassociated from the sources of knowledge. Individuals as well as contexts become predisposed to the cross-fertilization that naturally occurs as participants move across components of the system.

Superimposed over the educational system, this functional system encompasses every benchmark of the educational pipeline—preschool, elementary school, junior high school, high school, college, and adult education. Through participation individuals gain knowledge of what it takes to maneuver through the educational system and, by extension, other mainstream institutions. Importantly. institutional contexts such as the undergraduate course, the after-school site, and the collaborating institutions (i.e., the LCHC, Head Start, and the Boys and Girls Club) regain their utility in serving a diverse constituency as innovative institutional arrangements that make possible the flow of capital.

ELIGIBILITY AS CULTURAL AND SOCIAL CAPITAL

The institutional structures and practices that interrupt or deflect minority students' progress through the educational system are indeed formidable obstacles. Another significant barrier, one less studied and perhaps the most insidious, is the way in which eligibility to higher education is inscribed in the minds and policies of educational practitioners and reformers. Narrow and discrete definitions of what makes an individual eligible can play havoc in the ability of minority college students to enter into negotiations with institutions of higher learning. In fact, our research has led us to seriously question conventional notions of eligibility. Students who arrive at the university with the appropriate A–F requirements, adequate test scores, and proper grades are not necessarily ready to meet the demands of an academic cultural system. Although they may qualify on paper, their ability to felicitously maneuver through the system can be seriously hampered by their unfamiliarity and inexperience with the culture of the institution. In other words. they do not have adequate social and cultural capital to secure a position within the intellectual and social realms of an academic community

I propose a new conception of eligibility, one that locates social practice as the center of competence. Achieved through years of sustained interactions with institutional agents, eligibility as a social practice goes hand in hand with learning to "read" the norms and expectations of the university and thus bridges the distance between the university and community. Immersion in the social and cultural practices valued by both the community and the academy as early as preschool increases the likelihood that the individual will be able to find him or herself at home in institutions of higher education. This contention was resoundingly supported in 1999 by a 21-year study that followed 111 poor African-American families in North Carolina (Wilgoren, 1999). Those individuals who received high-quality intervention as early as day care were more than twice as likely to attend and remain in college. What these children learned early in life and then practiced along the way were the norms and expectations valued by a specific cultural system—higher education.

The work at *La Clase Mágica* has taught us that eligibility to higher education is not simply the performance of discrete academic skills, although these are also important. Rather, eligibility is having the means to negotiate the social and intellectual life of the academy. Broadly, it is a socially constructed competence gained through the practice of everyday life. Like Bourdieu's cultural capital, this competence is acquired over an extended period of time in sustained exposure to activities involving institutional representatives. Through meaningful relationships individuals learn approaches to meaning-making relevant to written and oral communication privileged in the academy, as a deeper sense of competence than to merely knowing the mechanics of how to study, fill out applications, and take tests. Fully eligible individuals, for example, readily understand and have the means to achieve the goals and objectives of the institution. They know the importance of and can act upon what is expected of a student in a course. They not only know how to write, read, and study, but also know that they must closely consult with professors, actively participate in class discussions, and skillfully dismantle written and oral arguments. In other words, they form part and parcel of cultural production of the class.

Although cultural discontinuity between minority student backgrounds and the school's personnel is widely documented, many minority-oriented supplementary programs focus on improving high school students' eligibility in the narrowest sense of the term. Such programs are designed to raise the student's grade point average and SAT scores; many focus specifically on college preparatory material. Little attention, however, has been paid to eligibility in its expanded sense. Outside of efforts such as AVID (Advancement Via Individual Determination) few, if any, programs exist that attempt to teach minority children the knowledge and skills they missed by being routinely shunted into low educational tracks (Mehan et al., 1996). If minority students do not have well-placed institutional agents in their immediate social networks from whom they can learn the institutional know-how for successful integration into academic life, they are likely to experience cognitive dissonance when they first face the culture of academia (Stanton-Salazar, 1997). The absence of shared cultural understandings makes it difficult for minority students to see themselves as congruent with other campus groups (Tinto, 1987). This emotional and psychological disorientation has serious consequences for a system interested in its diversity. Many minority students experience great difficulty fitting into campus life. They also have a difficult time figuring out how academic training relates to their life goals. Many, if not most, question whether the potential economic benefits of staying in college and receiving a diploma are worth the prolonged physical and cultural separation from their families and communities (Bernal, Saenz, & Knight 1991; Romo, 1984).

Following the logic of Bourdieu's arguments, we can assume that current interpretations of eligibility contribute significantly to the perpetuation of hierarchical and exclusionary practices within institutions. Policies that support interventions and admissions based on this narrow interpretation of eligibility bar large numbers of minority students from higher education. These policies also relegate the unique cultural and epistemological contributions of minority students as insignificant in value. Educational practitioners and policymakers who promote eligibility as a composite of mechanical and knowledge-based strategies are ill informed and unwittingly cause a tremendous amount of pain. Mastery of knowledge to transact the educational system and, by extension, other mainstream institutions is more than an accumulation of discrete skills that can be acquired in the last years of high school. Rather, it is an intrinsic understanding of the complexity of intercultural communication and its respective institutional norms and expectations. In effect, it mirrors the slow and lengthy process of cultural change and language acquisition.

The connection Durán (1995) has mapped between literacy and the "know-how" for participating in the everyday activities of social institutions helps round out the definition of eligibility used in this chapter. Bridging Bourdieu's concepts of cultural and institutional capital with the sociocultural view of literacy as the ability to interpret and assume new forms of communication and actions within a cultural and social community of practice, Durán proposed that institutions and communities embody and require different forms of communicative competence. Knowledge of basic literacy skills is not enough to be a "competent participant" in institutional culture. Individuals must be able to interpret and by extension "read" and act upon the underlying social relationships and norms of interaction inherent in institutional culture. In short, individuals must be "interpreters of culture," attributing precise meaning to oral and written texts that form the basis of intercultural transactions (Vásquez et al., 1994). This competence is carefully crafted in the interactional routines of undergraduate students and minority learners at *La Clase Mágica*. As these learners move through a prearranged series of activities especially designed to reflect the cultural knowledge of both constituent cultures, they learn the language and literacy practices of both communities. They learn to negotiate the academy without losing hold of their prior history. Next, I turn to the views of language and culture that frame both the new definition of eligibility and the rationale for material and intellectual organization of *La Clase Mágica*.

DOWN THE STREET BUT WORLDS APART: SEPARATED BY LANGUAGE AND CULTURE

This new conception of eligibility to higher education assumes the ability to mobilize tacit knowledge of how the institutions work. However, this kind of deep-seated knowledge is acquired through a socialization process few minority individuals have access to—long and sustained relations with acculturated members of the institution. Although favorable conditions for such knowledge building exists at school, those who already have a familiarity with the social and cultural capital of the institution, as Bourdieu and others point out, are given grater opportunity to access it. Minority students, on the other hand, have few venues from which to access this continual knowledge. The media, with its capacity to act as a socialization tool, more often that not, skews, fragments and/or caricatures its representations of life in academia, making it ineffective, if not dangerous, capital in the hands of the uninitiated. Furthermore, institutions are not prepared to bridge the gaps in knowledge and language of intercultural communication; instead, each institution insists that its clientele learn the nuances and implicit meanings that characterize its written and oral forms of communication. By default, then, it falls on minorities to gain the cultural and linguistic fluency they need in order to interact advantageously with mainstream institutions.

Thus, how can individuals who live down the street but worlds apart from mainstream institutions acquire the necessary knowledge and skills to adequately engage them? How can the gap between the capital needed to maneuver through a predominantly ethnic minority community and that needed to participate successfully in intercultural relations with representatives of mainstream institutions be narrowed? The structural and cultural distances between the communities pose seemingly insurmountable barriers. The difference in culture and language of the two communities is not the only disjuncture. the accouterments of space and the location of public and private institutions also widens the distance between the two groups. Minority enclaves, for example, are separated from the White, monolingual, and high-income communities that typically surround them. The effects of class, race, and history also mark every aspect of their difference—the space, patterns of interrelations, and personal narratives of the residents. These differences are real and influential, however, in the following section, I focus only on language and culture as the frame from which to examine both the structure and content of learning contexts. I select this narrow focus for two reasons: (1) class, race. and history are largely expressed in the language and culture of the learning context, and, (2) as action researchers these elements are what we can directly andactively manipulate in the interactional routines and curriculum of the activity.

Culture. It is well established that a very specific culture of learning operates in classrooms across the United States, if not across the world (Gallego & Cole, 2000). Moreover, it is widely held that this culture is also closely connected with middle-class norms and epistemologies. So strong is the influence of classroom learning that children frequently deploy school-oriented behavior in other learning contexts such as those found in church groups, after-school programs, and impromptu learning circles. A relevant example is the bilingual children who scolded others in the early stages of *La Clase Mágica*, "We speak English here!" or called the staff by the title of "*Maestra*" [Teacher]. These children juxtaposed the learning character of *La Clase Mágica* with the formalities of school. What these behaviors imply is that learning can only be accomplished in English and that adults can only be authority figures—two philosophical principles in complete contradiction with the goals of *La Clase Mágica* as I point out throughout this book. The course of action of first-grade children when paired with kindergartners for reading and writing is another example of the strong cultural norms operating in the classroom. Although not explicitly taught formal literacy strategies for teaching and learning, the older children reproduced these school based practices in cross-age tutoring routines with younger peers (Heath, Pease-Alvarez, & Vásquez, 1994). For them, reading was accomplished through sounding out letters and syllables in discrete and fragmented segments. Meaning and comprehension were not elicited in their lessons, in contrast to the goals and practices of teaching and learning routines of *La Clase Mágica*.

The adage, "I can't hear what you are saying because I am too busy watching," illustrates the power of action for immature learners. Children learn just as much if not more from what is done before their eyes than from what is said. Learning, in other words, is not disembodied from the ways in which it is ordered nor is it simply achieved through language. Although language can function as the medium and content of culture, the way we organize life also has a powerful affect on learning and development. According to Vygotsky, for example, culture is the "socially structured ways in which society organizes the kinds of tasks that the growing child faces and the kinds of tools, both mental and physical, that the young child is provided to master those tasks" (Luria, 1979, p. 44). Thus, the cultural context organizes what and how learners learn in a fluid exchange in what Bruner (1986) called an ongoing play. The cultural context specifies what is learned, who is learning from whom, and the tools that are needed to accomplish the tasks at hand. This theorizing, however, neglects the complexity and ambiguity that constitutes the cultural life of language minority learners. As the children cited earlier exemplify, multiple cultures tug at their comprehension of the world around them.

Other examples are the research on literacy (Heath, 1983; Vásquez, 1989; Vásquez et al., 1994) that illustrate the cultural incongruities between the literacy practices of mainstream institutions and communities who differ from middle-class norms and standard English. Durán, for example, echoed a concern for a broader understanding of how expectations by the mainstream far exceed the literacy skills of immigrant families. In order to participate successfully in intercultural relations with representatives of these institutions, individuals from diverse communities must first bridge a wide gap between the know-how required to transact their own community-based institutions and those out in the mainstream (Durán, 1995; Mehan, 1992a; Vásquez, 1989;). Most institutions are not prepared to bridge the gaps in knowledge and communication intercultural relations; instead, each institution persists in expecting its client population to learn the nuanced and implicit meanings that characterize that institution's written and oral communications. By default, then, it falls on minorities to gain the cultural fluency they need in order to interact advantageously with mainstream institutions. . In spite of this lack of relevant knowledge, community members make valiant efforts to pool the linguistic and social resources at their disposal to get their needs met (Vásquez, 1989). They set in motion elaborate systems of support to facilitate intercultural communication yet, rarely do they fully satisfy their need for services and information (Heath, 1983; Vásquez, 1989).

The cultural discontinuity between mainstream institutions and communities of color, therefore, pose formidable obstacles to addressing the demographic realities of the 21st century. The view of *La Clase Mágica* from this perspective is instructive in illustrating the social structures and social relationships by which nonmainstream groups can master the necessary mastery to participate in equitable relations with institutional representatives. At the same time, it illustrates the possibilities that are open to mainstream institutions for responding to language and culture outside of the mainstream norm.

Language.   Language plays a critical role in cross-cultural communication, both at the collective and individual levels. As the medium for communication and the context for cultural expression, language encompasses every aspect of human experience. It is "a powerful medium of socialization" (Shieffelin & Ochs, 1986) that is inseparable from culture. Language allows the exchange of ideas, and in conjunction with cultural practices, plays a fundamental role in shaping which ideas gain currency in a society. Reminiscent of Bruner's ongoing play, Ochs (1986) asserted the dialectical relationship between culture and language use:

> One critical area of social competence a child must acquire is the
> ability to recognize/interpret what social activity/event is taking place
> and to speak and act in ways sensitive to the context. (p. 3)

Ruiz's (1987) description of language as "a window into other cultures" effectively captured this view of language. In other words, people talk, tell stories, ask questions, and search for meaning in culturally specific ways.

Yet, there is much more than the reflection of culture in the ways language is used. Language also situates the self in dialogue with the processes of a group's construction and transmission of its traditions, history, and norms. Helen Keller's discovery of the relationship between the cool fluid flowing in her hand and the movements of her teacher's fingers directly impacts her concept of self (Percy, 1975). She becomes human when the amorphous continuity that has linked her to the world around her is ruptured by her discovery that the movements in her hand were a sign for water. Language separates her from the objective reality and gives her a distinct sense of self. She is Helen, a human being, and not the wild animal child that had terrorized the family. The triadic relationship among the self, symbol, and object grows out of this discovery shaping the vision seen through Ruiz's "window." The view, in other words, is not neutral. Language "completes the thought," of what is out there, as Vygotsky (1978) would have it, and paints the scene with the meanings and nuances of the speaker's history and culture. A separate consciousness is created through the continuous interrelation of language, culture, and self-identity.

Thus, language "links what is inside the head with what is outside" (Barton, 1994, p. 14), expressing much about who we are in relation to those around us. The ways we use language and the language we use reflects both subtle and explicit messages of group membership and social identity. Language conveys a sense of community, belonging, and solidarity, but it also simultaneously marks differences and provides a basis for exclusion. It distinguishes us from them in intercultural communication. Joshua Fishman (1985), for example, observed that language is a referent for strong personal and societal preferenes, ideals, and refusals. Carlos, a child participant of *La Clase Mágica* put it this way:

> "Aunque sepa todo y me case con una persona importante, soy Mexicano." [Even if I know everything, and I marry an important person, I am Mexicano.]

If language is a marker, allowing us to differentiate ourselves from them, what happens when a person, or even a community of people, speak more than one language? Most of the theoretical inquiry into the connections between language, culture, and identity assumes a homogeneous linguistic environment. Little is known about how a child develops a coherent concept of self when his or her social world is characterized by multiple viewpoints and conflicting language codes. We know that language contact affects both language and culture (Appel & Muysken, 1987) but not how it affects identity. Can we assume that multiple ways of thinking and doing are syncretized into one identity? Or, are they incorporated into a repertoire of separate identities that allow the individual to transcend sociocultural borders? In other words, is the self constant or is it variable? Or is there a third possibility in which the self is constant but composed of a multiplicity of related personas individually enacted according to the constraints of the social context as both Anzaldúa (1987) and Gleason (1983) pointed out?

Our work at *La Clase Mágica* suggests that language plays a critical role in calling forth and sustaining specific identities. A diachronic analysis of language use among long-term participants of the program confirmed Anzaldúa's (1987, 1990) contention that at any given moment the individual has multiple cultural possibilities at his or her disposal. Contemporary contexts embody choices that radiate out of historical trajectories in language, culture, and general orientation toward the larger society. How freely the movement across identities occurs, how many possibilities are held open, and how successfully the individual dons any given persona varies over a wide range of personal and societal factors. The life experiences of bilingual individuals highlight some of these factors.

BILINGUAL IDENTITY

The bilingual individual presents a special case of the relationship between language and identity. Anzaldúa (1987), Flores (1984), and others tell us volumes about a "native" identity struggling against hegemonic forces from an "embattled" position of power. A growing number of studies also point to the sociolinguistic forces that strengthen or weaken a bilingual's social identity on the basis of the status of his or her home language. It is likely, for example, that a bilingual's identity will be strengthened if (1) the language "closest to the heart" (i.e., the language spoken in the home) is the dominant language of the society (Rotheram & Phinney, 1987); (2) the second language is learned in a foreign-language classroom rather than acquired through socialization (Ruiz, 1987); and (3) the individual's bilingualism proves useful in resolving conflicts in group membership by serving as a bridge connecting two sets of norms and expectations (Heller, 1987). Bilingualism in these three instances is valued and desired. It situates the speaker advantageously; here the bilingual operates from a position of strength, similar to a majority position.

When, on the other hand, the language of the heart is a minoritized one, the legitimacy, authenticity, and virtue of a bilingual's social identity is vulnerable to attack. Lacking strong cultural support, the presence of a speaker of a minority language arouses an unease among the majority as encounter with an "alien among us." In the United States, and increasingly in Europe, the fear and resentment exhibited toward people who live in a given locale "but whose hearts are elsewhere" (Ruiz, 1987, p. 5) is evident in such public displays as separate educational placement (Mehan, 1992), language litigation (Crawford, 1992; Padilla et al., 1991), and exaggerated media reports of hate crimes and physical violence in minority communities (Reed, 1998). The response of the majority, however, is immaterial in comparison to the affront this reaction has on the individual's sense of self.

Not having the language or social experience to correctly interpret the world outside the home or community exposes the minority language speaker to cognitive dissonance. Adrienne Rich described this unsettling experience:

> When someone with the authority of a teacher, say, describes the world and you are not in it, there is a moment of psychic disequilibrium, as if you looked into a mirror and saw nothing. (Quoted in Rosaldo, 1989)

What are the short and long-term consequences of such disequilibrium? Does the lack of social support for one's identity lead, as Erikson (1963) suggests, to pathology and as a consequence to incarceration? Can the child offset this effect by discarding the old-world view and adopting an entirely new one? Or, does he or she add a new vision of self to a pantheon of identities? Anzaldúa's work (1987, 1990) helped answer these questions.

Anzaldúa (1990) proposed a meaning of identity that approximates the notion of soul. Driven by the need to give voice to the internal "subject of our discourses" and the need to cast off "masks" imposed by outside social forces, identity emerges in the "interfacing" of multiple personas. As individuals experiment with new conceptions of self in relation to old or new social situations, one or another identity emerges. A convert, for example, uses the ideological language of the conversion narrative to create a vision of the transformed self. The narrative itself also provides the context for resolving old conflicts that initiated the conversion in the first place (Stromberg, 1990). The "subject of our discourses," or in Erikson's terminology, the "unity of self," mediates all the possible vistas offered by any combination of language, culture and sense of self. Vague and illusory forms of self that do not re-affirm a unity of self are thus rejected.

In constructing a sense of identity, bilinguals have at least three options within a monolingual–multilingual continuum: they can form a strong ethnic identity, assume the identity of the dominant group, or develop a bifocal or multifocal view of self. Those who opt for the first alternative choose "well-defined, specific identities that act as protective cages hindering diffusion, depression, disintegration of a vulnerable personality" (LaPonce, 1987, p. 45). This strategy is especially probable when minority status and language are challenged and the individual retreats to an ethnic position. We recognize this identity as the "ethnic nationalist" ideal type personified by Malcom X, Reyes Tijerina (a land rights activists from New Mexicano), and Russell Means in contemporary American Indian history.

The second option available to bilinguals is assimilation into the dominant group. Richard Rodriguez (1983), Linda Chavez (1991), and Rosalie Porter (1990) are celebrated cases of individuals who have embraced the dominant, "public" identity and have rejected their cultural and linguistic distinctiveness to great personal advantage. Many others, however, find that trading in their ethnic culture and language exacts too high a cost. Among the Asian and Latino students enrolled in the practicum undergraduate course that serves *La Clase Mágica*, a strikingly high proportion lament sacrificing or "giving up" their native language and culture for that of the White, English-speaking majority. These students describe themselves as feeling adrift, not fully accepted in either culture.

A third identity option allows the self to flow in and out of two or more sets of norms and expectations. Although, the attempt to participate in more than one disparate cultural system, can leave the bilingual in a continuous state of psychological tension, there are also some benefits to this state of fluidity. Canadian French–English bilinguals, for example, regularly participate in two distinct social networks where activities and identities are often in competition. They must continually resolve conflicts that grow out of the clash between the two cultures of which they are a part (Heller, 1987). Although this daily exercise is stressful, it appears workable. According to Heller, Canadian bilingual adolescents lay "the foundation for the development of a stable position on the "frontier" between French and English by breaking down barriers with jokes and code-switching" (p. 195). This approach to intercultural relations accords these young people a sense of accomplishment and social ease.

Whether individuals choose a "native" sense of self or a shift to a "dominant" identity, or even assume a persona that is variable, they nevertheless experience both loss and gain. All three modes of adaptation imply an increased sense of belonging and solidarity; all three also suggest some level of sacrifice. The decision to assume either a native or dominant identity, for example, precludes other possibilities. Secure in his or her choice, the individual shrugs off feelings of guilt or disloyalty when confronting other possibilities. When the decision is imposed, however, as it is for minority students at school, the individual is compelled to assume a specific identity and has to reconcile to an absence of self; to a "darkened mirror" incapable of self-reflection. On the other hand, the decision to bridge cultural systems by developing two or more seemingly separate ways of seeing oneself also exacts a burden on the individual. Compromise yields deliberate and masterful participation as Heller (1987) pointed out, but it is the bilingual who is incumbent to make the shift rather than the monolingual or the social context. Still, of the three modes of adaptation, the last is the most desirable in terms of success in school. In spite of the potential tensions and stresses, this strategy represents a cultural gain, not a loss. This is especially true when the individual is not compelled to relinquish the language and culture "closest to the heart."

We might ask ourselves what the gains and losses might be if the context were one in which both languages and cultures held equal status? What sense of self would develop in this "third space," where opposing discourses merge in a transformative dialogue (Gutierrez, Rymes, & Larson, 1995)? Does the need for a unified self compel individuals to maintain a "native," "dominant" identity, or does a fusion occur, so that the self represents neither one nor the other but something new and transformed? A careful review of the data on two long-term participants of *La Clase Mágica* (see chapter 5 for a discussion on Rina and Carlos) helps us to understand the way learners might see themselves if their learning contexts were engineered to draw and build upon their background experiences rather than to reject them.

NEW VISTAS AND NEW EXPECTATIONS

Together the perspectives on aspects of *La Clase Mágica* that I have described allow us to reconceptualize an educational activity into a social action project. They provide us with the view of both the present state of things and the possibilities of what they could accomplish if we were to take into account the constituent parts and the multiple resources they make available for educating previously underserved populations. The project is no longer one that studies learning and development in a provisional time and context for the sake of research. Rather, it becomes a project that aims at reorganizing reality in a purposeful and expansive way. The vista, then, encompasses a community of learners constituted by participatory involvement by all members of the system. Although some roles are necessarily more asymmetrical than others, as Rogoff (1994) pointed out, the educational activity is one of active and transformative participation. The project moves forward in mutual agreement and input by members who are either mature or less mature; expert or novice, acculturated or not as acculturated. The learning that takes place for any of the participants is intricately connected to the purpose of the overall activity. All participant groups—the children, adults, undergraduate students, staff, researcher, and even the electronic entity—work together to form a concerted and forceful effort in bringing about substantive change.

It is worth noting, however, that institutional partnerships, in and of themselves, do not produce transformative and reflexive change. This type of change is achieved only through careful and deliberate action by the project's management team, who conceives and carries out the project's goals and objectives while maintaining its underlying principles. *La Clase Mágica* is about working in a community of learners that apply different frameworks for doing research, teaching, and service. The team must carefully observe that the project does not turn to "fixing the native" (i.e., changing Spanish-speaking individuals to fit a particular standard). Rather, conventional and inflexible structures of domination in language, action, and knowledge are replaced with new conceptions of what counts as knowledge, who imparts it, and how and where it is distributed. We expect that mutual relations of exchange among participants from different cultural contexts that constitute the intellectual fabric of *La Clase Mágica* will produce effective and sustainable change across each of the points of contact in which the three cultural systems—the university, the community, and the family—meet. Change is not only expected in the participants but in the contexts as well. To expect otherwise—that is, to expect change in the participants and not the contexts—is to hope for temporary and illusive change.

NOTES

[1]The National Center for Educational Statististics (http.//nces.ed.gov/pbus/9602.html) Comendium: Histotrically Black Colleges and Universities:1977-1994.

2

A New Identity and New Possibilities:
An Innovation of the Fifth Dimension

I arrived at the Laboratory of Comparative Human Cognition (LCHC) in the summer of 1989, as a UCSD Chancellor's Fellow. My interests in the home language and literacy practices of Mexicanos in other immigrant communities in California drew me almost immediately to the LCHC-sponsored Fifth Dimension. Locally, this computer-based after-school activity had already proven successful with Anglo, English-speaking elementary school children who were then its main participants. The team of LCHC researchers (headed by Michael Cole) and UCSD undergraduates who staffed the Fifth Dimension's three sites in north San Diego County had tried repeatedly, but unsuccessfully, to entice local bilingual children to join the program. Still, team members remained eager to "set up a system that would overcome existing barriers to participation in computer-based activity by minority group youths." [MA, Spring/1989]

Eventually, such a system did come into being, in the form of *La Clase Mágica*. This chapter recounts the complex process of shaping and reshaping the Fifth Dimension to accommodate the needs and interests of a *Mexicano* community, while also fitting the program within the institutional constraints of its host, a small Roman Catholic mission, and its sponsor, the University of California, San Diego (UCSD).

La Clase Mágica grew out of the conceptual and theoretical model of the Fifth Dimension rather than from an already existing bilingual computer program. I begin this chapter by briefly sketching the historical antecedents of *La Clase Mágica* dating back to its origins as a Fifth Dimension. In the following sections, I discuss the four key principles of Fifth Dimension on which *La Clase Mágica* is founded and explain their importance in the development of our project. I follow with a detailed discussion of the principles and processes that drove the development of a bilingual bicultural innovation of the parent project. I conclude with some final comments on what the adaptation process means for educating language minority populations.

THE FIFTH DIMENSION ORIGINS

I found the possibility of using the Fifth Dimension to create and study ideal learning environments for Spanish-speaking children irresistible. I was attracted by the model's deep commitment to pursuing children's optimal learning potential, an uncommon goal in the schooling practices of Spanish-speaking students in the United States. Moreover, as a design experiment, the Fifth Dimension would afford optimal conditions for developing and evaluating innovative learning environments (Brown, 1992). What would it take, I wondered as I contemplated involvement, to create a Fifth Dimension that would meet the needs of Spanish-speaking children from the local Mexicano community? And, equally important, what might a group of Spanish–English bilingual elementary school-aged children teach us about the use of the home language and culture as intellectual tools?

These questions subsequently shaped the decisions that led to the adaptation of the Fifth Dimension into a bilingual/bicultural project. They also played a part in the ongoing revisions and additions that have made, and continue to make, the program a suitable learning setting for participants from four different age groups who come from a wide range of cultural and academic backgrounds. Building on previous work (Vásquez et al., 1994), I set out, with the collaboration of key members of the service community, to create an environment that recognized the children's background experiences as intellectual tools for problem solving, negotiating tasks, and meaning-making. LCHC-sponsored research by Moll and Díaz (1987) had already pointed to the benefits of using the first language in reading activities; we sought a deeper understanding of the role(s) that language and culture (of both home and school) play in cognitive development, pedagogy, and social relations. Specifically, we wanted to know when and how the first language and culture functioned as a bridge, rather than an obstacle, to new academic knowledge and skills.

The Basic Design of the Fifth Dimension. In its earliest incarnation, the Fifth Dimension was a computer-based curriculum for academically challenged children attending an after-school academy housed in the library of an elementary school near UCSD. Efforts to develop a model system for the in-school study of learning disabilities eventually led LCHC researchers to after-school hours—where they would be free to manipulate the curriculum and relations of power to achieve maximum interaction between children and adult participants.[1] Building on the previously successful strategies of involving undergraduate students and computer-mediated games—observers had noted the "good interactions around arcade games" (p. 58), the researchers created a fictional world in which the power of adults was diminished in direct proportion to the increases in the power of the participating children (Laboratory of Comparative Human Cognition [LCHC], 1982).

As originally conceived, the fantasy world of the Fifth Dimension was loosely based on "Dungeons and Dragons (D & D)," a self-directed role-playing game that first became popular in the early 1980s. In both D & D and the Fifth Dimension, players assume the role of a character journeying through an adventure-laden fantasy world ruled by a powerful magical entity. Supported by text-based materials and engaging in continuous interaction with the magical being, participants move through a series of adventures. In Dungeons and Dragons, the adventures take place entirely in the players' imaginations; in the Fifth Dimension, the computer and board games provide the context for each adventure. In the latter, adults collude with the children in constructing a fantasy world. In both activities, the object is for each player to build his or her character into a champion of sorts who accomplishes great feats of fancy.

The fantasy world of the Fifth Dimension is represented by a maze with 20 rooms often constructed on poster board or printed on a page. To "win," a player (in the guise of a particular fantasy character) must make her or his way successfully through every room. Each room has two to three games assigned to it.[2] Each game is accompanied by specially designed "adventure cards" that detail the goals and tasks that must be completed in order to finish each particular game. Because each game may be played at any one of three levels of expertise—Beginner, Good, or Expert—the tasks and goals vary in difficulty. The role of adult collaborators (mainly UCSD undergraduates and the magical, electronic entity called "Wizard" in the Fifth Dimension) is to provide sufficient material and intellectual resources to support the children's active involvement in directing his or her progress through the task-laden labyrinth. They are encouraged (but not required) to make all game-related decisions. They decide the path they want to take through the maze, the game(s) they want to play in each room, and the level of difficulty at which they want to engage the game(s).

The Fifth Dimension design is gender neutral, challenging boys and girls equally. Moreover, because progress through the maze is self-paced, the program is accessible to children whose academic skills are limited, as well as to those who are already proficient. The Fifth Dimension is also fundamentally a social, collaborative experience; children and adults work together in a freely chosen partnership. The collaborative nature of the activities is especially important. It encourages children to believe in their capacity to act and achieve beyond their actual level of development (Litowitz, 1990). Acting as adventurers, the young players take on new roles and acquire more powerful identities (Bruner, 1990). And, because ideas and information are exchanged in a relationship where the traditional status hierarchies between children and adults are deliberately undercut, adults learn to see themselves as "older siblings" rather than as teachers or sources of final authority. They may point the way for children who want help, but they are not allowed to "take over."

Internal Modifications. In 1986, with funding from the Spencer Foundation, Michael Cole modified the program to meet the needs and interests of children from his home community in north San Diego County. The majority of this group of elementary school-aged children were Anglos from middle- to upper middle-class backgrounds.[3] Cole transplanted the organizational structure and the fantasy component of the Fifth Dimension to three sites: a boys and girls club, a daycare center, and a library. To draw the community into the operation of these sites, he conducted community-based seminars designed to create a shared knowledge base and a superstructure for linking various community organizations with UCSD's research/teaching program.[4]

In relocating the Fifth Dimension, Cole (1986) was also indirectly testing its adaptability. He hoped to assess the "potential of new information technologies to create powerful new educational systems" (p. 6) and to evaluate their effectiveness and sustainability in new institutional settings, with new populations. As part of the new initiative, Fifth Dimension programs opened in African-American communities in Chicago and New Orleans; and in Moscow, Russia, at the Institute of Psychology. The success of the new sites suggested the usefulness and appeal of the Fifth Dimension in diverse racial and linguistic communities. These locations did not, however, test the program's potential to evolve into a fully integrated, culturally relevant educational activity. Although the activity changed to accommodate the conditions of the host institution, none had bilingualism or biculturalism as its goal: Fifth Dimension participants adjusted to the activity system's underlying mainstream cultural assumptions and its monolingualism.[5] Whether the program could reflect its participants' cultural and linguistic resources or preferences remained to be seen.

From Modification to Adaptation: Laying the Groundwork for Innovation. Fortuitously, the Mexicano community of Eden Gardens (see chapter 3 for a description of Eden Gardens) is located less than a mile from the Fifth Dimension at the Boys and Girls Club, the remaining site of the original three Fifth Dimensions in 1989. Although Cole's students had surveyed the community and found it receptive and in need of educational services, attempts to draw Mexicano children into the nearby Fifth Dimension (the Boys and Girls Club site) repeatedly failed (Megi, 9/12/89).[6] Convinced that the Fifth Dimension offered a unique possibility to create "powerful educational systems," I was undaunted. Confident that the community would rise to the occasion, I set out to find a way to gain and sustain neighborhood interest in the project.

An obvious entrée into the community was St. Leo's Mission, a small Roman Catholic facility ministering to a large Spanish-speaking laity from the local neighborhood and the surrounding agricultural areas. St. Leo's is the heart of community life for *Mexicanos* in north San Diego County, drawing large numbers of people for *la misa en español* [Spanish Mass] and numerous other social and religious activities.[7]   Several undergraduates and I "hung out" at the mission for most of Fall Quarter, 1989. After Mass, we joined members of the congregation, many of whom stayed to have menudo [tripe soup] or pan dulce [sweet bread] for breakfast at the mission's kitchen and to visit with friends. We also spent time in the parking lot, visiting the mercado ambulante [market-on-wheels] that sold fruits and vegetables. These outings were useful for documenting the language use of the parishioners and identifying the leading figures in the community.

    We found that the Spanish-language Mass was the singlemost important draw for the Spanish-speaking laity.[8]   Every Sunday, in near-native Spanish, the attending (Anglo) priest at St. Leo's delivered a "homily-lecture."[9]   Stepping down from the pulpit, with a felt-tipped pen in hand and still speaking in Spanish, Father Kaicher outlined the structure of the mass and its significance on a posterboard located in front of the altar (MRA 10/28/89).[10]   In addition to the obvious importance of Spanish in the Mass, we found that it was also the language of conviviality among the congregation. Greetings. gossip, jokes—all the before- and after-Mass exchanges—took place in Spanish.

    Through our presence in the community on Sundays, we were able to enlist the support of María Lourdes Durán, the catechism director, and María Nuñez, the mission's receptionist, two high-profile leaders in Eden Gardens. These women were at the pulse of community activity, familiar with children's school schedules and well-known and respected by children and adults alike. Mrs. Durán and Ms. Nuñez immediately perceived the educational value of our proposal and offered to broker negotiations for space and equipment with Church personnel. Their excellent relations with Fr. Kaicher clinched the decision to open the new site at St. Leo's Mission and—more importantly—fixed "las computadoras" ["the computers," as the program was initially called] in the future of mission activities. The new program was given a temporary location inside the mission itself while the house trailers located on the mission's property were being remodeled. Once the trailers were ready, las computadoras would share the new space with a local Head Start program that the mission also hosted.

The Early Sessions of the New Site.   On Tuesday, January 23, 1990, after weeks of preparation, during which Mrs. Dúran and Ms. Nuñez were trained (at LCHC) to use computer and telecommunication technology, the new Fifth Dimension opened as *La Clase Mágica*. In numerous preparatory sessions with children and their parents, the Fifth Dimension had taken on a different character. as these community members took an ever-increasing role in planning for the new site. Early in the proceedings, Mrs. Durán and Ms. Nuñez suggested a name change, explaining that they found the notion of a "fifth dimension" ambiguous and difficult to explain. It was a change that propelled the new "fifth" into a new dimension, radically affecting the make-over of the maze which embodies the fantasy world of the Fifth Dimension. Spanish-language names and titles of historical figures in Mexican culture began to appear on the map of the maze. In taking such an active part in the development of the new site, these parents and children (i.e., "the community") had begun what we eventually came to recognize as the critically important process of redefining *La Clase Mágica's* approach to its own longevity.

On the afternoon of the first session, 22 elementary school-aged children spilled off a district school bus, running and chattering noisily.[11] They were eager to "play computers"—which at the time consisted of four Apple 2Es, one IBM computer, and a Texas Instrument game, all cobbled together out of bits and pieces donated from other sites in the area and assembled on four tables in the aisle directly in front of the mission's alter. Children crowded around the computers, squeezing in at the foot of the altar and filling the pews behind the computers. Three UCSD students "borrowed" from Cole's undergraduate course were invaluable in helping to harness the exuberance of the children and diminish some of the chaos that swept through the normally quiet sanctuary that first afternoon.[12] The students' ability to work effectively with children, noted by LCHC collaborators in the early stages of the Fifth Dimension, and at other sites, was again observed as they patiently and ever so tenderly attended to the multitude of eager children.

We were confronted with a wide array of problems in the initial stages of program implementation. Some sessions went relatively smoothly; others were chaotic. However, limited resources—discussed further in the following section—was the problem that both the student assistants and the research staff agreed was most pressing. Not having a permanent space was a great burden, as well. For 2 years, we had to assemble and disassemble the site for each of the three sessions we ran per week. During the first year, when *La Clase Mágica* was set up in the aisle in front of the alter, we stored our equipment in a candle closet at the side of the sanctuary. When we were relocated to the mission's kitchen the following year, the equipment had to be stored outside, in a shed. Technical problems with the hardware or the software or both continued to plague many sessions. Communication, typically conducted through telecommunication with the Wizard (later called *El Maga* at *La Clase Mágica*), was sporadic as well. The first exchange between a participant and the Wizard took place almost a month after the program began as we sat on the priest's bed—he had loaned us his telephone line. A student's fieldnotes reported that a child wrote to the Wizard to ask "him" questions about the computer game, "Match Game," and about "his" personal life [AB, 2/19/90].

The undergraduate assistants played a critical role in the adaptation process. Their sometimes startlingly naïve perspectives, often informed by popular culture and relative inexperience with minority populations, pointed the research staff toward areas that needed further development and consideration. For example, when students innocently referred to *La Clase Mágica's* young participants as "my children," and "my tutees," the research staff reconsidered the mechanisms operating at the field site that supported the role of the student assistant as an authority/teacher/tutor instead of a collaborator. When students noted fluctuations in the number of children attending the sessions and in the level and degree of engagement among those who did come, we respected their insight and used their judgments as a foundation for shaping solutions to the problems they were identifying at the site. When they repeatedly observed that "children are not following the maze," that the "site activities are too disorganized" and that there were "too many children per undergraduate student," we reviewed the evidence and decided that these were "growing pains" typical of the start-up phase of any new program, rather than being symptomatic of more serious problems. And, when the same comments were voiced later by visiting undergraduate students who normally assisted at the Fifth Dimension down the street, the research staff concluded that the students' comments reflected a cultural difference between the two sites: relatively higher levels of noise and activity was interpreted as confusion and disarray. Importantly, the students also helped us to understand the cross-cultural stereotypes that were operating in placing students in a minority community with a reputation for violence and drugs. Fueled by the media's skewed portrayal of Latino communities, many students were initially afraid to enter the community. Many still had joined the project thinking that the conditions of the home and community unequivocally explain underachievement and social behavior. Many of the first quarters were spent separating truth from fiction with selected students conducting a variety of studies on safety and interethnic relations in the community.[13]

LA CLASE MAGICA'S DOUBLE IDENTITY

After many additions and revisions, *La Clase Mágica* both endured and thrived. The reasons for its success are complex and interdependent, but for analytical purposes, they may be divided into two broad categories. First, *La Clase Mágica* is more than simply "modeled after" the proven structure of the Fifth Dimension. It is an innovation of the Fifth Dimension. The process of adaptation took on a life of its own, dramatically affecting the goals and design of the overall project, yet, many of the basic features of the Fifth Dimension remain solidly in place. Paradoxically, it is these same features that have also given rise to *La Clase*

Mágica's individuality—its identity as a culturally relevant approach to pedagogy, research, and ultimately to social action.

The second important source of *La Clase Mágica's* success is the cultural relevancy the program acquired in its dynamic, open framework used to adapt the Fifth Dimension to the local community. *La Clase Mágica* blends interests, goals, and practice in a continuous process of adaptation, implementation, and innovation. Initially, it also represented the coming together of a small group of talented and progressive young people who served as the project's staff. The young staff brought a commitment to innovation and diversity and the willingness to discuss and debate ideas openly at a very critical time of the adaptation process.

Next, I begin by outlining the features shared by *La Clase Mágica* and the Fifth Dimension and then move to a discussion of the features that sustain *La Clase Mágica* as a unique, culturally relevant project.

Building on the Fifth Dimension Model. *La Clase Mágica* naturally builds on both the organizational and theoretical framework of the Fifth Dimension model. It retained four key principles of the Fifth Dimension in its transformation to a new identity and new possibilities:

1. A protean nature that adapts to local conditions;
2. A mixture of play and education instantiated in a computer-based fantasy world;
3. A culture of collaborative learning; and
4. A focus on learning and development.

Each of these principles is discussed separately.

The Protean Nature. The ability of the Fifth Dimension model to adapt to the local conditions made it possible for *La Clase Mágica* to accommodate both the new institutional context represented by the mission and the non-Anglo cultural and linguistic characteristics of its new constituency. Moreover, many of the structural changes discussed in the next chapter are directly related to this flexibility. The successful addition of new aspects of *La Clase Mágica* (e.g., the Wizard Assistant Club, the adult computer class, and the Head Start program) underscores the Fifth Dimension's inherent ability to adapt to the local conditions.[14] This flexibility is essential. Whereas the constraints of the new environment and target population might have spelled the end for a more conventionally structured program, *La Clase Mágica* could respond creatively. As long as tables and chairs, computers, and a telephone line were available at the mission, we could convene our activities in front of the altar, in the kitchen, in the storage closet, or in any of the trailers situated on the grounds of the St.

Leo's property. Similarly, the activities and artifacts can be (and are) continuously re-arranged to suit the changing context and changing needs of participants (Cole & Nicolopoulou, 1991; Nicolopoulou & Cole, 1993); at the same time, the project as a whole can (and does) change form and content.

Over the 22 academic quarters covered in this book, *La Clase Mágica* developed in depth and breath from its predecessor. The first adaptations were cultural and linguistic in nature attempting to reflect the background experience of the population we were targeting. The curriculum materials and interactional routines developed beyond the focus on mainstream culture and English language of the original model and incorporated aspects of Mexican culture and history as well as Spanish language, the chief characteristics of the community we were attempting to serve. The second adaptations were structural as we responded to the social climate of the community and the work of the UC Latino Eligibility Task Force.[15]   In 1993, the Task Force requested us to step back and reflect upon the impact of our efforts on K–12 achievement and the underrepresentation of minorities in the UC system. This reflection expanded the breath of the project's goals. In answering that request, we began to reconsider the structure and outcomes of the adaptation process, evaluating their potential as a framework for pursuing our great goal of affecting change in minority student achievement.

The changes in the organizational structure led us to re-examine the seminal work of Moll, Anderson, and Díaz (1985) on institutional relations. The ingenious design of the horizontal and vertical integration of resources developed by these scholars formed part and parcel of the organizational structure of the university—community partnerships that constituted the Distributive Literacy Consortium, and the collective Fifth Dimension projects to which *La Clase Mágica* belonged. The cross-system structure was designed to funnel resources to local minority children by organizing the resources of relevant institutions and training minority undergraduate students in a rigorous academic program that would place them back in the community to help others. They envisioned intervening at specific mediational points and "making sure that the activities that benefit students in one context are linked through related activities to other contexts of importance to students' advancement" (Moll et al., 1985 p. 12). Superimposed over the expanding organizational structure of *La Clase Mágica*, this framework brought into view a "pipeline of qualified students" partnered by a series of interconnecting age-appropriate activities. For *La Clase Mágica*, connecting "relevant contexts for student achievement" as Moll, Díaz and Anderson proposed meant connecting the activities of preschool children in the Head Start version of *La Clase Mágica* with separate activities designed for elementary school age children, adolescents who had advanced to second level participation, and adults from the local community. The fifth age group, the undergraduates along with the academics participating in the LCHC seminar made explicit the recycling of knowledge and other understandings that were taking place across age groups, institutions, cultures, and languages. Prompted by this perspective, we saw the age-appropriated activities of *La Clase Mágica* as beneficial to the children's academic progress in the schooling system.

This conceptualization of our efforts shifted our perspective to a life-span approach, linking intergenerational levels of participants in mutual relations of exchange (see Fig. 2.1). In each context (e.g., site, seminar, undergraduate course, seminar), the participants' intellectual and material resources are brought to bear on context-specific issues related to minority education. As the researchers move across the cultural systems of the university and community, the leading activity of each of the embedded contexts changes from research to teaching to learning, and back again (see Griffin & Cole, 1984 for a discussion on leading activity). For the child participants, the leading activity cycles back and forth from play to mastering any number of skill-building activities, such as literacy and computation, to the social roles they play in assisting adults and peers. Opening zones of possibilities in which the individual and the context can achieve an optimal potential according to the demands of the moment (Moll & Díaz, 1987; Moll & Greenberg, 1990) became the goals of the methodology, theory, practice, and in particular, the interactional routines of *La Clase Mágica*.

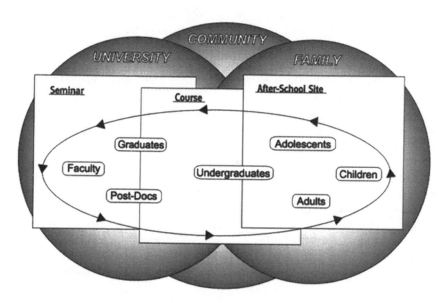

Figure 2.1. Intergenerational process of exchange.

This framework fosters system-wide change by creating a two-way flow that transforms the relevant contexts in all three cultural systems. Represented as the encircling arrow in Figure 2.1, this change occurs at the organizational (i.e., the contexts and cultural systems) and the individual level among the participants. Organizationally, the program gradually begins to reflect more and more the effects of the multiple perspectives, goals, and resources embodied by the diverse groups who are its participants. Individually, people engage in dynamic relations of exchange that help them to interpret and act upon the underlying social relationships and norms of the institution and the Mexicano community. For example, in the interactions with their older collaborators, the youngest participants acquire a familiarity with and an enthusiasm for higher education at the same time that the insights gained by the researchers, undergraduate, and graduate students are cycled back into the adaptation process, impacting the research focus; the structure and content of the undergraduate course; and the discourse of the community of scholars to which we belonged. Eligibility to higher education for prospective students from diverse backgrounds is made possible as well as some degree of qualitative change in the educational contexts that receive them—the home, school, and community—as well as the university.

The Computer-Based Fantasy World. The use of the maze to represent the fantasy world of the Fifth Dimension is a key element in *La Clase Mágica's* success. *El Laberinto Mágico* [The Maze], was adapted to include Spanish language and Mexicano culture, became the first and most important artifact to promote change in both the program and the children. As in any other Fifth Dimension activity, the maze organizes the activities at the site; but, in addition, at *La Clase Mágica*, it provides a framework for referencing the children's background experiences—creating the possibility of linking old and new knowledge crucial for language and cognitive development (Krashen & Biber, 1988). The maze demonstrated the positive impact of such links early on, and thus led us to make other changes. For example, we revised accompanying artifacts (e.g., constitution, task cards, journey log) to more explicitly integrate the children's multiple resources.

In many respects, it is the adapted maze that makes possible an environment in which bilingualism and biculturalism are the norm. When the children take on the role of "actor" (Bruner, 1990) and begin moving through the many rooms of the maze, making choices and completing tasks, they do so in a bilingual fantasy world. Rather than experiencing a sense of lack, as English learners typically do at school, children at *La Clase Mágica* can cast themselves as masters of reading, writing, and game playing in either language. Fantasy allows them to see themselves as invincible, or at least as more capable than they really are (Litowitz, 1990). At minimum, the adapted maze allows the children to view their background experiences as intellectual resources that are valuable assets in their fantasy quests.

The segment of video transcript reproduced below demonstrates the position of power children assume as they move through the maze. In this excerpt, the speakers are Natalie (N), a 7-year-old Mexican origin female from Eden Gardens, and LB, a male, African-American UCSD graduate student in his late 20s. The two have just settled down to play Language Explorer, a Spanish-language, reading-readiness computer game in which the players match words with their corresponding pictures. Even though her literacy skills are not fully developed, Natalie, a long-time participant of *La Clase Mágica*, is making use of the resources available to her—her own oral fluency and literacy in Spanish:

LB:	Have you played this before?
N:	Uh-huh. Tell me. Next.
LB:	Uhhhm. This one.
N:	What does it say?
LB:	El cono.
N:	El cono. Which one of these?
LB:	Uhm, the cone. That one.
N:	This one?
LB:	Uh-huh.
N:	You're wrong. I know these answers.
LB:	I think I'm right.
N:	Ok, this one now. This one.
LB:	What's that? La flecha.
N:	Flecha. Ok, which one now? But it is right there. Which one you think it is?
LB:	I don't know what that word means, though.
N:	Flecha. It's (drawing in the air) . . . arrows.

In the remainder of the interaction (not reproduced here), the collaboration continues, deepening as the two move through the game. Even this short segment above makes clear that it is Natalie who is in control. She directs LB to do the reading for her and asserts her mastery by proclaiming, "I know the answers." Her Spanish skills are important. The ability to draw on Spanish as a tool to make meaning gives her the upper hand over LB, whose limited knowledge of Spanish sometimes makes him uncertain how to proceed. Natalie, on the other hand, simply skips over a question when she is unsure of the answer. She pushes on, "Ok, this one now. This one."

Culture of Collaborative Learning. The exchange between Natalie and LB also highlights a third principle that makes *La Clase Mágica* a Fifth Dimension and at the same time demonstrates its special cultural relevance. The "virtual culture of collaborative learning" (Nicolopoulou & Cole, 1993) describes a system of relations that is made possible by a unique coordination between theory and practice. The organizational structure and the fantasy component of the Fifth Dimension create a "third space" (Gutiérrez, Rymes, & Larson, 1995) in which adults and children can re-negotiate meaning as equal and collaborative partners. Knowledge and skills drawn from the worlds of childhood, university life, ethnic group affiliation, and mainstream (Anglo) culture are dynamically exchanged between adults and children and made one's own. Adults share their wider knowledge of the world and more sophisticated problem-solving techniques, whereas children exchange their more detailed knowledge of the cultural conventions of *La Clase Mágica* and of their cultural group.[16]

The convergence of these multiple worlds and the leveling of hierarchical relations among the players is further ensured by the presence of an electronic entity called the "Wizard" in the Fifth Dimension and "*El Maga*" in *La Clase Mágica*. Multilingual, ageless, and of indeterminate gender, *El Maga* is the only authority figure in the system. By reducing the residual hierarchy in adult–child interactions, *El Maga* makes possible mutual relations of exchange between two age groups that conventionally assume a hierarchical relationship in learning settings.

Besides facilitating the co-construction of knowledge, as exemplified by the interaction between LB and Natalie, these relations foster the emergence of a new picture of the "other." For the adults, minority group members cease to be the threatening, unacculturated aliens portrayed by the media. And the children come to see the adults, often Anglo or Asian, and occasionally, African-American, as people with whom they may talk and play freely, breaking down the traditional barriers based on age, social position, and ethnicity. Importantly, these same conceptions of equality and full participation are carried over into the other contexts in the activity system of *La Clase Mágica*. Thus, for example, community representatives and university personnel meet at the negotiation table as equals. With the community and the university perceiving one another as valued and respected partners, active participation and interest on the part of the community is sustainable. This, in turn, further legitimates *La Clase Mágica* as a culturally relevant approach to learning and development.

A Focus on Learning and Development. In the Fifth Dimension, all elements of the activity system are committed to promoting children's intellectual and social growth. This focus also characterizes the efforts of *La Clase Mágica* and contributes to its uniqueness as a culturally relevant program. In both systems, adult–child interactions are organized to function within the individual learner's zone of proximal development, a space Vygotsky (1978) defined as the difference between what a child can do alone and that which he or she can do in collaboration with a more knowledgeable partner. At *La*

ClaseMágica, the adults ask questions, help identify the main idea, define technical vocabulary, provide visual representations, and trade roles with the children to help them achieve their "grandiosity and omnipotence" (Litowitz, 1990, p. 137). Children come to see themselves as more capable when they are genuinely involved in directing their own development rather than simply being recipients of information(Cole & Nicolopoulou, 1991, p. 41). All efforts are made to promote children's growth according to their own aspirations and abilities rather than through an "imposition from above and from outside" (Dewey, 1938, p. 18).

In the context of *La Clase Mágica*, the focus on learning and development centers on enhancing cognition by building on the children's prior experiences and linking these to new information to create new understandings. In contrast to the typical classroom, the primary concern of *La Clase Mágica* is not to help "children learn English so that they can be successful in mainstream society." Rather, the aim is to maximize cognitive development by engaging the children in the task of verbally posing and solving problems that emerge out of game-play. Silence, whether it is owing to absorption in the activities or to limited fluency (in either language) is discouraged. It does not matter which language or combination of languages the children use to express themselves; what is important is that they learn to talk through their game-play using Spanish or English as resources.

Shaping a Bilingual–Bicultural Innovation. The four key characteristics outlined before made it possible for us to adapt the new Fifth Dimension to the local conditions. More was needed, however, to develop a unique, culturally relevant project, namely an ongoing orientation toward and commitment to ethnic and linguistic diversity. Our specific focus on Spanish–English bilingual children from a *Mexicano* background greatly influenced the approach we took in shaping a design experiment relevant to the new context and target population. Although the immediate goal was to create an innovative learning environment for local bilingual children, the longer-term objective was to address the persistent and widespread history of failure experienced by Mexican origin children in American schools (Stanton-Salazar et al., 1995; Vásquez, 1996). Our goals were not only to help the children we were working with, but also to go beyond our day-to-day activities to formulate ways in which elementary, middle, and high-school level teachers would come to better understand and appreciate bilingual learners. The UC Links project detailed in chapter 3 demonstrates the possibilities for realizing this long term goal through a systematic and comprehensive approach.

Five principles specific to *La Clase Mágica* distinguish it from previous re-iterations of Fifth Dimension. These extensions to the parent project support its efforts to create the infrastructure capable of interrupting the continuous cycle of academic failure among minority learners in the United States. Not only do these new principles shape the projects' cultural and linguistic relevance, they also shape our approach to research, teaching, and service, the threefold mission of the University of California:

1. A recognition perspective in research and practice
2. A focus on multiplicity and diversity
3. A commitment to deliberate and continual change
4. A partnership with community members themselves
5. A multigenerational approach

A Recognition Perspective. Building on previous efforts (Vásquez et al., 1994), we approached the adaptation task from a perspective that emphasizes the cultural and linguistic resources intrinsic to the given social situation as well as the underlying dynamics that mobilize them. Rather than using a framework that showcased the gaps and flaws in the intellectual development of social actors, we wanted to document the multiple knowledge sources that converge in interactions with bilingual participants. Thus, we began by recognizing the social realities of bilingual children and the multiple learning experiences they encounter as they moved across the various cultural settings that are part of their daily lives. We believed that if the new learning environment was to reflect the lived experiences of these children, it had to recognize "the dynamic interactions of exchange between two or more cultures rather than focus on two opposing, mutually exclusive systems" (Vásquez et al., 1994, p.12). This perspective necessarily locates our efforts at the boundaries of two cultures and languages rather than only in the home or school. This vantage point prompts us to ask what a child can do rather than what he or she cannot do. Subsequently, it leads us to account for the range of resources these children bring to the learning setting and helps us build them into new social conditions. We are able to "capture similarities in language use across various contexts, the convergence of multiple knowledge sources in a single context, and the uniqueness of language use practices fostered by Mexicano culture" (p. 11).

A Focus on Multiplicity and Diversity. This recognition of the multiple cultural and linguistic resources of bilingual–bicultural children has shaped the focus of our inquiry from the beginning (Vásquez, 1989; Vásquez et al., 1994). We have paid close attention to how, when. and why the children at *La Clase Mágica* draw on their first or second language and their home or acquired culture as they solve problems. Placing restrictions on children's choice of language or on cultural referents would not only contradict our basic premise that children's background experiences are valuable intellectual tools, but would also contradict our goal of enhancing the children's cognitive development in favor of assimilation. Supported by Krashen and Biber's (1988) assertions that comprehensible input (use of language children understand) leads to second language acquisition, we gave Spanish language and *Mexicano* culture a status equal to that of English and mainstream culture. The principle of collaborative learning also prompted us to support children's choice of language use regardless of their fluency in either English or Spanish. Our concern was not with privileging one language over another but with providing children access to the most effective and readily available tools. Thus, for example, if a child chooses to use English, despite having a greater fluency in Spanish, we support that choice just as fully as the decision to use Spanish despite English competency.

This aspect of our theoretical orientation has had far-reaching effects on the project as a whole. In discussions among *La Clase Mágica's* small staff, the commitment to multiplicity and diversity prompted on-going deliberations about the design, goals, and effects of our efforts. As a result, our program is marked by ongoing cycles of innovation, reflection, and transformation. The desire to identify and understand the resources that the children draw on in interactions that occur at the site led us to an intense scrutiny of every level of the system.

During the phase in which we made the most extensive revisions in the new project, the staff consisted of four undergraduate women (one Anglo, two Chicanas, and one Mexicana), Mrs. Durán and Ms. Nuñez (both Mexican nationals) and me, a Chicana professor. The staff members' understanding of and commitment to each other and to the recognition perspective was crucial to sustaining the philosophy of inclusion that characterized the efforts of *La Clase Mágica*. Our discussions, often painful, bore little resemblance to the standard— and paradoxical pattern of academic exchanges: Namely, that teachers should validate others' personal experiences from a distant, "objective" position, if at all. Integrating the goals and objectives we had for the children and community into our own behavior was the first of many occasions in which we "collapsed the paradox" (i.e., went beyond a vicarious experience and actually played out the theoretical objectives ourselves: see chap. 4 for details) at *La Clase Mágica*. Our basic assumption that all children have valuable background experiences forced us first to examine and then to extract our own diversity for the language and cultural resources we needed as we groped our way toward making *La Clase Mágica* culturally relevant.

Diversity, however, can be a double-edged sword: Great possibilities for understanding and achieving multifaceted perspectives are often coupled with great opportunities for disagreement and misunderstanding. Fortunately, team members opted for working "through issues together, coming to a deeper understanding of their own cultures and identities" as Tricia Henry (1993) pointed out in a paper she delivered at the National Association for Chicano and Chicana Studies Annual Conference. It was a choice rather than to attack each other for their differences. This approach to decision making served as a prototype for subsequent meetings with institutional and community representatives: We set aside a great deal of time to establish open, cordial interpersonal relations, and we asked participants to share their personal histories in order to build a common understanding and trust. Most importantly, we accepted disagreement as part of the collaborative process (Matusov, 1996). This approach also specified that the adaptation process would be based on the resources available in the local setting, a strategy that accords with Ferdman (1990) and McLaughlin's (1989) prescriptions for effective first-language literacy programs.

A Commitment to Deliberate and Continual Change. Changes, small and large were made deliberately and continually across the first 22 academic quarters of *La Clase Mágica's* operations. We learned early and conclusively that stasis was neither attainable nor advisable. The changes we undertook involved more than the simple act of translating materials from English to Spanish. Over time, we revised the philosophical and pedagogical foundations of our program. The adaptation we set into motion did not then, or later, seek to substitute one culture for the other. Rather, the goal was to create optimal possibilities. We shaped the language we used and the actions we took to reflect an overarching commitment to and respect for diverse views and experiences. Along with the modifications we were obliged to make as part of the Fifth Dimension's accommodation to its new setting, we deliberately fine tuned the language and activities to fit our program's specific goals and objectives. Thus, the process of fitting the program to the local community simultaneously transformed *La Clase Mágica's* philosophical and material fabric.

A careful review of data[17] collected between fall quarter 1989 and spring quarter 1996 reveals three major phases of adaptation. In the first revision (1989–1990), we changed the names of the rooms of the Fifth Dimension maze from countries of the world to Spanish words that referenced Mexican history and culture (see Fig. 2.2 for the two mazes used at the time). For example, we re-labeled the room called "Australia," making it "Garibaldi," the name of a public square in Mexico City well known for its Maríachi bands. The changes in terminology were aimed at giving the children access to the cultural world of their ancestors as a resource they could draw on as they made their imaginary journey through *El Laberinto Mágico*. We hoped that substituting their own cultural history for the Fifth Dimension's references to a largely unfamiliar international geography would help the players make a connection between the world of the games and their other sources of knowledge.

Our hopes were confirmed in practice. Even when Spanish was only "sprinkled" through the accompanying materials, its presence prompted children to use their background experiences to personalize and visualize the games they were playing. The next example, an excerpt from an undergraduate student's fieldnotes, is representative of how the adapted materials accompanying the

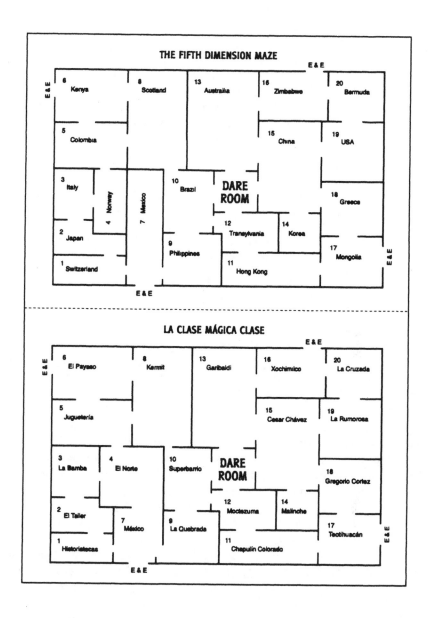

Figure 2.2. Fifth Dimension and *La Clase Magica* original mazes.

games facilitated children's use of prior knowledge. The fragment relates dynamics that took place around the English language-based computer game, Botanical Gardens. We had renamed the game as *El Jardin de Abuelita* and had added a few Spanish terms to the task cards that accompany the game.

> We first went to the seed room so that the girls could choose a seed to grow María wanted the "Matrushka," which sort of looked like a bush. I asked María , "How come you decided to choose that one?" María replied, "Porque se me hace bonita. Y cuando vamos a Mexico yo miro esas plantas (Because it seems pretty to me. And, when we go to Mexico I see these plants)." That seemed like a logical explanation to me. Lisa decided to choose the Seattle Rose because, as she claimed, "Las rosas me encantan [I love roses]." [IT/03/06/90]

Including Spanish words and references to Mexicano culture clearly made the material more comprehensible to the children.[18] A question that troubled the research staff, however, was how much incorporation of the children's home language and culture was "enough" to make a difference in their learning, language maintenance, or identity formation? At the time, we had neither the financial nor the linguistic resources to translate all the materials into Spanish. And, even in the absence of such restrictions, we were not convinced that it was necessary to undertake a complete translation. Our goal had been to create opportunities for children to access their prior knowledge as a link to new information. We were not trying to foster either language acquisition or language maintenance, although we were in full support of both. We were also well aware that successful participation in social and civic life in the United States dictated the acquisition of English as a desired outcome. What remained unclear was how much effort we would need to commit to translating the materials in order to produce the desired result of improved cognitive development.[19]

To answer the question of how much change was enough, we initiated a second round of revisions beginning in spring quarter 1991. This time we made deeper structural changes, focusing our attention on the "task cards" or guide sheets that accompany the games in each room of the maze (see Fig. 2.3 for a sample of a card used during this time period). The task card for "Marketplace," a computer game in which children must take on the role of vendors, for example, was moved to a more thematically appropriate room entitled "Xochimilco" (Henry, 1993).[20] We re-labeled the game MARKET PLACE/ PLAZA DEL MERCADO and changed the context section of the task card from evoking a world of selling for profit to an experience at a farmers' market, common in the lives of the children from Mexicano backgrounds. To evoke the marketplace, we included an example of the sing-song street poetics of vendors: "Vendo manzanas, vendo plantas, vendo limonada. Cual te falta?" [I sell apples, I sell plants, I sell lemonade. Which one do you need?]. This type

XOCHIMILCO   ROOM 13b
MARKET PLACE/ PLAZA DEL MERCADO

Vendo manzanas, vendo plantas, vendo limonada. Cual te falta? You are about to
open a stand at the open market. As a group project you will be selling apples,
plants or lemonade. Try to find the best selling price for your product. Read the
instructions for each level so you can get all the HINTS to reach your goal.
BUENA SUERTE! HAPPY SELLING.

BEGINNER: In this level you will sell apples (Choose #1) to pay for the folkloric costumes you will be using at the Cinco de Mayo Fiesta. After you decorate your sign with your name you are ready to sell apples!! Try different prices to figure out the best price. Keep experimenting with the price until you make at least 8.00 dollars profit.

When you've made that much, write to El Maga bout how many apples you sold, the money you charged, and your best price. Tell El Maga about the costume you wore and the region of Mexico it belongs. Which costume in your group was the most expensive and why?.

GOOD: For this level you will be selling plants (Choose #2). Your classmates have slected you to be the class business manager. You will need to make to make enough of a profit for your class trip to a live performance of Don Quijote.

You will have the opportunity to advertise your plants. Pay special attention to the number of signs you will need to use. When you've made a profit of at least 10.00 dollars write to your Wizardly business partner, El Maga, and tell whether the number of sings affected your profits and why.

EXPERT: Your church group has decided that they want to eat pan dulce and chocolate after church to celebrate la fiesta de la Virgen de Gualalupe. They decide to sell lemonade after church (Choose #3). Your goal is to make a profit of 15.00 dollars. When you've made that much write to El Maga about plants for the fiesta and what you will need.

Do you think spending money on advertising was a wise business choice? Tell El Maga about your best sign. Was this the best way to attract customers?

Figure 2.4. El Mercado task card.

55

of vendor's litany is regularly heard in predominantly Mexican neighborhoods in this country and in Mexico.

During research team meetings, we discussed the labeling and the content of each card in order to arrive at a framework that satisfied our standards without overstepping our limited linguistic and economic resources. Even with the support we received from our sister team in the Bilingual Partnership of the Distributive Literacy Consortium, tailoring the Fifth Dimension materials to capture the context of the lives of the children at our site was slow and labor-intensive.[21] We added several more games in Spanish and we introduced two rooms specifically designed to give children opportunities to incorporate games and activities from their homes. We also created two noncomputer activities and placed them in different rooms. In Historiateca (a neologism for story room), children are asked to share stories from home, school, or community, or to create their own tales. Actividades tradicionales [traditional activities] contains a variety of traditional Mexican games such as Escaleras y Serpientes [Snakes & Ladders] and lotería [a bingo-type picture-board game].

During the latter part of this phase of adaptation, we sought to integrate Spanish more evenly across the four-level structure of the task card—the title, the context paragraph, the play level, and the reflection section (see the left column of the sample task card in Fig. 2.4). We added Spanish terms in each of these sections, often renaming the game and contextualizing the game environment in relation to Mexicano culture.

The play level is an important section of the task cards. It signals to the player the level at which the activity can be performed—beginner, good, or expert. We revisited this section of each of the task cards and adapted it to reflect the cognitive ability of younger children who were attending the site. Spanish terms and, when appropriate, cultural referents were included but the text stayed closely linked to the world of the games. The adaptation of the reflection section of the task card, on the other hand, contextualized the game's tasks even more specifically to the kinds of activities Mexican origin children often participate in during their daily lives at school and in the community: watching a folkloric dance troupe, taking a school field trip, and celebrating the fiesta of the Catholic Virgen de Guadalupe [Virgin of Guadalupe, the patron saint of Mexico]. This fourth section of the task card provides a clear example of how the Fifth Dimension's design lends itself completely to bilingual–bicultural adaptations by motivating children to reflect on their own actions and to engage in literacy-mediated activities with the Wizard. Keying the adaptation to the children's background experiences allows them to use these experiences as stepping stones to new information and skills—in the case of *La Plaza del Mercado*, the terminology and math skills required in business.

A third revision in 1995 was completed over a period of 6 months. We fine-tuned the previous structural changes we had made in the task cards and

You are a Zookeeper at the San Diego Zoo, y acabas derecibir una promoción que te obligará a viajar a México a trabajar en el Zoologico de el Parque de Chapultepec. Antes de ir a México, necesitas aprender los nombres de los animales. Este juego te ayudará. El objeto de este juego es practicar el vocabulario Español

BEGINNER

1. Este juego es para practicar el vocabulario en Español. Primero hay que practicar, esto se hace operimiendo el ratoncito en la palabra Practise

2. Para practicar nomas oprime el ratoncito en algun lugar en el zoologico y veras como la computadora te dice como se llama en Español.
--Para regresar al principio o seguir adelante, oprime el ratoncito en las flechas que estan a los lados----

---si quieres puedes regresar al principio y leer las instrucciones oprimiendo el ratoncito en donde dice Instructions-----

3. Cuando ya te puedas mover por todo el zoologico escribele a El Maga y asi terminaras el beginner level,

GOOD

1. Felicidades por haber llegado a este nivel!!
2. In order to advance to the expert level, learn 3 other cage's of animals and their names. First review your cages of choice, and begin to learn the names of the individual animals.Once these names become familiar get ready to test yourself.
3. Go for it ! Now test yourself on those same 3 cages.(Click onto instructions for the test mode. When you are ready, click onto "TEST", begin to play!
4. When you have successfully learned 3 whole cages animal's names, you are ready to become an expert zookeeper!

EXPERT

1.AWESOME!
2.Congradulations you've made it to the Expert level
3.With all of your "expert" knowledge you are on your way to learning Spanish!
4.Find an amigo or amiga that has never played El Zoologico, and teach them about the game. If you can teach them how to play the game, that is your first step to finishing this level.
5. To become a 100% expert, you need to know all the words in the diccionary!
-go back to the instrucctions and click on diccionary to get the list of words.
6.Write to El Maga about your experince playing and teaching El Zoologico, be sure to include your name and the name of your amigo or amiga because El Maga may write you back!

Figure 2.4. The Zoo task card.

added many more games (and accompanying task cards) in Spanish (see Fig. 2.4). By fall quarter 1996, we had 15 Spanish-dominant task cards and 15 English-dominant ones. Seven cards now contained an equally balanced use of both languages. This round of adaptation differed from previous ones in two important ways. With most of the labor-intensive changes out of the way, we could now turn our attention to the incorporation of Spanish-language materials. We conducted an extensive Internet search and located 13 new bilingual computer games and activities to add to the maze. Additionally, Mrs. Durán's newly developed expertise in literacy, computer use, and pedagogy now made it possible for her to participate actively in curriculum development, a task she took over from then on.

Several other changes also took place in the intellectual orientation of *La Clase Mágica*. The terms we used to designate the community, adult collaborators, the electronic entity, and even the children themselves altered. These changes underscore the attention the research team gave to correlating language with actions. It was not sufficient to say that we were applying a new framework for understanding children's learning and development. The language that we used had to explicitly and implicitly support the new conceptions we were committed to implementing. When Spanish or Mexicano culture limited the use of a word translated from English, we concocted a new term. When an English term was close to what we wanted, we "tweaked" its meaning to better serve our purposes.

One of the earliest revisions of the vocabulary used at *La Clase Mágica* centered on the structure of the relationship between the children and the undergraduate assistants. When we first began the program, the undergraduates entered *La Clase Mágica* as "Wizard Assistants." They were asked to assist the children with the games, in a capacity much like older siblings. We soon realized, however, that this role carried with it a residual hierarchy that encouraged a didactic stance. In the early fieldnotes, undergraduates referred to the children as "my students," "my kids," and "my pupils," and they saw themselves as "wizards," "teachers," or "tutors." The undergraduates were primarily concerned with helping the children succeed in school and in mainstream society. The children, in turn, saw these young adults as "teachers" little different from the authority figures in their classrooms. Changing the college students' title to "Amigos/as" [Friends] opened up new possibilities for the students to see themselves as the children's friends and to act like playmates.

This new self-perception helped erode traditional status hierarchies and encouraged a more open and closer relationship with the children, one that allows for an exchange of world views. The following passages, excerpted from two undergraduates' fieldnotes, demonstrate the flow of information that the new relationship facilitated:

> I got a chance to talk to Norma for quite some time as we discussed
> the filling out of her form. We talked about her favorite pastime,
> horseback riding, and she was enthralled when I informed her that my
> roommate, Tracy, teaches horseback riding. I felt privileged when she
> wrote my name in the space for the question, "What makes you
> happy?" [KG/01/25/93]

> Out of the blue, Nina asked me if you need a computer to do your
> work on at college. I thought to myself what an impact college
> students have on these children, they are already thinking of college!
> I told her that some people have computers to do papers on but others
> use typewriter just as well. I also told her about the computers that
> you can use on campus. She asked me if I had a computer and I said
> yes. Then she asked me what I wanted to be, "like a doctor or
> something?" I told her that I wanted to be a psychologist. She asked
> me what that was and I told her that I wanted to help people who have
> troubles. She started telling me what she wants to be. "I want to learn
> as many languages as I can, and become a doctor and then go to
> places like Africa and help the people there." I was so impressed with
> this goal! [AD 10/22/93]

The role of Amigo/a frees the undergraduate students to enjoy
themselves too, to see the children as they see any other youngsters in the society,
and to also view themselves as learners. KG, an Anglo Amiga, expresses this
quite well:

> I thoroughly enjoyed my first encounter with *La Clase Mágica*, and
> am very excited to begin the program with the children. I hope that
> the children feel comfortable with me and that I am able to present an
> approachable and helpful amiga. I am interested in learning more
> about multiculturalism in the classroom and how different cultures
> can be integrated into the curriculum. . . . I also hope that the children
> will help me to retrieve my Spanish skills that I once had. At the
> moment, I feel a little self-conscious about speaking Spanish with
> those who are native speakers of the language. [KG/01/12/93]

In addition to assigning the undergraduates a new name and reaffirming
their role as collaborators, we also revised the terms the children used to refer to
themselves. In the Fifth Dimension, children are represented as "cruddy
creatures" as they move through the maze. We were unhappy with this self-
imagery because its Spanish translation, "criaturita," connotes smallness and
defenselessness, directly contradicting the strong, positive self-image we wanted
to encourage in the children. After several unsuccessful attempts to positively
align token and affirming representations, we gave up and changed the children's
designation to Amiguitos [Little Friends]. This self-ascription deliberately

complements the undergraduates' title and reinforces the children's organizational position as equally powerful to their adult partners in the journey through the maze.

We completed the leveling of traditional status hierarchies in *La Clase Mágica's* organizational structure by renaming the Wizard to *El Maga*. A literal translation of wizard would have required identifying the system's only authority figure as male. Using the construction "*El Maga*" mixes genders and thus avoids specifying one or the other and also avoids reducing the entity's power over the whole system.[22] Although the term often trips native Spanish speakers, who favor using *La Maga* or *El Mago* (the Spanish gendered equivalent to Wizard), the neologism prompts children to continuously ponder and inquire about *Maga's* gender.

The flexibility with language that the notion of *EL Maga* encourages was brought home to me in a comical way one afternoon when I was working at the site. One of the young boys, approaching me with a sheepish grin on his face, asked, "Olga, are you bi?" Startled, but mentally acknowledging the play on words (bisexual–bilingual), I waited a moment before responding. Sure enough, he filled the pause with a triumphant shout, "-lingual!" Of course, this youngster knew very well that I spoke both English and Spanish. What he was hoping to confirm was his belief that I was *Maga*. In a previous electronic "chat" with *Maga*, the boy had posed the inevitable question, "*Maga* are you a boy or a girl?" When *Maga*, just as inevitably, had responded, "Neither," the youngster had concluded his message, logically, with the assertion, "Then you must be bi." However, in playing with the bisexual connotation, the young boy was suggesting that he knew I was the *Maga*, an accusation I was repeatedly subjected to when I visited the site.

A Partnership With Community Members.   Another important reworking of the concepts we used at *La Clase Mágica* reflected the integral collaboration we had with the members of the community. We redefined the meaning of "community" to specify the constituency of the host institution rather than its administrative hierarchy. Unlike the Fifth Dimension program down the street, which worked closely with the administrators of the Boy's and Girl's club that hosted the program, we side stepped the St. Leo's administration.[23] We forged our partnership instead with the Spanish-speaking laity, formalizing the relationship through the establishment of a parent advisory group and an adult computer class. Targeting community members as partners in such social action was a risky innovation. The *Mexicano* community had had relatively little power or resources throughout its history in Eden Gardens (see chapter 3 for details on the history of Eden Gardens). Their working-class background, limited English fluency, and low educational attainment detracted from the community's power and status in a partnership with the University of California, an institution top-heavy with resources and institutional hieracrchy.

Yet, the way we chose to define "community" directly impacted our goals for making *La Clase Mágica* self-sustaining. We aimed for an up-take of the goals and objectives of the project by the participants rather than by a formal host institution. In other words, we hoped the community members who participated in the activities of *La Clase Mágica* would be willing to support the program with their active involvement. We sought a level of involvement that went beyond ad hoc participation. My reasoning was that if and when the program faced a crisis, adult participants would not only be willing but also able to contribute time and effort to perpetuating the day-to-day computer activities. This eventuality was made real because of my tentative status as postdoctoral fellow in the early stages of the program and later as my tenure was not a guarantee. The degree to which community members internalized the principles of *La Clase Mágica* has yet to be fully examined, but by 1996 parents had taken a more active role than ever before. From 1993 to 1996, the community had become fully responsible for running one of the three sessions that *La Clase Mágica* offered per week.[24] In addition, many parents had taken active roles in fund-raising and participated in activities cosponsored with the Fifth Dimension nearby.

A Multigenerational Approach. The uniqueness of this enterprise is not that we simply address the entire life span but that various leading activities—such as research, electronic communication, literacy, collaboration, and curriculum development—provide meaningful and effective articulation across important contexts relevant to student achievement. The pipeline of qualified students that Moll, Díaz and Anderson envisioned is effectively created through a dynamic intergenerational process of exchange that socializes children and adults to adequately handle the knowledge and skills found in various parts of the system.

These leading activities are not mutually exclusive and, for the most part, are inseparable except for heuristic purposes. For example, research as a leading activity across the contexts of the LCHC seminar, the undergraduate course, and after-school site best exemplifies the dynamic intergenerational process of exchange that typically takes place among and across novices and experts, simultaneously driving a transformation and innovation of the pertinent contexts. As faculty research pushes our understanding to greater levels, it also provides the means for training and enculturating graduate students, and occasionally postdoctoral colleagues, who in turn work closely with the undergraduates enrolled in the course. The cycling back and forth of learning and teaching continues for the undergraduate students, children, and adults in the community. Ever so imperceptibly participants are affected by the contexts which are themselves changing in response to the growing understandings shared across participants. Thus, in the natural flow of life, without marking knowledge as correct, complete, or profitable, participants learn new ways of seeing, doing, and saying.

The research activities have had a significant role in the development of intellectual and material resources available to all levels of participants in the project. Besides providing new insights into creating innovative learning environments where all participants can have the opportunity to achieve their optimal potential, the research activities of *La Clase Mágica* have been instrumental in enhancing access to educational resources and institutional support. These efforts have helped trained many undergraduate students for graduate school and for teaching careers at the same time that their research topics have fed back into the adaptation of the organizational structure and content of the curriculum. One of our undergraduate students, for example, was able to show how a child was incorrectly considered "learning disabled" by other undergraduates because he retreated into silence or physical violence for being called "shy." The reflection essays of undergraduate students at the end of the quarter invariably document the life-changing insights that students have as a result of their participation in the project. Not only are these important contributions to the evaluation, pedagogy, and research of the project, they are also important feedback to the participants' own sense of self.

LESSONS LEARNED ABOUT CULTURAL RELEVANCE

Over the 22 academic quarters of fieldwork and teaching the undergraduate field course connected to *La Clase Mágica*, we learned that developing culturally relevant learning environments involves an on-going, deliberate, and open-ended process. It is not possible to use a prepackaged program aimed at a putative group of learners. To be successful, as well as culturally relevant, the program must directly address the local sociolinguistic context, assess the availability of socioeconomic resources, and remain continuously open to a broad range of educational possibilities. These are not easy requirements to fulfill. For every effort to stake out new territory, to undertake new risks for the sake of innovation, there are concomitant forces linked to deep-rooted intellectual and institutional traditions that continually push the process back toward what is known and proven. It is very difficult to advocate uncertainty; very hard to resist the impulse to tie up "loose ends," at whatever the cost. Thus, in discussions with and among students, research staff, and members of the broader research team, ambiguity and multiplicity is conti-nuously contested—and often misunderstood and misrepresented—even with several years of experience behind us. Old intellectual habits die hard.

        To summarize, a fully integrated model of a culturally relevant approach to teaching and learning was pieced together as the research team pursued the adaptation of the Fifth Dimension. This model argues for an inclusive, collaborative, and flexible approach to a full range of educational practices, including pedagogy; training of adults working with children; and parent involvement. Although learning and development are its premier goal, the model has far-reaching implications for social change and educational reform. It proposes a paradigm shift that emphasizes multiple perspectives (Greenfield, 1994) on the educational project. The learners' home language and culture are viewed not as lamentable impediments to be overcome, but as valuable intellectual resources to be tapped (Moll & Díaz, 1987).

        It will be a few more years before we know the full impact of participation in *La Clase Mágica* on the children's progress up through the educational system. We do know, however, that the adaptation of the Fifth Dimension into *La Clase Mágica* provides equal access to and equal status for both English and Spanish, and that participating children are more successful in acquiring their second language and maintaining their first language than their peers in a more traditional public school bilingual program (Vásquez, 1993). The warm and supportive environment of *La Clase Mágica* facilitates trusting relationships that make it possible to intervene in the children's identity formation and help them learn to view themselves as valid and contributing members in problem-solving processes (Stanton-Salazar et al., 1995; Vásquez, 1995). The dynamic relations of exchange with institutional agents (in this case, the undergraduate students) are an important component in shaping the way children perceive university life. Moreover, these relations enhance the acquisition of social and academic skills and the accumulation of resources that will someday facilitate these learners' success in a university setting.

        Definitive statements concerning the effectiveness of *La Clase Mágica* as an aid to increasing the likelihood that its young participants will eventually choose to attend college must await the results of long-term evaluation studies. Our preliminary findings, nevertheless, indicate that all the long-term participants who stay in the program into their high-school years enroll in college preparatory courses, pointing to higher education as a future option. Other findings offer important insights on creating innovative educational activities for learners from diverse backgrounds. Culturally relevant education and the notion of transforming the educational pipeline go hand in hand. It is not enough to adapt the child to the pedagogy, the pedagogy must adapt to the child. Regrettably, as Reyes (1992) so poignantly objected to in the field of literacy, the application of one form of pedagogy is more often not applied to all students. The bilingual, bicultural adaptations of *La Clase Mágica* attempt to adapt the pedagogy to the child. And, in doing so, the program has created a ripple effect that has already qualitatively improved the learning experiences of participating children and adult representatives of the community and university.

NOTES

[1]The Fifth Dimension was first conceived as an in-school activity; it became an after-school program because of conflicts with school personnel at the target site. On December 7, 1981, Delf College (pseudonym), a San Diego County private, after-school academy for learning-disabled children, piloted the Fifth Dimension as a way to improve the children's reading levels. Of the 24 children who participated in the program, 13 fit the clinical definition of learning disabled. Most Participants were Anglo and middle class.

[2]Some of the games are arcade-variety and contain little or no written text. Most, however, are commercially available educational software requiring advanced literacy and critical-thinking skills.

[3]Cole retreated to his home community in protest over UCSD's failure to support the retention of several minority scholars who had contributed to the early design of the Fifth Dimension and to LCHC's focus on diversity (Cole, 1984). By concentrating on his own cultural group and refusing to be a surrogate for minority researchers, Cole hoped to make clear to UCSD administrators that their decision would replace the rich contributions of a minority perspective with a void.

[4]A university course on the uses of technology was designed to provide the workforce for the field site and for collecting data through written observations (see chap. 3 for details about the course).

[5]Staff at the Moscow site translated all of the materials from English to Russian. Although the children were picking up and using English-language computer terminology, their language-use patterns as they moved through the maze were not systematically observed because the researchers' interests lay in tracking cognitive development, not second-language acquisition (personal communication with Irina Venerikima, Moscow site project director, February, 1997).

[6]Several of Cole's Latino students, as part of their course projects, approached members of the community. The students did manage to recruit several children, but once the quarter ended and the undergraduates left, these youngsters dropped out of the program.

[7]For example, the mission had recently been a center for the community's campaigns against drugs, gangs, and abortion. And, during the amnesty program for workers without green cards, efforts undertaken at the mission had enrolled hundreds of undocumented individuals.

[8]The group did not attend any of the other English-language services at St. Leo's, nor did they attend any services at the Catholic Church located nearby (in an affluent part of the city).

[9]Few priests in the mission's history had served the Mexicano community of Eden Gardens as selflessly and warmly as did Father Kaicher. However, because he had violated probation for blocking entrance to an abortion clinic, he was jailed for 45 days during the early period of *La Clase Mágica*. Despite the widespread support of the community, he was reassigned to a parish near the border. With him left the open-door policy for *La Clase Mágica*. Access to the mission's resources was limited by his successor, a cloistered nun who reportedly held a doctorate in bilingual education. She provided symbolic support for the project, but she invested the bulk of her energies in the mission's traditional, church-related activities.

[10]Members of the research team identified the priest's Spanish-language homily lecture as the first case they observed of the use of participants' linguistic resources to mediate the acquisition of new knowledge. This same strategy came to define the way *La Clase Mágica* approaches its participants' background experiences.

[11]Although we had arranged with the school district beforehand to have the children dropped off at the gate of the mission, it took several weeks before the new route was running smoothly. Several times, I had to collect the children from their regular bus stops and bring them to the mission.

[12]Scott Woodbridge, who had been enrolled in Cole's undergraduate course and then became a member of LCHC's staff, was instrumental in getting the new site started. He also helped train the community representatives who were brought to UCSD for computer training. His level of commitment is best described in his own fieldnotes for November 2, 1989:

> . . . how do I fit in? Good question! I was asked by Olga to help in the organization/development of the site. I consider this time a volunteer effort for the community as well as the education of myself. Having experience with the Fifth Dimension, and missing my work with the kiddies. I am refamiliarizing myself with the activity, taking the opportunity to learn Spanish and reinforce my notions and experiences with the theories of Vygotsky and ZOPED development.

[13]The focus of the early courses that dealt with literacy issues in the community and communication in the community lent itself to such studies, however, my own ethnographic survey of the community deemed it safe for my undergraduates. Its reputation of violence and drugs, I found was outdated by about 10 years.

[14]Although a goal from the very beginning, the inclusion of a modified version of *La Clase Mágica* for preschool children attending the Head Start program was not achieved to a satisfactory degree until our seventh year of operation. We simply did not have the resources to systematically supervise the undergraduate students assigned to Head Start or to provide them with the same kind of experience other students in the class were having in both *La Clase Mágica* and the Fifth Dimension.

[15]See chapter 3 and Hurtado et al., (1996) for a further discussion on the UC Latino Eligibility Task Force. As a representative of UCSD, I joined the task force at its onset and was later commissioned to examine how our efforts at *La Clase Mágica* and AVID (Advancement Via Individual Determination), directed by Hugh Mehan, affected Latino eligibility to higher education.

[16]Every academic quarter (i.e., every 10 weeks) a new group of undergraduate students comes to *La Clase Mágica* unfamiliar with the culture of the Fifth Dimension and with the games and task associated with the rooms in the maze. Thus, children are in a much better position to be the "experts" in *La Clase Mágica* activities.

[17]The analysis focused on fieldnotes written by the research team, copies of field-developed materials, and staff reports, and debriefings.

[18]The children at *La Clase Mágica* draw on their multiple knowledge sources to make meaning in the same ways that we observed among children in the Northern California community of Eastside (Vásquez et al., 1994). In both groups, the children relate the content of the tasks at hand to their own previous experiences in Mexico, as well as in their local communities and homes.

[19]The issue of the use of standard Spanish vs. Spanish dialects—of which there are many varieties (see Elias-Olivares, 1977)—was repeatedly discussed in our research staff meetings. Several staff members voiced the concern often echoed by educators who see the use of "nonstandard" Spanish as according incompetence to speakers and writers. Others in the staff voted for a closer representation to the use of Spanish in the community.

[20]Xochimilco is a park of floating gardens in the southwest corner of Mexico City. The park is named after a Náhuatl tribe which, according to legend, was the first to leave the mythical Aztec homeland in the north.

[21]For more than a year, Dr. Margaret Gallego's Michigan team and our staff traded adapted task cards. Two staff members worked closely with Mrs. Durán and Ms. Nuñez during an entire summer.

[22]*El Maga's* power is substantial. For example, once, when frustrated with the electronic responses of several members of the telestructure, he/she/it cut these members off from further correspondence until they expressed remorse. On another occasion, *Maga* challenged the key figure in the Fifth Dimension universe, Michael Cole, who adroitly deflected *Maga's* wrath through humor.

[23]This strategy, like many other's, were influenced by the socioecological nature of the institution. Although neither the Boy's and Girl's Club nor St. Leo's Mission are in the business of education, the goals of the former are more aligned with the goals of the after-school activity. St. Leo's was willing and able to commit little more than space and other equipment for *La Clase Mágica*.

[24]For a discussion of the enormous contributions Mrs. Durán has made to La Clase *Mágica*, see chap. 6. Volunteering her time before Monies became available Mrs. Durán has been a key figure throughout the life of the project. Today she coordinates all the activities pertinent to *La Clase Mágica*.

3

A System of Relations for Acting Locally, Thinking Globally, and Planning Long Term

As discussed in the previous chapter, *La Clase Mágica* staff and participants altered the Fifth Dimension's design in content and structure to accommodate the educational needs and characteristics of the local community. We made curricular adaptations to reflect the cultural and linguistic character of the target population—Spanish-speaking children living in the adjacent *Mexicano* community. Without the same kind of deliberate resolve, yet with the same impact, we also made changes to the Fifth Dimension structure by expanding its system of relations to include contexts and constituencies relevant to minority student achievement. Although functioning independently and embodying separate agendas and separate foci, these adaptations dialectically formed a separate model system of institutional relations. As such, they approximate what Griffin and Cole (1984), called a "functional system" made up of complex yet flexible constituents working together "as the needs and opportunities arise to perform the function of development" (p. 49). In the process they gave rise to a form of social action that sought a more comprehensive way to enhance the educational achievement of linguistic minority students.

The revisions on the structure and content of the project were intertwined; alterations inevitably had ripple effects that led us to sharpen our research lens and our practice. For analytical purposes, I have taken what is a complex web of change and teased apart some of the most significant strands to examine separately. At the most general level, I have chosen to isolate institutional modifications from content changes, in hopes of showing the comprehensiveness and multidimensionality of the changes needed for effective social action (see chapter 2 for a discussion on the changes in content). My goal is to make the interrelationship between the macro–micro processes clear enough to demonstrate the range of possibilities that exist at the boundaries of two disparate and often hostile cultural systems. More importantly, I hope it will show how *La Clase Mágica* is in a position to disrupt the current cycle in which dominant groups accumulate ever-greater amounts of cultural capital while minority groups are divested of the little capital they do possess.

By reorganizing social structures that have historically obstructed minority populations from gaining access to educational resources and institutional support (Stanton-Salazar et al., 1995), the expanded structure and goals of *La Clase Mágica* redefined institutional relations and the distribution of power. It spawned new questions about what knowledge is valued, where it is acquired, and who possesses it (Nocon, 1997). These questions in turn, generated new strategies for understanding and acting upon the multiplicities embedded at every level of the system. More importantly, it led to the consideration of the model as a viable alternative to the Affirmative Action strategies that were being dismantled in the UC system at the time.

I begin with a brief sketch of the history of social relations between a wealthy, predominantly White community and another that supplied it with low-income, mostly language minority workers. Microcosms of the society at large, these two communities, the city of Solana Beach and its division, Eden Gardens, provided *La Clase Mágica* with the symbolic and material conditions of conventional intercultural relations between *Mexicanos* and mainstream American. Three cultural systems: the University of California, San Diego (UCSD), the laity of a small Catholic Mission in Eden Gardens and the *Mexicano* family, however, were complicitous in disrupting the status quo. These 3 institutions formed a unique and an unlikely partnership in which the *Mexicano* family played an integral role. Later, I follow with a description of the institutional contexts and activities that make up the university and community side of the partnership, with the understanding that the *Mexicano* family has a defused affect throughout the community side of the partnership. The model system of relations that Michael Cole and I hammered out at UCSD to address issues of K–12 achievement and the underrepresentation of minorities in higher education gave birth to UCLinks, a consortium of university–community partnerships I describe in the following section. Finally, I conclude with the new vistas we gain from a macroperspective and lay out the impact we expect our efforts will have in the not so distant future.

SEPARATE STORIES OF SHARED SPACES: UCSD AND EDEN GARDENS[1]

To the untrained eye there are only two communities brought together by *La Clase Mágica*: a wealthy, predominantly White community and a small working-class *Mexicano* community. However, when one looks beyond conventional formulations of componential elements, a more apparent complexity comes into view. Even the research team worked under the assumption that UCSD and the Eden Gardens communities were the only two components of the partnership for an extended period of time. However, the difficulty and ambiguity of referencing "the community" led us to re-examine who and what exactly was the community. This period of reflection led us to the following conclusion: The research team was the university partner representing UCSD and St. Leo's Mission was the community partner but, surprisingly, it was the *Mexicano* family that was the third operating cultural system.[2] Working together, across language, class, and ethnicity, these cultural systems make up the life-blood of the functional system created by *La Clase Mágica*. At every level of the new system, *La Clase Mágica* initiative weaves in the cultural norms, knowledge base, and language of all three partners into the discourse and artifacts of each constituent institutional context and activity.

In general, UCSD and the *Mexicano* community of Eden Gardens have little in common besides their relative proximity and early beginnings. The two cultural systems have developed independently and in dramatic contrast. Both are insular communities symbiotically related to the larger civil society, yet unlike UCSD, Eden Gardens is marked further by class and ethnicity. From the beginning, the university established a pattern of relations with its immediate surrounding area; however, outside of menial jobs, those contracts, interactions, and exchanges included few, if any, members of the *Mexicano*/Latino community. Minorities, and, in specific, Mexican origin individuals have been and continue to be severely underrepresented in the staff, faculty, administration, and student admissions at UCSD. Labor has closely related the two communities to the greater society, however, UCSD has historically enjoyed a broader, proactive town and gown relations with the San Diego civil society, than Eden Gardens, which remained practically isolated from the surrounding community aside from sharing its labor force. And, although positive media coverage of UCSD has fluctuated over time, with very few exceptions, Eden Gardens has repeatedly received anything but negative coverage from the city newspaper.

UCSD: From Outpost to a Sixth Campus of the UC. Like other institutions of higher education that sit adjacent to language minority communities, UCSD historically has had little or no relations of exchange with the *Mexicano* community of Eden Gardens, just 8 miles to its north.[3] Although, both cultural systems sprung up around the same time in nearly the same geographic space, there is no record of social or labor relations since its early history. At the turn of the century, in its earliest incarnation, UCSD was an outpost for oceanographic research; Eden Gardens was a work camp for *Mexicano* railroad and field laborers. The recorded history of the area surrounding the university and St. Leo's, the Catholic mission that hosts *La Clase Mágica*, is a "history of Anglo Americans," according to two undergraduate students who investigated the subject for more than a year (Andre & Melton, 1992). Any cross-cultural mixing that occurred before the 1970s, in both settings, took place along class lines. During the Great Depression, for example. destitute "Archies" and "Oakies." fleeing the economic hardships of Arkansas and Oklahoma of the 1930s settled in among the working class *Mexicanos* of Eden Gardens. At UCSD, there is no evidence of any *Mexicano* presence in the early years. Statewide, Latinos were virtually absent for the first 100 years (1868–1968) of the University of California's history (University of California, President's Task Force, 1975). Spanish-surnamed individuals who graduated during that time were most likely foreign-born students from wealthy, Latin American backgrounds.

Thus, across history, the differences in class, culture, and language have played a critical role in sustaining the separation between the two communities. The university's views on diversity across time have also played an important role. For example, the Educational Opportunity Program initiated in 1965 by the University of California President in conjunction with the Regents responded to the sociopolitical climate of the times and the new definition of diversity ushered in by the Civil Rights initiatives (University of California, President's Task Force, 1975, p. 37). According to a framework supplied by the President of Harvard University (Harvard University, 1993–1995), the UC replaced differences in opinion, interests, or talents with race and ethnicity as the prevailing categories in admission policies with its new resolve to "remedy the long standing injustice toward disadvantage sectors of the State population" (p. 37). In doing so, it cracked open one of the last social institutions to minority integration. Accounts of those "tumultuous years" clearly suggest that the university was hardly ready for the differences in experiences, needs, and visions of the incoming minority students and other student activists (McGill, 1982).

Long periods of planning by local and state officials preceded the establishment of the sixth campus of the University of California system. Its early history can be traced back to a UC Berkeley research outpost established in 1892 in La Jolla. This marine field station gradually grew into the internationally acclaimed Scripps Institution of Oceanography. After years of behind-the-scenes negotiations, civic and political leaders received the boost needed to rally public support for a new campus when the Russians launched the Sputnik satellite in 1957. The "Sputnik Incident" catapulted the country and the state into a frenzy of activity to seal the gap in science and engineering made evident by Russia's lead in technology. The demand for "bigger and better science, and to crank up across-the-board funding to unprecedented levels" was a windfall for the new campus (Anderson, 1993, p. 48). As a result, the Regents authorized the Institute of Technology and Engineering in 1958 and the following year authorized it and its burgeoning area as a general UC campus.

For its first decade, the fledgling campus focused solely on science and engineering, attracting some of the most recognized scientists in the country. By the 1980s, UCSD could pride itself of 64 members of the National Academy of Science, eight Nobel laureates, six winners of National Medals of Science, two

Pulitzer Prize winners, two Field medalists in mathematics and six MacArthur
Foundation fellows (Anderson, 1993). A truly elite body—mostly White, male,
and wealthy—with lofty goals of distinction graced the "Cathedral on the Buff,"
as Roger Revelle, one of the university's strongest supporters and early architect,
conceived the new university. Built from the top down and from the inside
outside, Revelle believed the university was like a cathedral, "the center to which
all men turn to find the meaning of their lives and from which emanates a
wondrous light, the light of understanding" (p. 37). Its distinguished faculty, its
creativity and innovation justly fulfilled the University's goals for diversity
(Kerr, 1961).

The turbulent 60s, however, ushered in new definitions of diversity and
new mandates for representation in every aspect of the university operations—
membership, curriculum, and service. As a radical force swept across the
nation's campuses, the UCSD's administration came face-to-face with "black and
brown students [who] wanted no more than an institution to serve their needs as
they set about claiming what had been denied to their forebears" (McGill, 1982,
p. 153). Among the foremost political and social goals of the time was an end to
the segregation that characterized the nation's secondary institutions (Morris,
1995). At UCSD, the conflict centered on the symbolic and academic plans for
founding the university's third college initially designed to focus on "historical
study" and "contemporary social issues" (McGill, 1982, p. 114). Black and
Chicano students aggressively proposed other goals for the college; that it:

> be devoted to relevant education for minority youth and to the study
> of contemporary social problems of all people. . . . This college must
> radically depart from the usual role as the ideological backbone of the
> social system, and must instead subject every part of the system to
> ruthless criticism. (Lumumba-Zapata Demands, quoted in McGill,
> 1982, p. 115)

Born in controversy, the "minority college" slowly lost its idealistic charge as the
fervor of the 1960s waned. By the 1990s, finally named Thurgood Marshall
College, the third of what are now five colleges emphasized a social science
curriculum (University of California, Campus Planning Office, 1992). The
legacy of those troubled times can be traced to the curriculum of one of its many
programs entitled, "Dimensions of Culture" (DOC). All students in the college
must enroll in a three-quarter course that variously examines diversity, the justice
system, and cultural history of American society in relation to cultural minorities.

Many changes are evident today in the post-Affirmative Action era of
the 1990s, however, adequate representation is still an illusive goal. Alarmingly,
as the UC system leads the country in instituting new definitions of and new
strategies for achieving diversity, campuses across the UC system have
experienced a dip in the admissions of Blacks and Hispanics who are choosing

more favorable learning environments. At UCSD, the presence of Mexican origin students, on the other hand, has crept slowly each decade since the 1970s (4% to 5%, 7% to 10.2%, respectively). Those who manage to enroll, however, do not perform as well as their Asian and White counterparts, taking a year or so longer to complete their education (Mehan et al., 1996). This disproportion is also reflected among the faculty, which in 1995 constituted 4.4% of the ladder rank faculty; Whites constituted 83.7% of the total population. A report to the Academic Senate by the Committee on Affirmative Action (1997) noted that "twenty departments have no Hispanic ladder rank faculty."

Located less than 25 miles north of the Mexican–U.S. border, in a county where approximately 20% of the population is Chicano/Latino and where 35% of the student population in the city schools is Chicano/Latino dictates an immediate and incisive action to rectify the underrepresentation of this population (Chicano/Latino Concilio, 1995). Action-oriented programs with such decisive goals are few and far between. *La Clase Mágica* is one such program. AVID (Advancement Via Individual Determination) is another (Mehan et al., 1996; Stanton-Salazar et al., 1995). The university itself also has several outstanding outreach programs and plans for a charter school loom in the near future.

Eden Gardens: From Work Camp to City Division. The *Mexicano* community of Eden Gardens is a subdivision of Solana Beach, a midsize Southern California city located in the northern portion of San Diego County. It is encapsulated in the middle of a one-square mile area surrounded by increasingly higher priced homes and multiplex apartments radiating out into its periphery. Its outer boundaries are framed on all four sides by major thoroughfares. In 1967, Highway 5, one of the main arteries that flow up and down the state of California, slashed Eden Gardens in half, separating the *Mexicano* residents away from Anglo neighbors on the East. The freeway, a stone's throw away from St. Leo's Mission, *La Clase Mágica's* host, also closed-off entrance into the area from the east. The intersections of Steven's Road—running North and South on its west border—with two off ramps of Highway 5 effectively framed the area *Mexicanos* have called *La Colonia* for almost 100 years.

Outsiders, other than the UCSD students, go to Eden Gardens to worship, eat, and play sports. They come to visit three Mexican restaurants, two churches, and a park situated at the heart of the community. Unlike other minority enclaves (Vásquez, 1989; Vásquez et al., 1994), local business establishments do not cater in any significant way to the *Mexicano* residents. St. Leo's Mission is the only establishment that attracts a visible *Mexicano* following for most of its services. In effect, intercultural relations inside the community remain instrumental. Under these structural relations, it is likely that visitors see only poverty and difference rather than experience the sense of "warmth" and "family influence," Steve Melton was able to detect after having spent several quarters listening to the oral histories of long-time residents. Meaningful relations with these old-timers allowed Steve to see beyond the exterior of his initial perceptions to the rich social relations of the tightly knit *Mexicano* community.

The *Mexicano* community of Eden Gardens has maintained a stable presence in the area as far back as the late 1800s, when Mexican laborers, working for the Santa Fe Railroad or the nearby ranchers, immigrated to the area. The immigration signaled a shift in cultural and economic power of the area from Mexican to American, as the land grant system gave way to the onslaught of the westward movement spurred by the Gold Rush and Manifest Destiny. It was the third such shift and one that has lasted into the present; each succeeding power subjugating its predecessors economically and culturally and permitting relatively little intermingling (Andre & Melton, 1991). First, Spain seized control of the area from the native inhabitants, the Yuman Indian tribes in the 1700s. Spain established its cultural and economic supremacy in the area through the San Luis Rey Mission, one of 21 California missions it built to govern its new land holdings. The second shift in power was marked by secularization of the mission system following the Mexican War of Independence when Spain ceded its territories in the New World to Mexico. Like other missions and surrounding land, the San Luis Rey was dismantled and subdivided into a series of rancherías [ranches], displacing both the native peoples and Spanish residents. Lasting approximately three decades, this second era gave way to American corporations and development. Thus, when Eden Gardens first sprouted, the area was completely under Anglo American control, the Native Americans were relocated in reservations, and *Mexicanos* had become the new work force. These new conditions gave rise to "two different cultures, two different economies, two different standards of living and two different communities that have persisted into the present: Solana Beach and Eden Gardens" (Andre & Melton, 1991, p. 20).

Across time, the interrelations between the two ethnic groups have been distant and intermittent. Unlike the city of Solana Beach, which was designed (Andre & Melton, 1991), Eden Gardens simply evolved, remaining in relative isolation for many years in a kind of benign neglect by city officials. The reasons for such differences in the developmental patterns of the two areas are structural rather cultural. Until the late 1960s and early 1970s, individuals of Mexican descent were unable to acquire bank loans, even if the property they wanted to buy was within Eden Gardens. Also, Mexicans and their descendants were not allowed to own or occupy property outside of Eden Gardens until the early 1970s, when legislation made it unconstitutional to reject prospective buyers on the basis of race, gender, or religion. In fact, before the 1970s, *Mexicanos* and other minorities could enter properties outside Eden Gardens only as "employees or servants of the owner" (Wiersema, 1984, p. 8), institutionalizing a symbiotic relationship between Whites and *Mexicanos* that has been sustained over the years. To this day, intercultural relations between *Mexicanos* and Anglo residents of the surrounding areas are fettered to labor market needs. *Mexicanos* have supplied the labor force behind the development of much of North San Diego County and the now wealthy community of Solana Beach.

What we know of the history of Eden Gardens today is based almost exclusively on its residents' oral histories, collected periodically by newspaper reporters, and by *La Clase Mágica* staff. If it were not for these efforts, there would be no record of the community (Andre & Melton, 1991). Mainstream accounts of San Diego county, Solana Beach, typically make no mention of this *Mexicano* enclave, despite its longevity and many contributions to the development of the surrounding area. When official documents such as school records and land deeds do mention Eden Gardens, it is to note the need for 'separate arrangements. For example, school records of a P.T.A meeting on January 13, 1928, discussed the "Mexican problem" and the need to separate the children at once. A land deed of the time stated outright:

> Neither the said premises nor any portion thereof shall ever be conveyed, transferred, demised to or held, occupied or owned by or resided on by Mexicans, Indian Mexicans, and Mexicans directly descended from the Indian stock of the Republic of Mexico and also by any person or persons not of the white or Caucasian race. But persons of any race may be on said land as employees or servants of the owner. (Quoted in Wieresma, 1984, p. 8)

The separation between the two communities was heightened between 1928 and 1949, when Mexican children were schooled separately from Anglo children so that the former could learn English and become part of mainstream culture. Although the prevailing attitudes behind segregation saw these children as unclean, disease-ridden, and amoral, their ability to provide cheap labor also featured prominently in decisions to school them separately. According to Donato (1997):

> On the surface, educators maintained that segregation at the elementary level was best for Mexican American children in order to serve them properly when in fact the goal was to keep them apart from white children and, ostensibly, to maintain a supply of cheap labor in their communities. (p. 17)

This is an aspect of the community's history that still rankles with some of the old-time residents. Ironically, this "Americanization school" was located on the same block where *La Clase Mágica* resides today (Wiersema, 1984).

The late 1960s and 1970s brought a period of unrest for the residents of Eden Gardens as real estate developers, drug dealers, and new immigrants moved in en mass. Many of Eden Gardens' original families moved away in the 1970s, selling their homes in response to pressure from developers and city planners. A feature article on the community published in the San Diego Union reported that "[w]hole sections of its perimeter went commercial and industrial. An acre off Ida Avenue purchased for $4,000 in the early '60s today is worth $320,000" (Wiersema, 1984, p.13). Nothing threatened the community's well-being, however, more than the period it suffered under the grips of drug dealers. It took almost a decade before the community would win back its streets and many more years before it would lose its fame for being the headquarters of the cocaine trade.

Still, Eden Gardens continues to flourish. Some streets are inhabited entirely by families whose members have been in the area for generations. Other streets were populated by individuals with no previous ties to the community. A community survey by *La Clase Mágica* staff (conducted between Spring Quarter 1994 and Winter Quarter 1995) found that slightly more than half of Eden Gardens' residents arrived after 1970. A steady stream of immigrants, particularly those from Mexico, continually replenish the community with Spanish-speaking residents, housing 2 to 3 families in the relatively few single family dwellings available in the area. The participants of *La Clase Mágica* come from this group. Notably, newcomers who are more transient and single males often are not welcomed by long-time residents, who perceive them as the cause of the community's high rate of rental properties and pattern of transience. As one old-timer of *La Colonia* pointed out:

> When they first come to the Mission, or when they first come here, one of the things I notice is the tremendous isolation from society and from each other. . . . And, there's a certain amount of prejudice, not from the Anglo society as much as from the Hispanics already living here. [AY:3/15/93]

Today, according to the 1990s census, Eden Gardens is composed of 52% Hispanic and 45% White. At its core, however, the ratio of Hispanics to Whites is much greater— 85% to 15%. Judging from the findings presented in student research papers across the 6-year span, interracial contact among residents continues to be intermittent or nonexistent (Franke & Janikas, 1992). Whites who reside in the community tend to live in gated-complexes, townhouses, and condominiums clustered at the community's periphery, where land prices are "cheap" by comparison with rates in other sections of Solana Beach and nearby communities. An Anglo resident's confession to a staff member of *La Clase Mágica* that he "didn't know it was the bad part of town" before he moved into his new home in Eden Gardens illustrates the relatively low visibility of the area's *Mexicanos*. It also illustrates the endurance of a negative image the community acquired as a "drug infested barrio."

The Mexicano Family: From Invisibility to Front and Center. The life-span approach, parent involvement, and the large number of siblings that participate in the activities of *La Clase Mágica's*, places the "family" at the center of the institutional relations between the community and the university. Although not all participants exhibit kinship ties nor have they all been residents of Eden Gardens, all have been closely linked by the same community institutions—St. Leo's Mission, Head Start, and the public schools. If participants are not associated through kinship or fictive ties, they certainly belong to the family's social networks of support. For example, many of the participants were drawn to the mission's social and religious activities by active layleaders. For a period, Mrs. Durán (the program coordinator) and her husband were actively involved in the ecclesiastic activities of the mission. Mrs. Durán was the director of the catechism classes involving 12 teachers and 200 children when I first stepped into the mission grounds back in 1989. Mr. Durán was the president of the *Padres de Familia* that oversaw the fund-raising activities of the mission.

La Clase Mágica sits squarely in the middle of activities in which participants take part as a function of life in the community. It draws the same children and their families who attend Church functions, cultural events, Head Start, and numerous entertainment activities such as the Mexican folk dance classes offered in and around the mission. The families share a history, language, and the same social concerns as first-generation immigrants. On many occasions, the issues of the day, whether they were related to the family, the church, or the community, accompanied the participants to the door of *La Clase Mágica*. For example, during a particular period of displeasure with the church administration, the concerns voiced at the meetings of Los Padres de Familia were invariably revisited as parents came and went with their children to *La Clase Mágica*. Patterns of social relations at *La Clase Mágica*, also reflected the social relations of the families. Mrs. Durán, a leading figure in the community, was accorded the same deference and acquiescence in *La Clase Mágica* as she received as the catechism director and teacher.

With very few exceptions, the families mirror the demographic profile of first-generation immigrants. They are young, Spanish-speaking, working-class, and for the most part came from a two-parent home. Informal data confirmed that these families also experienced a low rate of delinquency, less psychological distress, and more marital stability as has been found among first generation in comparison to second and third generation immigrants (Buriel, 1993). Generally, adults were born in Mexico and had migrated to the United States less than 20 years before. Children were U.S.-born and attended primary grades in U.S. schools. Spanish was the primary language of the home and fluency in English of the parents was basically instrumental. The family was exposed to English through the children's participation in the school system and minimally from the adults' employment.

The tight knit community and the demographic characteristics of the participants reinforced *Mexicano* family values and responsibilities in the activities that constituted the daily life of *La Clase Mágica*. Independence, responsibility, and deferred gratification, found to be encouraged by first-generation parents (Buriel, 1993) played a critical role in the way children and adults took to the activities and goals of *La Clase Mágica*. Older children often watched over their younger siblings, helped run the Friday session of *La Clase Mágica*, and found the employment by the project as a way to help contribute to family resources.[4] The responsibilities assigned to long-term participants known as Wizard Assistants (discussed later) were roles these children had previously experienced in their homes and communities. As translators, many of these children were experienced in negotiating the needs and interests of their families with mainstream institutions. Encouraged to be self-reliant and independent, these children nevertheless observed *Mexicano* values of parental authority. Their respect for the adults at *La Clase Mágica* was never breached even though at times they found themselves in complete disagreement with the terms set by someone like the coordinator or myself.

In its present location, *La Clase Mágica* mediates the transitioning of Mexican born residents into mainstream culture and its institutions. Importantly, it is a place where parents and children can acquire the experiences and competencies associated with information-based society and thus helps them circumvent the "cultural schisms and synergisms" that plague second generations as a result of intergenerational discontinuity (Buriel, 1993; Buriel & Cardoza, 1988). Children and their families can come in contact with U.S. English-speaking society, have access to computers and telecommunication technology, as well as acquire the use of inquiry and praise associated with critical thinking practices privileged in the schooling system.

A FUNCTIONAL SYSTEM FOR SOCIAL ACTION OR "UN SISTEMA DE INCORPORACIÓN DE ESFUERZO"

Although partnerships between the university and the various branches of the private and public sector have gained momentum since the 1980s, few have fully aligned their mission to that which defines the university: research, teaching, and service. Few, if any, have involved minority community participation as the partner in the enterprise. A review of the literature reveals numerous partnerships yielding worthwhile social and academic gains, however, research or minority control is ostensibly absent. In most instances, the partnership aims at unilateral change in the target population (e.g., students or teachers—or at institutional practice—curriculum development, resource distribution, and student placement; Wilbur & Lambert, 1991) rather than affecting systemic change in both partner institutions.

The university–community partnership forged by collaborators of the Laboratory of Comparative Human Cognition (LCHC), a research unit at the University of California, San Diego (UCSD) shows much promise for systemic change. This model system of institutional relations lent itself to modifications that opened partnering institutions to evident need for change in content and structure. In the reiteration that formed the systems of relations of *La Clase Mágica*, the LCHC model provided the framework for connecting the ground level work of serving a local minority population to greater social issues of K–12 achievement of minorities and their underrepresentation in higher education. Thus, the commingling of the activities and resources of both the university side of the partnership and the community side brought into focus both the local and global perspectives of the issues of minority education. Importantly, it captured a broad-based effort that involved cultural systems, institutional contexts, and activity systems. Next, I describe the nodes that constitute university side of the partnership and then move to describe the components that make up the community side of the initiative, although the distinction between the two is often fluid and indistinct as notions of community membership are blurred or redefined.

La Clase Mágica became an innovation of its predecessor in both local and global goals and objectives. Locally, it expanded the LCHC model by linking three prominent socializing institutions with no history of interrelations. The three institutions created a unique system of collaboration best characterized as "un sistema de incorporación de esfuerzo" [a system of collaborative effort] in which each institution contributes the resources at its disposal. The university contributes its technical and educational resources. The community provides the physical space and furniture for the after-school site, and the family contributes its human and cultural capital.[5] Throughout the day, all three systems come together in the instantiation of a learning activity especially designed for a particular age group. In the mornings, preschool children attending Head Start work in the same computer room that their older brothers or sisters and possibly their parents used later in the day. Thus, regardless of whether representatives of all three cultural systems are present in the computer room or any of the other activity systems, their knowledge, language, and intellectual resources are present in the materials and intersectional routines of the participants. When they do come together, they do so as equal partners of the collaborative process.

The points of contact where the university, the community, and the family have the opportunity to come together include a research seminar, a weekly staff meeting, an undergraduate course, an after-school site for elementary school aged children, a club within a club for adolescent children, an adult computer class, and a preschool activity for children from the adjacent Head Start Program (see Fig. 3.1). When we align these activities together, they touch all but infancy and old age in the developmental cycle, even though they are at different levels of development and often have different origins (e.g., the Head Start adaptation formed part of the original plan yet it was the least developed at the time of this writing). The built-in interrelationships within and across each activity engenders multiple and varied opportunities for the exchange of intellectual and material resources that enriches the experiences of all those involved. As affiliates of the community and university come together repeatedly in these settings, a new set of relations is cultivated, offsetting the imbalance in social and cultural knowledge existing between the two groups.

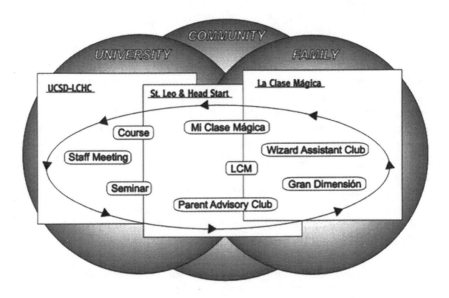

Figure 3.1. System of Collaborative Effort.

This organizational structure deliberately links many of the contexts that are known to affect student achievement (Moll et al., 1985). In place of the traditional series of rigid educational benchmarks, it creates a flexible structure composed of separate but associated settings that prepare individuals to conduct successful and meaningful transactions in both the dominant and home culture. Rather than advocating the primacy of one perspective or one knowledge base over all others, this structure recognizes the value of multiple epistemologies by tapping diverse forms of knowing. The collective in all its forms and functions is privileged over individual forms. The result is a continuous process of change, occurring at both the individual and the institutional level and entailing continuous adaptation, reflection, and more adaptation.

At the global level *La Clase Mágica* is unique in its goal to bring about systemic change in the allocation of and access to resources by minority populations. Theoretically, change is made possible in every nook and cranny of the system through XMellon or Mellon Patch, as the multilayered communicative system that linked all sites and facilitated, access across and among all types of participant groups: researchers, community members, children, students, and funding agency, was affectionately called. The effect on *La Clase Mágica* is notable and immediate as the isolated concern for the schooling practices of local minority children is taken up by a geographically dispersed research collective of similar nodes (see Fig. 3.2).

Collaboration across contexts, populations, and disciplines elevates the issues of access and equity for Spanish-speaking students from a local condition to a global process. Intellectual resources and materials developed by other research teams to address problems or goals of research and educational practice facilitate the ability to understand and build on areas that are outside of *La Clase Mágica's* foci or our research agenda. In turn, *La Clase Mágica* contributes insights into pedagogical practice and inquiry related to the use of the learner's background experiences as critical intellectual tools for learning and development. The exchange between *La Clase Mágica* and other members of the Mellon Patch has also had a reciprocal impact in shaping the system-wide research, evaluation, and dissemination. Although still in its infancy, this high-level form of collaboration promises new ways to conduct research and to forge well-informed solutions of ongoing problems in educational practice through multiple perspectives.

The University Side of the Partnership: Local Action With Global Impact. By the time I joined the Laboratory of Comparative Human Cognition (LCHC) in the summer of 1989, its collaborators had already made major strides in developing linkages across institutions that had had no previous relations. LCHC had sponsored, or encouraged, partnerships between university and community institutions worldwide. Despite their diversity, these efforts had a common background: All were related, some directly, some indirectly, to the after-school, computer-based program known as the Fifth Dimension and to a specially designed undergraduate practicum course taught at the respective universities. The two focal points required systematic involvement of university personnel, students, and community members in the task of coordinating activities and resources, thereby promoting mutual relations of exchange across the three cultural systems. By focusing their efforts on after-school activities, LCHC researchers demonstrated the practicality and benefits of using community-based centers as live laboratories in which to conduct research and to practice innovative pedagogy with cross-aged groups (Cole, 1991a, 1991b; Nicolopoulou & Cole, 1993). At the same time, both systems provided a unique form of service that allowed both institutions to benefit from the other's contribution.

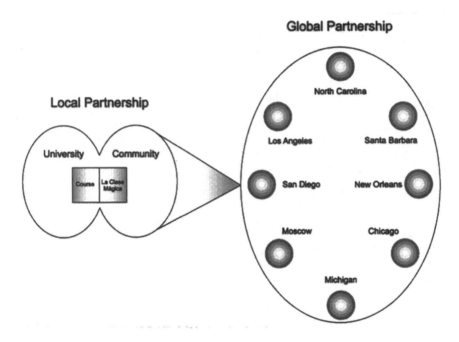

Figure 3.2. Local and global perspectives.

These accomplishments had been achieved largely through several linked components that are at once locally situated and globally dispersed. At the local level, a weekly research seminar, an undergraduate course, and, most importantly, an after-school site were organized around the research interests and pedagogical innovations of sociohistorical theory in the area of cognitive development as a social phenomenon. Globally, the Distributive Literacy Consortium, a research collective of community–university nodes similar to the partnership between UCSD and St. Leo's Mission at Eden Gardens, drew on the expertise of leading national and international scholars from a variety of disciplines, working in diverse contexts with diverse populations (Cole, 1991). The design links the university and community most visibly through the undergraduate course and the after-school activity, but the seminar and research collective also play significant, supportive roles, providing forums for discussion and reflection on all aspects of the course and site activities.

The multidimensional character of the LCHC model, which serves the needs and interests of each of its constituent parts, encourages an active, fully committed form of involvement. The after-school program provides a research site for faculty and researchers; an educational activity for children, including a hands-on learning opportunity for undergraduate students; and a safe, "fun place" for the community's youngsters to be during after-school hours. This design also makes it possible for both institutional partners to contribute to and draw from a mutually created pool of resources that, in addition to physical materials and finances, includes important intangibles, such as shared attitudes of cordiality and respect and greater and more positive visibility for each institution. The connection to members of the research collective whose interests in cognitive and academic development provides a forum for testing of new ideas, setting new goals, and establishing new working relationships.

In the form of *La clase Mágica*, these relations of exchange formed a comprehensive culturally relevant approach to social action, one that sought to enhance minority student's eligibility to higher education and to retained them once they were admitted. I describe these Next.

The Weekly Seminar. In 1978, when Michael Cole joined the faculty of the Department of Communication at UCSD, he brought with him LCHC and its on-going weekly seminar. Focusing on development in diverse contexts, the seminar traditionally drew participation from the local UCSD faculty and graduate students.[6] Periodically, scholars, distributed nationally and internationally also participated in the seminar through a variety of electronic lists; one of which is dedicated to the Distributed Literary Consortium, called XMellon because of its funding agency, the Andrew Mellon Foundation. On many occasions, this distributed group of scholars greatly enriched the experiences of the local participants by actively participating in course discussions and even coauthoring articles. Connected through telecommunication, local participants gain the opportunity to test their ideas in a greater context and form collegial relationships with scholars in different parts of the world.

Across time, the seminar has also benefited by and helped to support the participation of minority scholars. American minorities, like myself, have periodically joined LCHC as postdoctoral fellows dating back to Rockfeller, its previous institution. In this respect, the seminar forms a key context in which reciprocal relations of exchange enrich both the participants and the context in a transformative way. Most of us have integrally incorporated into our own research the ideas of sociohistorical theory elaborated during the weekly seminar. Minority participation, however, has also influenced innovations that have grown out of the seminar. A notable example was the incorporation of the notion of vertical and horizontal integration of resources developed by Moll, Anderson, and Diaz as a foundational element of the organizing structure of the university–community relations of the Fifth Dimension model and subsequently that *La Clase Mágica* initiative. The role of the seminar as a relevant context for minority student achievement was especially evident in the fall of 1995 when Dr. Margaret Gallego, a research associate and former director of *La Clase Mágica*-Midwest, and I offered a course on issues of development in multicultural settings, detailing the lessons we had each learned in our respective sites. Teaching the seminar gave Gallego and myself an opportunity to carve out the intellectual content of our respective manuscripts. But, it also gave us the opportunity to draw on the expertise of nationally known scholars such as Bernard Ferdman, Kris Gutierrez, and Gabriel Gorenzki, who participated periodically throughout the Quarter. The participation of undergraduate students (a rare occasion) and graduate students working as staff members on the research team of *La Clase Mágica* during this Quarter achieved the ideal goals of the intergenerational mentoring process I describe in the previous chapter. Each context of relevance to student achievement in the university and the community was systematically connected by the common goal of enhancing minority student achievement (Moll, Anderson, & Diaz, 1985).

The Research Staff. On the ground, the component that came to represent UCSD in the day-to-day interactions with the community representatives was the research staff. Much of the success of *La Clase Mágica* can be directly related to the talented individuals who made up the initial research team. Limited by funds to support graduate research assistants, I was forced to draw on a pool of undergraduate students enrolled in courses I taught through the Department of Communication. Mostly women and bilingual, these individuals served as the backbone of the research initiative. Their idealism and social consciousness steered the conceptualization of our work as a social action initiative, leaving an indelible mark in the adaptation and development of the project.

What guaranteed success of the adaptation and the program in general was the dynamic open-ended approach to research and program implementation that developed among this small team of undergraduate student staff. On-going staff deliberations about the design, goals, and effect of the adapted materials set in motion a continuous process of innovation, reflection, and transformation that not only permeated every level of the system but also "inspired new levels of thought which contribute[d] to a greater understandings of ourselves and the project" (Henry, 1993, p. 17). The staff members understanding of each other and the goals of the project were crucial to the philosophy of inclusion that embodies our culturally relevant approach. Often painful, the discussions among this diverse research team—which at the time consisted of Anglo, Chicana, and Mexicana young women along with a Chicana professor and Mrs. Dúran—collapsed the paradox expected of teachers in the school, which is to validate others' personal experience from a distance. Our diversity and limited resources forced us to look upon one another for the language and cultural resources to build the knowledge base of the adaptation process.

Across time, other talented undergraduate and graduate assistants have joined the research. For the most part, they are selected from the undergraduate course or in the case of graduate students, for their interests in issues of minority education. Each contributes special insights into the growing envisionment of how best to access educational resources. Each leaves better prepared to seek his or her own accomplishments in a variety of fields. At the time of this writing most of the undergraduate assistants had gone on to pursue graduate level training.

The Undergraduate Course. The three-quarter undergraduate course is one of the key components of our design experiment. It is the university counterpart to the field site in the community. It coordinates the efforts of both partner institutions in providing a unique and culturally relevant education for our future leaders, providing the latest in research and theory and a field site to apply it. It is a context where the critical exchange of the expertise of the professors and the novel and ingenious expressions of the students, feeds a continuous adaptation of the innovation. New ideas are tested, unworkable ones rejected, and on-going change is promoted as students put into practice their learning of technology, child development, and ethnography as child-collaborators and class discussants. At the end of the Quarter, invariably almost 99% of the students claim it to be one of the most important and relevant experiences in their undergraduate careers.

Each Quarter the course alternates focus, variously touching upon three aspects associated with inequality in the education of language minority students: technology, gender and language, and culture.[7] A set of core readings across the three quarters, however, covers all three areas. In 1997, the three-quarter course, Practicum in Child Development, was offered jointly by the departments of Communication, Psychology, and Child Development Program. The 30 or so students who took the course for six units were placed in the various sites that sprung up in North San Diego County, including *La Clase Mágica*.

Theoretically and pedagogically, the course offers one more context for experimentation. Continuously, I have attempted to close the gap between theory and practice by using a pedagogical strategy I call "Collapsing the Paradox," in which the classroom materials and organization replicates the roles students play at the after-school site. In a nonhierarchical context, students take over the responsibility of presenting the course readings with the rest of the class propping their presentations with scaffolding strategies that increase the clarity and quality of the presentations. The students experience first hand how it feels to achieve their optimal performance through each other's scaffolding. They learn to provide one another the right amount of assistance without taking over the task and importantly learn to both trust and respect each other's contributions. Part of the class session also provides for reflection on both their learning in class and at the site. Thus, by the time the students work with the children, they are well informed about what to expect and how to interpret it. As a result, the students' fieldnotes following their observations at site reflect a rich understanding of some of the most difficult concepts of sociohistorical theory: the zone of proximal development, leading activity, and scaffolding.

Importantly, the undergraduate course also expands the conventional framework of child development by integrating language and culture as key aspects of sociopsychological growth. Making these components a central focus of the undergraduates' fieldwork and course readings helps the students grasp the variability of developmental goals and the complexity of culture acquisition in different societal contexts (Greenfield, 1994). Students acquire a greater understanding of cultural diversity as they probe the empirical and theoretical basis of such perplexities as language use and culture construction. Many course papers of students assigned to *La Clase Mágica* have focused on some aspect of the role of Spanish and *Mexicano* culture on social, cognitive, or academic development.

The Distributive Literacy Consortium.   At the system level, the Distributive Literacy Consortium (DLC) is the university component that facilitated the development of a global perspective on local issues. Funded by the Andrew Mellon Foundation, the DLC builds on LCHC's long history of focusing on development in diverse contexts and community-based institutions as educational sites. Loosely organized as a consortium of nine university–community nodes initially paired into three partnerships, the DLC began with a focus on the acquisition of literacy among three distinct populations—Anglo, African-American, and Latino (Cole, 1991).[8] Although locally based and remotely integrated, each node autonomously designs, implements, and evaluates its own version of the common activity. The collective voices of the project directors, students, evaluators, and representatives from the funding agency, each with his or her own stake in the project, co-construct norms and expectations of this distributed community through. The directors periodically report electronically on the trials and tribulations, victories, and setbacks of the local initiatives as well as tackle broader community issues such as evaluation, dissemination, and joint meetings.

Although discussions on this elaborate telestructure do not always result in consensus across its vertical and horizontal lines of communication, they do bring to bear a wide range of resources to understand and act upon issues of practice, research, and theory. Consortium members share knowledge gained through the local experience at site and build on each other's theoretical and methodological experiences and insights. New understandings are distributed across the consortium and are used to construct and revise research objectives. Many different perspectives come together as a function of the list serve discussions. Researchers are thus well positioned to critically assess the merits of a wide range of educational approaches, methodologies, and evaluation procedures.

Although it has shifted in focus across time, the consortium has been committed to diversity at every level of the intellectual enterprise. From its inception, diversity has featured prominently in the conceptual and organizational design, whether the focus has centered on literacy development, institutional sustainability, or the dissemination of innovation, the leading activities of the consortium's three funding cycles. Across its tenure (1991 to 1996), minority representation has been consistent in both the target population and participating researchers. Two of the consortium's initial partnerships, the Bilingual Partnership and the Literacy Partnership, focused on regionally dispersed Mexican immigrant and African-American populations; the third focused on English-speaking children of Anglo background in Southern California. Although the Bilingual Partnership dissolved in the reorganization of the consortium in 1994, the focus on culture and language was retained in the broader system with the inclusion of an outside evaluation team focusing on language and culture and a new member of the consortium, the UC Santa Barbara team headed by Dr. Richard Durán.

The reorganization of 1994 also brought with it a focus on community up-take better known as sustainability. The focus on up-take prompted each research initiative to set new goals to secure the institutionalization of the course and field site by the end of the 3-year cycle. Situated at the hub of the consortium activities and having had a head start over other team members, the two teams at UC San Diego managed to secure support for the three-quarter course very early in the process. Cole's decade-long involvement with the local boys and girls club gave him the leverage to negotiate the up-take of the Fifth Dimension by the community institution. *La Clase Mágica*, on the other hand, having targeted the constituency rather than the administration of its host institution, was on a precarious course. Without outside funding to support the salary of the site coordinator, *La Clase Mágica* was poised to turn to parent volunteers for the management of the site activities. The coalescing of numerous representatives from several relevant community agencies into a formal coalition precluded *La Clase Mágica's* next step in its sustainability plan. Beginning with the immediate crisis at hand—finding funding for the *La Clase Mágica's* coordinator—the coalition quickly moved to a broader agenda: to recruit funds and take up the responsibility of overseeing the operations of all after-school field sites in the community, which had grown to three by 1996. The formation of the coalition moved the Fifth Dimension and *La Clase Mágica* closer to one unified effort at the same time that it jettisoned our sustainability plans to have the "community" take up the day-to-day responsibility of the operations of *La Clase Mágica*. The new source of funding created an interesting problematic but it also assured the continued funding of the community side of the costs.

The Community Side of the Partnership: Founding a New Institution.
When I first entered the *Mexicano* community of Eden Gardens from UCSD, I brought with me the organizational structure of the Fifth Dimension, expecting to implement a program similar to one already operating among predominantly Anglo children in a nearby boys and girls club. However, as the staff and I drew community representatives into the design, implementation, and maintenance of the after-school educational activity, we opened the Fifth Dimension model to reflexive and transformative change that set off a series of modifications dramatically affecting its goals and objectives as well as its structural features. As we began to negotiate for a space to set up our new site, we found ourselves including parents and preschool children in our project goals. By the time we opened the site, the transformation of the Fifth Dimension was well on its way to becoming a social action initiative that aimed at changing the social and academic conditions of bilingual learners, both young and old. Its new name, *La Clase Mágica*, not only reflected the shift in language; it also reflected the integral involvement of a voice seldom heard in educational reform efforts—the community.

The changes that took place in the "community" component of the partnership made *La Clase Mágica* unique and multifaceted. Rather than recognizing the administration of St. Leo's Mission, the host institution, as the collaborating partner as organized by the Fifth Dimension structure, *La Clase Mágica* recognized instead a historically disempowered constituency: working class, Spanish-dominant, *Mexicano* parents as its community partner. In so doing, it recognized the parents and leading members of the community. They were the ones that took on the responsibility of negotiating fiscal and administrative arrangements with the university team rather than the administration of the host institution. Although the church officials have consistently allotted space, office equipment, and a telephone for *La Clase*

Mágica activities, over time their level of interest in *La Clase Mágica* has waxed and waned. Similarly, the relationship between *La Clase Mágica* and Head Start, a federally funded program for preschool children, which shares space with us has varied until 1996 when Head Start became one of its funding sources.

Following, I describe the component parts of the community side of the university–community partnership.[9] I focus principally on the points of contact that developed within and across the three cultural systems and discuss their importance to the overall project of enhancing eligibility to higher education institutions. Some of these contexts developed in tandem with the development of the after-school activity; others, such as the Wizard Assistant Club and the adult computer class, grew out of the changing needs of the program participants. To avoid redundancy I have chosen to leave out a separate discussion of the core activity (i.e., *La Clase Magica*) initially designed for elementary school aged children. With the exception of the parent component, all other activities are modeled after this activity.

The Parent Component. The parents, on the other hand, acting through a loosely organized parent group, have been consistent and enthusiastic in their collaboration with *La Clase Mágica* staff throughout its existence. Initially, community representation in planning for *La Clase Mágica* included adults from the local elementary school, church, Head Start, university, and parents of the children attending the after-school program. However, as the group accomplished its primary goal of deciding how Head Start and *La Clase Mágica* would share space at the mission, collaboration among this group fizzled out.[10] The parents of the children who participated in the site activities remained the most active and consistent participants. Over time, this involvement has taken two forms. First, they regularly participate in a loosely organized yet formal gathering once or twice during a quarter and in times of crisis readily heed a call to meet with the research and implementation staff. They also informally participate in site activities—parents play computer games alongside their children and, attend special gatherings (e.g., end-of-the quarter parties, *Maga's* birthday celebration, meetings with visiting dignitaries, the Friday afternoon sessions of *La Clase Mágica*, and fundraising activities. Parents have responded consistently, although in varying numbers, to requests from the research staff for input on decisions related to the design, implementation, and sustainability of *La Clase Mágica*. Although not all parents attend each of the program meetings every time, all parents at one time or another take part in these activities.

Our experience confirms other evidence that, barring conflicts in work schedule or family responsibilities, *Mexicano* parents from working-class backgrounds will participate in activities related to their children's educational activities (Delgado-Gaitan, 1990, 1996). From the very beginning, our staff not only encouraged parents to attend meetings but also systematically sought to include their suggestions and cultural resources in the on-site materials and activities. By repeatedly encouraging parents to actively participate in all aspects of the operations of the after-school site, we attempted to side-step the hierarchy that teachers maintain when they involve parents in their classrooms (Lareau, 1989). We solicited help with mundane tasks, such as providing snacks, but we also actively asked parents for advice in planning and problem solving.

In preparation for parents' eventual up-take of site operations, the research staff devoted some of the evening parent meetings to in-service training on the technical and pedagogical components of the program.[11] Our goal was to help the parents develop into full partners with the university, thus positioning them to take over site operations as university and the Mellon funding tapered off.[12] We hoped that by training the parents, they would not only become familiar with and integrate into their lives the pedagogical tenets of *La Clase Mágica*, but would also train others, producing a stable pool of committed and skillful staff from the community. Beginning in Winter Quarter of 1995 (the program's 18th academic quarter), parents assumed full responsibility for the Friday session of *La Clase Mágica*. In conjunction with most of the Wizard Assistants, and an occasional undergraduate, parents took over full responsibility for running the site for at least one session per week.

Communicating the goals and objectives of *La Clase Mágica* to parents has been an ongoing, open-ended process. Even in the absence of a full understanding of the program, parents have been quick to grasp the importance of our aims of supporting the program's bilingualism. As one parent aptly stated in an impromptu note written after one of initial early planning sessions:

> En nuestras juntas en unión con Olga se toco el tema de poner nombres para clasificar este projecto y se elijieron nombres de México y su cultura porque la mayoría de los pequeños estudiantes son hispanos y para tratar de acerles recordar más fácil su cultura y sus raíses y logren tener un futuro mejor. [SOC/12/89]

> [In our meeting with Olga we dealt with the topic of selecting names to catalog this project, and names of Mexico and its culture were selected because the majority of the little students are Spanish-speaking and so that they easily recall their culture and their roots and to help them achieve a better future.]

Whether or not this parent understood the full implication of using the children's language and culture as a basis for further learning, it is clear that she under- stood our goal of making Spanish and *Mexicano* culture prominent features in the children's learning activities. She also aligned the goals of *La Clase Mágica* to "help them achieve a better future" with her own personal goals of bettering their economic and social conditions.

Another indication of the parents' awareness of the importance of the program was their willingness to rally en mass to support *La Clase Mágica* every time a crisis arose. For example, the comment "nosotros sabemos lo importante de las computadoras" [we know how important the computers (*La Clase Mágica*) are] was often voiced during negotiations for space with Head Start personnel and church representatives (see later for details on the relationship between *La Clase Mágica* and Head Start). This awareness and commitment to "las computadoras" was tested in Fall of 1996 when *La Clase Mágica's* future teetered in the balance. At the time, neither the community nor the university seemed likely to be able to raise sufficient funds to pay the site coordinator's salary, as stipulated by the funding agency's goals for institutional uptake. The Fifth Dimension site housed at the nearby boys and girls club had received funding from its host institution. For *La Clase Mágica*, the options were volunteerism or closure. The parents' response to this impending crisis was strongly supportive. Having been sufficiently involved in the operations of *La Clase Mágica*, a good number of parents were prepared to staff the site as volunteers not simply on Fridays, but on the other two weekdays that the program normally ran. as well. In the end, this alternative went untried, however. In responding to pending closure, representatives from community institutions involved in the larger project, formed a new group to help support *La Clase Mágica*. The Solana Beach Coalition's first agenda item was the salary for *La Clase Mágica's* program coordinator. Fortunately, two private donors contributed enough funds to cover her salary, simultaneously giving the coalition the time to gain its footing.

La Gran Dimensión [**The Great Dimension**]. From the initial stages of the project the research team recognized the wide dissemination of computer and telecommunication technology in American society and its inaccessibility in minority contexts. Early on they raised the concern of making the computer room available to Eden Gardens adults. Parents, too, after seeing and trying out the computers their children were using. periodically inquired about using computers when the children were not present. In February of 1993, two undergraduate students in collaboration with members of the research staff launched the first computer class. In practice, few parents attended the classes. Instead, these training sessions drew members of the community-at-large. many of whom were parents of preschool children in the Head Start program, our future constituents. Recognizing the importance of computer technology, these parents often bought computers at garage sales and later brought them in during the day to *La Clase Mágica* or *La Gran Dimensión*. the activity that was organized for adults. At the time finding classes where they could learn to use their newly acquired hardware was more of a challenge than finding the computer equipment itself. Between 1993 and 1996, we offered six introductory computer courses. The essence of these classes is captured in the following segment from a fieldnote written by a staff member at one of the first sessions:

> The classes began the 1st of February and are held Tuesday and Thursday evenings for an hour. We were lucky enough to round up eight Macintosh computers for our course—many were the students' [community adults] own home computers—and have focused our efforts on teaching familiarity with Macintosh programs and functions. The four programs we are using are MacWrite, MacPaint, Type!, and Tetris. The class has so far attracted about 7 or 8 enthusiastic attendees, though more have sat in for a class or two.
>
> The ethnic composition of the class is very diverse. Of the eight "regulars," two are Vietnamese immigrants, one is a South African immigrant, four are Mexican immigrants, and one is Mexican-American. Some are monolingual Spanish speakers, some bilingual Spanish–English speakers, and some English–Vietnamese or English–Afrikaans speakers. In terms of gender, the class has attracted more women than men. However, the women have brought their husbands with them on several occasions. One husband and wife team is included in the eight "regulars."
>
> In addition, the level of computer experience varies from student to student, though none have worked on a Macintosh computer before. A few have never seen a typewriter, so working on a computer keyboard is a completely new experience for them. One woman had worked on a bilingual computer for a translator in Mexico, while most others had seen computers in the workplace but never used them. When asked why they were interested in the class, reasons cited were for future work, to help a child with homework, and to teach others how to use computers. [TH/2/10/93]

Notes taken periodically by the students enrolled in the undergraduate course echo this description. They point to the value of the computer course for introducing computer and telecommunications technology to a sector of society with little other opportunity to join the information-based society. Many of the participants in *La Gran Dimension* were using a keyboard and typing letters for the first time in their lives. In the quarters following my leave of absence to write this book, adults who attended the computer program were also taught Website technology.

An important goal of *La Gran Dimension* was to provide one more context in which university and community representatives could engage in meaningful and practical interaction. The sessions provided community members with access to computer resources and training while at the same time giving undergraduates the opportunity to negotiate the theoretical propositions of the practicum course in a setting where the participants' ethnicity and ages varied widely. The sessions offered the undergraduates experiences much like those that their classmates were having during the other age groupings, but with an older group. The fieldnotes submitted by staff and undergraduate assistants attest to the benefits accruing to all parties. The following "reflections" section of an undergraduate student's fieldnotes is representative of the learning that took place among the students and adults. Here, an adult, male, working-class Latino and a middle-class female undergraduate of Asian/African-American background share their respective knowledge. The student frames the interaction within Vygotsky's (1978) notion of the zone of proximal development as she examines her role as a "scaffolder."

> I felt the "AHA" experience and felt a "click" [referring to the term for selecting icons on the computer desktop] today with the adult class. I found that even though JD [technician offering the course] is speaking Spanish and teaching the basics in Spanish, that I should feel comfortable enough to just speak English. I just feel that computers are overwhelming enough, that I should try to speak Spanish and not make the process even more difficult by making them try to understand what I mean in English. I was taught a little lesson in that when Eduardo taught me a little Spanish as I was trying to communicate with him and [he] didn't understand a word. This is a prime example of how I am learning from this whole experience and I am still able to share my knowledge with someone else. I was almost underestimating how much they [other adults] were both understanding of what I was saying until Esteban was playing the game by himself and winning big. I saw my role as "scaffolder" and was able to sit back and just prompt both of them instead of doing the task myself.

Further research and resources directed at evaluating the computer classes will help shed more light on the efficacy or relevance of this context for enhancing the intellectual or technical knowledge and skills of Spanish-speaking adults. Even at this preliminary stage, however, we do know that the participating adults and university students are acquiring valuable experiences. The adults are also learning to negotiate entré into a society, especially those newly arrived immigrants who arrived at *La Clase Mágica* from Mexico or other Latin American countries.

Mi Clase Mágica [My Magical Class]. At the other end of the age span, Mi Clase Mágica or MCM serves the youngest group in collaboration with Head Start, a federally funded program sharing space with *La Clase Mágica* at the mission. Head Start and *La Clase Mágica* came to St. Leo's at approximately the same time and waited for 2 years before they settled into a permanent joint space.[13] Targeting a different age group, the two programs coexisted sharing the same space at the mission and serving basically the same families but at different timing periods: Initially, *La Clase Mágica* opened at 4:00 p.m., after Head Start had closed for the day. Although both programs shared the same goals for a holistic and multicultural approach to development, it would be long before the two programs joined efforts. Head Start's stated philosophy closely resembles *La Clase Mágica's* culturally relevant approach. Its program is founded on the belief that:

> 1. A child can benefit most from a comprehensive, interdisciplinary program to foster development and remedy problems expressed in a broad range of services; and that
>
> 2. The child's entire family, as well as the community must be involved. The program should maximize the strengths and unique experiences of each child. The family, which is perceived as the principal influence on the child's development, must be a direct participant in the program. Local communities are allowed latitude in developing creative program designs so long as the basic goals, objectives and standards of a comprehensive program are adhered to. (Head Start Program Performance Standards, 1992).

Both programs seek to enhance the cognitive development of children primarily through the use of the community's own resources, nonstratified grouping, multicultural curriculum, and bilingual instruction. Both also involve parents integrally as staff, volunteers, and learners.

Along with these similarities, there are also important differences in each program's efforts to bring about substantive social change; perhaps the most basic of these differences is that Head Start focuses on preschool children and provides medical and dental services. These differences alone would not impede a strong working relationship between the two programs, however. What made collaboration difficult, especially in the early stages, were the sharp differences in the amount of funding that each program received and in the specific problems and concerns that the two staffs faced as they tried to launch their respective programs. Finally, the fact that the two programs in the beginning operated at different times and from different locations at the mission added to the independent evolution of each. During the 2 years that we waited for the completion of the facility that was slated to house both programs permanently, Head Start offered two sessions for the community's preschool children in a small trailer at the back of the mission grounds. *La Clase Mágica* held its sessions inside the mission itself, at first, and then later in the kitchen of the mission.

As the new facility was being readied, church officials and representatives from both educational programs met to discuss time schedules and the allocation of resources. Fieldnotes from this period indicate that *La Clase Mágica* staff repeatedly tried to establish a closer collaboration with Head Start. The follow-through was sporadic, however. In return for using Head Start's new and esthetically pleasing space that Head Start was renting from the mission, *La Clase Mágica* offered the staff use of the computers for their class time, undergraduate student help, in-service training, and the potential for cross-age tutoring [SM/9/6/91].[14]   In practice however, institutional constraints, such as limited resources, federal guidelines, and a series of new Head Start site directors, precluded all but the most informal kinds of collaboration between the two programs, even after they moved into shared quarters.

In Fall 1995, the newly appointed Head Start site director stunned *La Clase Mágica* staff with the request to vacate the premises by the beginning of the new year.[15]   Up to this time, relations between the programs had been amicable and workable, if somewhat harried (*La Clase Mágica's* sessions began, literally, as soon as the Head Start activities ended for the day). Up until then, periodic meetings had been held to dispel the inevitable tensions that accompany the sharing of quarters. Joint projects had been successfully undertaken now and again. For example, for three Quarters, both program directors worked closely to introduce computer technology and games to the Head Start teachers and children. And, for more than a year, an LCHC postdoctoral fellow worked closely with the Head Start director to develop computer activities for the program's children and teachers at the same time as she tracked the effects of bilingualism on child development. This history of mutually beneficial relations between the two programs was lost on the newest Head Start director. She found the relationship unworkable and noxious to the esthetics and orderliness of the Head Start program, not to mention the violation of federal and safety guidelines.[16]

Church officials backed the new director's decision and gave *La Clase Mágica* two options: (1) The program could move to the parochial elementary school located in an affluent community about a mile and a half from the mission. (2) It could separate the children into three different groups and spread *La Clase Mágica* throughout the mission grounds, using small spaces available in the kitchen, the clinic, and the back office. Neither option was tenable. Either move would subvert the culture of collaborative learning that had taken root at *La Clase Mágica*, and both would curtail the acquisition and distribution of knowledge that now occurred through expert–novice peer interactions. Moreover, the ease with which parents could "drop-in" on *La Clase Mágica* would be lost if either option were implemented. We had already seen the devastating effects of severed connections when the mission's catechism program was relocated to the parochial school—the number of participants dwindled from a teeming 200 or more children to less than 50.

Parents rallied to *La Clase Mágica's* support. Led by Mrs. Durán, the site coordinator and respected community member, they appealed to each succeeding level of the Head Start administration until they reached the chief area director, Jack Foster. At the parents' request, I approached Mr. Foster, who was a seasoned facilitator of intercultural relations. He not only reversed the site director's decision but also readily perceived the potential benefits of cross-system collaboration.[17] To ensure a successful working relationship between the two programs, he personally mediated the terms of the collaboration, which were worked out in a series of joint meetings at his office. Thus, instead of moving, fragmenting, or closing, *La Clase Mágica* opened the new year with a new goal—to develop an age-appropriate version of its fantasy world for preschoolers. Together, *La Clase Mágica* staff members, Head Start teachers, and a small number of UCSD students began reconceptualizing the site activities in terms of the needs, capabilities, and interests of 4 and 5 year olds. In 1996, this endeavor was still in progress. It would take several years before we would achieve a well-working design for both preschool and elementary school age children. We were confident, however, that improvements in funding ushered in by the new community coalition would guarantee success.

The Wizard Assistant Club. This activity was designed to give children who completed a prearranged set of activities a new purpose for their participation. In the few quarters of the program, two children who had advanced to expert level left *La Clase Mágica* because they felt no particular need to stay. They had completed what was expected of them and no one knew what role they would play from then on. The loss of these participants' accumulated knowledge and assistance was a substantial blow, one that made it clear we needed to develop a new status for children who had participated in the after-school activity long enough and skillfully enough to navigate their way through all 20 rooms of the maze. We created a second tier of participants, with the designation of "Wizard Assistant" (WA). We implemented this new designation and organized special activities for members of the Wizard Assistant Club not only to provide something new to stimulate the interests of our long-term participants, but also because we were keenly aware how much the program benefited from these children's acquired expertise in the specific activities and in the overall technology.

Beginning in Winter 1993, two undergraduate students per quarter were assigned as managers of the Wizard Assistants. The trials and tribulations associated with this position are detailed in the students' fieldnotes and course papers, where they express the difficulty of working with children who are full of contradictions. The students described the children variously as "helpful," "unresponsive," "spoiled," "energetic," "independent," "cocky," "obnoxious," "self-directing," and "self-assured." The managers' task was to create a role for these children who were highly experienced in problem solving, negotiating skills, and directing their own activities. After several quarters, the under- graduate managers devised a set of expectations for the Wizard Assistants that intersected with *La Clase Mágica's* goal of community uptake. This was accomplished through a number of artifacts and specially designed activities for the age and expertise of these participants—a contract with *Maga*, a maze called the Attic, and Internet access.

The Wizard Assistants are recognized as experts in the culture and technology of *La Clase Mágica*. They provide assistance with the overall telecommunications technology and with the individual computer games that are featured in the maze. They are well-versed in the workings of *La Clase Mágica* and are expected to help first-level children and often the undergraduates comply with the norms of the site. A typical example of how these children scaffold the undergraduates responsibilities is by letting the newcomers know what they can and cannot do. "We cannot get into a car without written permission," "we have to play computers half and hour before we can play outside," and "we get to decide where we want to go on field trips." Their role is defined to include most of the same tasks and responsibilities as those assumed by the more experienced undergraduate students. The WAs, as they are most commonly known, help parents run the site during the Friday sessions, they speak at conferences and university classes, and they give orientations to the new set of undergraduates who arrive at the site each quarter. In Winter 1996, the WAs were paid to help out with a new Fifth Dimension site that opened in the local elementary school. This special status has had a strong holding power over the children who become Wizard Assistants and it has inspired other children to follow the rules of *La Clase Mágica* so that they, too, can achieve such rewards.

As we continue to develop age-appropriate adaptations for each of the contexts mentioned earlier and systematically link them into a concerted effort, we get closer to our goal of jump-starting a steady flow of qualified students who can successfully and meaningfully negotiate the various benchmarks of the educational system. These community contexts have made it possible to target key stages of the developmental cycle where institutional support and educational resources are of greatest need. Much more has to be accomplished before a system of reciprocal relations is functioning effectively and systematically. The process is long and labor intensive but well-worth all the investment in time and energy. As I prepared to finish this book, all of the WAs who had reached high-school age were enrolled in college preparatory courses.

These community and university institutional arrangements and separate components create a pipeline, section by section. Aligned by common goals and objectives, that is, enhancing the academic achievement of Latinos—the weekly seminar, the university course, the after-school activity for elementary children, the Wizard Assistant Club, the parent component, the Head Start initiative, and the adult computer classes—each represent benchmarks of the educational system, beginning in preschool and linking elementary, junior, and senior high school, through adult education and higher education. As we continue our deliberate and continuous development and study of how each of the points of contact is systematically and instrumentally interconnected, we get closer to achieving the goal of supplying a "steady flow of qualified students" along an educational pipeline that Moll, Díaz, and Anderson envisioned in the early 1980s.

The institutional relations that evolved in each of the points of contact described earlier position the university and community as equal partners in a collaborative effort. The two institutions combined their interests and resources in developing unique educational experiences for their respective constituencies. The collaboration on designing, implementing, and sustaining *La Clase Mágica*, gradually leveled long-standing distinctions between members, contexts, and goals to produce steady but fragile working relationship. With changes in the content and language of the materials used at site come deeper changes in the relations of exchange between the partner institutions. The direction of the research and of the pedagogy (discussed more fully in the previous chapter) evidenced a slow but deliberate shift. We moved toward a sharper focus on the points of contact between the two institutions, studying the broader learning possibilities of the various contexts and the participant groups.

Revisions have been intertwined; alterations on either side inevitably produced a ripple effect leading to new understandings and further changes. For analytical purposes, I have taken what is a complex web of change and teased apart some of the most significant strands to examine them separately. At the most general level, I have chosen to isolate institutional modifications from content changes in this chapter in hopes of showing the comprehensiveness and multidimensionality of the change that must take place if effective social action is to occur. More importantly, I hope that separating structure and content will make the interrelationship between the macro–micro processes clear enough to demonstrate the range of possibilities that exist at the boundaries of two disparate cultural systems.

SEEING THE FUTURE IN THE PRESENT

The future comes into view when we examine our efforts from this macro-level perspective: it shows us what it would take to make institutional changes to the system and what is possible when we begin to apply the approach widely.

Rethinking the connections and interrelations between each of the relevant points of contact raises the issue that much more than individuals are moving from one context to the next. The ways of thinking and doing practiced in each of these contexts form the foundation for action in subsequent settings. This accomplishment is readily apparent in the adoption of the model by a UC system-wide collective of scholars interested in K–12 achievement of minority students and their adequate representation in higher education. The collective, described next, was appropriately called UCLinks.

UCLinks: An Experiment in Scaling Up. In the fall of 1996, the model described earlier was taken to new heights when UC research teams representing each of the nine campuses in the UC system embraced the model of institutional relations and the possibilities it offered for studying the multidimensional aspects of minority education. Seeing the need for new ways to maintain diversity at the university, given the Regents decisions to eliminate Affirmative Action, the then Chancellor of UCSD, Richard Atkinson, funded Michael Cole and I to explore the possibility of a system-wide consortium. We traveled to each of the campuses and met with colleagues whose work addressed the multiple minority populations underrepresented in the UC system.[18] At each campus, the project piqued the interest of colleagues with a long history of research, teaching, or service in minority populations. The following year, having moved to the presidency of the UC system, Atkinson, again gave his full support to the fledgling consortium appropriately called UCLinks.

The UCLinks system opened with nine UC and CSU (California State University) teams whose task was to examine issues related to academic achievement among minority populations, especially African-Americans and Latinos. Like members of the Distributive Literacy Consortium, each team created a rich environment in which to apply theory and practice and at the same time form part of a comprehensive effort to understand and act upon the multidimensional nature of minority underachievement and underrepresentation. Adopting features of the Fifth Dimension design, each team created after-school learning environments where children and undergraduate students would gather to engage in computer-mediated activities

UCLinks systematically linked local efforts in various minority communities with university students and personnel across all nine UC campuses and several collaborating state university campuses. Each of the university–community nodes established through UCLinks developed and studied an educational activity specifically designed for minority children. Importantly, decisions regarding which point(s) of contact between the university and community would be targeted for research were made according to the needs and interests of the researchers at each node. Thus, the perspective on the problem of minority achievement and underrepresentation in higher education were as varied as the individual interests, academic disciplines, and career trajectories of the participating researchers would allow. Taken together, however, they constituted a concerted effort to effect change in the ways research, pedagogy, and service were conducted in support of diversity. Thus, UCLinks offers a possibility of reaching a much greater number of children across a wider age span by involving other campuses and other communities. Over time, then, this system of relations could encompass students along the full length of the educational system.

UCLinks also offers new hopes for substantive social action in increasing the underrepresentation of minorities in higher education. In committing to UCLinks, the University has taken an active and innovative role in meeting its own goal of recruiting a broader, more culturally diverse student body. This step makes the university a full-fledge member in defining and supporting a culturally relevant approach to education needed to rectify the imbalance in resources and participation so prevalent in present day society. There is much to be learned about whether such an extensive effort can maintain its focus on enhancing minority participation in higher education, but for the moment, the university has established its leadership in meeting the challenges of diversity.

Of course, regardless of how energetic and creative the many participants in UCLinks may be, strong and steady institutional support is critically important if real change is to be sustained over time. The relationships, activities, and outcomes described in this book generate two main recommendations for the UC system in the context of its support for UCLinks. These are:

1. Long-term support for the continued implementation and evaluation of the participating UC teams and lobby funding agencies to help shoulder the burden of financing for the field courses, such as the practicum in Child Development; teaching assistants in each field course to assist with site coordination and fieldnote retrieval (downloading), grading, and archiving; and for the acquisition of up-to-date computers and telecommunication technology to use in the courses.

2. A program to guarantee admission to all long-term participants of the after school sites who meet specific qualifying criteria when they graduate from high school.

WITH GREAT EXPECTATIONS

The example of *La Clase Mágica* suggests hope for the future. The social exchange between a university student and an elementary school-aged child is an excellent place to cultivate a vision of higher education. We are hopeful that in the next 15 years, many of the 200 or so children who have participated in *La Clase Mágica* up until 1996 will be among the 700,000 students who will be ready to enter California's state college and university systems (Assembly Committee on Higher Education, 1994). We expect, as well, that many of the hundreds of graduate and undergraduate students who have collaborated with these children will be among the faculty, researchers, and other institutional representatives who will be in place on campuses throughout the state to welcome the new college entrants. We also expect that these new students and institutional agents will be well informed and prepared to meet the social and intellectual challenges of participation in both institutional contexts: the university and the minority community.

Every child, student, and adult who has participated in the project has gained much more than the academic training provided by the course and site activities. All have gained a unique experience in multicultural education and important insights into the value of diversity. The dynamic relations of exchange that constitute *La Clase Mágica* socialize participants not only to the social norms, attitudes, and skills that are the core of academic life, but also to the kind of social world that recognizes differences as a resource and as an opportunity for growth. Our experience at *La Clase Mágica* has taught us that transforming the educational pipeline means much more than increasing the number of minority students enrolled in higher education. It means creating innovative contexts where all individuals are valued for their contributions to the construction of knowledge.

Today we are in the final stages of our sustainability goals for operating both the site and undergraduate course without outside funding. Over the next couple of years, as I fully divest myself of my leadership responsibilities as head researcher, we will learn what kind of up-take the community and the university will implement in their respective educational settings. At least part of the success of the program as a whole is attributable to its relatively straightforward, observable advantages to both the community and the university. Because reciprocal relations of exchange and the co-construction of knowledge, both integral to problem solving have real, observable consequences. participants on both sides of the partnership recognize the advantages of pursuing joint efforts.

For individual participants, this kind of partnership creates a setting in which a sense of personal empowerment and mastery is not only possible but also likely. No longer is the individual child or adult restricted to the culture he or she was originally socialized into; at the same time, no longer is a foreign and inaccessible culture imposed from above. Individual children and adults are free to pool experiences and resources from multiple domains to construct a new, hybrid culture of possibilities. It is not surprising, then, to find that children who participate in *La Clase Mágica* or, hopefully, in similar programs at other sites, co-construct new images of themselves that afford them higher status among their peers at school (Montes, R., personal communication, October 12, 1995). Granting minority children and their parents ready access to the same kinds of institutional funds of knowledge that members of the dominant culture have always been able to tap helps "level the playing field" in everyday transactions with mainstream society. Gaining cultural fluency allows minorities to "decode the system," by making sense of the cultural logic of the mainstream institutions that most directly affect their lives. This mastery, in turn, yields an expertise that guarantees minorities a more equitable bargaining position vis-à-vis the dominant culture (Dúran, 1995; Stanton-Salazar & Dornbusch, 1995; Stanton-Salazar et al., 1995).

University personnel, for their part, begin to see minority populations in terms that go beyond the singular dimension portrayed by the media or the quaint stereotypes of folk knowledge. Through their field participation as "amigos" rather than as tutors or teachers, university students acquire a consciousness about their own role in boundary-setting in interethnic communication. They learn the crucial role language plays in perpetuating misguided conceptions of cultural and linguistic resources. For example, they become conscious of the negative framing of such concepts as "language barrier," and the damaging effects of labels like "lack of motivation," "disadvantaged," and "at risk." Importantly, they come to question the value of conventional educational practice as they discover, firsthand, its role in producing passive learners. So when students proclaim in their end-of-the-quarter self-reports that the course and site experience was one of the most rewarding experiences of their college career, they are testifying to the role they played as active doers and thinkers.

The partnership between UCSD and St. Leo's Mission also suggests that non-school based community institutions have a role to play in promoting systematic social change. By collaborating with a college or university, a community institution that is not specifically educational in nature or mission can provide the institutional support that local children and their parents need to acquire the kinds of knowledge and skills that are essential for educational success. A community institution can play an important role in helping parents become partners in their children's education by making possible a context in which parents and children come together in after-school hours to engage in learning activities. Through a reciprocal relation with the university, a noneducational community institution can offer undergraduates a unique opportunity to access the kinds of community knowledge and skills that students increasingly demand as basic to a relevant, quality education.

In the next chapter, I delve deeper into the workings of *La Clase Mágica* and examine the tools we have used to create and evaluate this culturally relevant environment. I use the notion of the maze as the representation of a fantasy world to view *La Clase Mágica* as a cultural object from which we can examine cultural production and socialization. I have chosen this approach to engage the reader in a vicarious journey through the fantasy world of *La Clase Mágica* and therefore portray more intimately the experiences of the child participants.

NOTES

[1] Separate Stories of Shared Spaces comes from the work of two undergraduate students—Steve Melton and Tim Andre—who studied the written and oral histories of the city of Solana Beach where the *Mexicano* community of Eden Gardens is located.

[2] The *Mexicano* family and *Mexicano* community are used interchangeably because project participants are drawn from the community and their characteristics are continous with those of the larger group.

[3] A case in point is the historically nonexistent relations between the University of California, Santa Barbara and the adjacent *Mexicano* community of Isle Vista. In 1997 when I was in residence at the Center for Chicano Studies, administrators were unaware of any sustained set of relations with the community nor of any of its members enrolled at the university.

[4] Long-term participants were paid for their assistance at the other after-school programs in the community.

[5] While the small Catholic mission that hosts the after-school site is often referred to as the "community" for administrative purposes, its laity of Mexican descent, in the guise of the Parent Group, more adequately represents the second partner in this three-way relationship.

[6] See Cole's report to Rockfeller in 1984 and his decline of an award by the Council of Anthropology in Education in 1989 denouncing the lack of attention to minority scholarship.

[7] In 1994, Cole and I were compelled to consolidate into one, the independent courses we had each been teaching in association with our respective sites. Teaching three courses a year focusing on our field research constituted two thirds of our teaching responsibilities. The load was professionally and personally taxing. It was also not cost-effective for our department nor advantageous for our intellectual pursuits. We drew support from the Psychology and Communication Departments (the new Child Development Program supplied some funding for a third quarter), and scheduled ourselves to teach the course at least once a year. Mindful of other sensitive contradictions—the asymmetry of an older male and senior professor and a junior Chicana assistant professor—we managed to balance the curriculum foci to support the theoretical emphasis at both sites. Deliberate action was taken to guard against default to the intellectual content of either course.

[8] The configuration changed dramatically after the first level of funding when three sites closed as a result of insufficient insitutional support by the university or community or both—the Chicago site, the New Orleans site, and Michigan sister site of *La Clase Mágica*-west. The idea of

a two-team partnership was abandoned and three new units were added in Santa Barbara, North Carolina, and Whittier, California.

[9]Because a detailed discussion of *La Clase Mágica* site activities, including the context and transformation of the after-school program, is given in chapter 2 and throughout, I do not include *La Clase Mágica* in the description of the component parts of the university–community partnership presented here.

[10]In fairness to the other institutional representatives, it should be noted that parents were much more easily and readily accessible to the research staff. For example, when parents dropped off or picked up their children, staff would remind them of particular tasks or responsibilities they had agreed to undertake and would encourage them to attend upcoming meetings, etc. These informal exchanges contributed directly to a closer, more mutually rewarding relationship between staff members and parents.

[11]Since I opened the field site as a postdoctoral fellow with no guarantee of a permanent position, parents were prepared from the beginning for the eventuality of my departure.

[12]From the beginning, *La Clase Mágica*, like other Fifth Dimensions, was designed to eventually become self-sustaining. The goals of the Distributive Literacy Consortium specified that the community institution would take up the funding responsibilities of the costs for site operations, specifically the coordinator's salaries and the up-keep and replacement of computer hardware and software. The sustainability goals for the university involved the institutionalization of the practicum course. Thus, as long as the community was able to fund the operations of the field site, the university would support it would students and expertise of its involved faculty.

[13]Initially, church officials guaranteed space for both programs but as it turned out Head Start ended up paying rent for the space *La Clase Mágica* would come to share with them.

[14]*La Clase Mágica* stood to gain more than attractive surroundings if it shared the new space with Head Start. The new location would finally afford the opportunity to leave the computers and related activities set up and ready to use, from day to day. This would dramatically reduce the time we spent on "mechanics" and physical preparations for each session.

[15]By this time, *La Clase Mágica* was occupying a large part of a small house trailer at the mission that housed the Head Start office. The year before, the previous director had negotiated with the parents to move *La Clase Mágica* to the small trailer so the Head Start program could apply for an excellence award. It was agreed that *La Clase Mágica* would move to the small trailer and that it would not have to move again. The new director chose to ignore that agreement and she convinved church officials to support her position.

[16]She charged that *La Clase Mágica's* tables and chairs were too high for preschool children, that the room was too crowded, and that the wall posters were inappropriate.

[17]The parents' achievement especially impressed long-term members of *La Clase Mágica* staff. Involving Head Start intregally in the activities of *La Clase Mágica* had been a goal from the onset of the project, but lack of resources had prevented a systematic relationship. Most recently, LCHC has made efforts to widen and deepen the collaboration with Head Start by incorporating help from other San Diego area universities. In Fall 1997, University of San Diego professor Steve Gelb offered to provide UCSD students assigned to Head Start with telecommunication access to his courses on child development, which focus on preschool children.

[18]Cole, Scott Woodbridge (graduate student in Santa Barbara and long-time member of the LCHC staff), Charles Underwood (Office of the President) joined us as we criss-crossed the state proposing the new consortium.

4

A System of Arifacts
for a Methodology inAction

The cultural and physical location of *La Clase Mágica*, as well as its position between fantasy and reality, poses unique methodological challenges for traditional evaluation. Funding agencies, review committees, parent groups, and newcomers want to know what *La Clase Mágica* is and what it does. The context and the listener necessarily shape the explanation. Some hear the short of it: *La Clase Mágica* is a computer club for bilingual children (see Fig. 4.1).

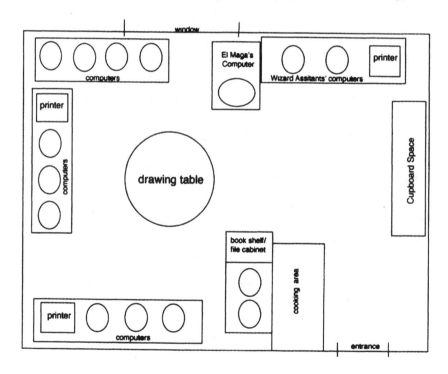

Figure 4.1. Map of site.

104

Others hear the long of it: *La Clase Mágica* is an innovative, after-school educational activity that links university and community institutions in partnership to funnel educational resources and institutional support to local bilingual children. Between these two broad characterizations are numerous accounts that focus on specific aspects of *La Clase Mágica*. This book, for example, provides four other distinct perspectives that shed light on the institutional relations, curriculum, language use, and participation structure of this ever-changing project.

In this chapter's telling, I focus on the project's system of artifacts. These were designed to accomplish two purposes: to enhance the development of the participants and to study the program's own "internal transitions and transformations" (Leont'ev, 1978). Both material and symbolic, these artifacts organize life at the intersection of multiple borderlands that include space, language, generation, ethnicity, class, and identity. Specifically, they help construct a world at the nexus of fantasy and reality in the minds and social relations of children from a *Mexicano* community and adults representing the university. It is a world of worlds where bilingualism and multiple knowledge sources facilitate everyday literacies and an unusual conceptualization of a multicultural identity. The merger of these multiple worlds is clearly evident in a clip from a widely distributed video on *La Clase Mágica*. In the video, an Amiguito [a child participant] and an undergraduate Amigo [friend] ponder the problem of how to get to the other side of the river in the computer game "Oregon Trail. " The following exchange occurs:

Amigo:	Oh, we'll need a ferry to cross here.
Amiguito:	A fairy? A fairy to drive us?
	[pause] Oh, yeah. With dust.
Amigo:	Dust? Dust? How does that work?
Amiguito:	Dust. You put dust on the wagon and it flies.
	Then, it gets out wings.
Amigo:	Oh—fairy dust.
Amiguito:	Yeah, dust. (unintelligible)
Amigo:	That's incredible!

This intricate interweaving of multiple worlds is a fundamental characteristic of *La Clase Mágica*. Resources and possibilities for being are drawn from many different venues, including the children's home culture, their host community, *La Clase Mágica*, and new sources that are generated from multiple combinations. It is a cultural system that prepares children and adults for multiple possibilities through what Vygotsky aptly described as the:

> . . . socially structured ways in which society organizes the kinds of
> tasks that the growing child faces and the kinds of tools, both mental
> and physical, that the young child is provided to master those tasks.
> (Luria, 1979, p. 44)

In other words, the children at *La Clase Mágica* can imagine themselves
traversing a fantasy world because of the substance that is given by the cultural
artifacts and the corresponding social relations that arise from the use of these
artifacts (Holland & Cole, 1995).

The way in which the system of artifacts interacts with the everyday
life at *La Clase Mágica* is one of the project's most interesting characteristics
but it is also one of the biggest liabilities with regard to standard evaluation
procedures.[1]   Our work closely parallels the theoretical and empirical goals
of the classroom-based design experiments conducted by Brown (1992),
however, this interaction between artifacts and reality precludes meeting
all aspects of an experimental design. For example, distinctions between
researcher–implementer, learner–expert and creator–observer of culture,
essential divisions for objective measures of assessment, are blurred in an
activity structured to level the power structure and allow equal participation by
all those involved. Thus, asymmetrical power relations, an informal learning
environment, and magical realism, key features of the Fifth Dimension structure
upon which *La Clase Mágica* is built, present insurmountable challenges to a
traditional experimental design. Even the standard approach to measuring
individual achievement is inconsistent with the project's voluntary, collaborative,
and egalitarian character. On occasions when we have submitted to pressures for
"objective" evidence of program impact, components that have been intricately
woven into every aspect of the project—such as individual choice—have proven
incompatible with control conditions. A related element, voluntary participation,
produces such pronounced selection bias that generalizable results are
impossible. Over time, we have conducted matched comparisons and within-
group comparisons on second language acquisition and language maintenance of
the treatment group over the control group, however, our results cannot be used
to draw empirical conclusions about *La Clase Mágica's* because of this selection
bias. What we can do, however, is trace the participants' developmental
trajectory in bilingualism, biliteracy, and computer skills as well as note their
acculturation and identity formation.

Rosaldo's (1989) critique of classic social analysis has been a source of
support in pursuing the evaluation of program effects on learning and
development. We have viewed life at *La Clase Mágica* as in continual flux, "not
fixed and constraining," as the dominant positivist approach assumes (p. 32).
Rather, it is in a state of becoming, constantly changing in response to
new understandings and newly formed conditions. On-going research and

discussions among the adult participants (e.g., in class with the undergraduates and in staff and parent meetings) have repeatedly pointed to the ephemeral quality of hard facts from *La Clase Mágica*. For example, when we take time, as researchers, to appraise our understandings, we find that we can only describe a given moment in time. By the time we return to the activity as implementers, our current understandings frequently are outdated. Conditions have changed, the children have moved to a new level of maturity and new goals have been set in motion.

Another obstacle to providing a definitive assessment of what *La Clase Mágica* is and what it does is the project's unique borderlands character. Life at *La Clase Mágica* is situated halfway between home and school and links Spanish and English, adult and child, minority and mainstream, low income and middle class, and *Mexicano* and American in multiple and complex ways. Participants use multiple epistemologies and multiple knowledge sources for meaning making and problem solving inevitably making it almost impossible to secure a neat measure of achievement. For example, assessment tools typically determine achievement in a single language only. The norms of communication of *La Clase Mágica*, in contrast, involve an intricate combination of both Spanish and English. Under these conditions, a monolingual approach is inadequate for assessing a child's actual level of performance (the goal of current educational practice); it also lacks the ability to distinguish between what an individual can accomplish individually and what he or she can accomplish in collaboration with a more experienced partner (the goal of sociohistorical theory). At best, monolingual tools can claim certainty regarding only a very narrow definition of children's abilities.

Although cultural fluidity of *La Clase Mágica* thwarts the possibility of project evaluation free of circumspection, it does lend itself to tracking the processes by which participants become active members of the culture. Achievement, in this case, is not measured by an arbitrary mark on a piece of paper, or by the ability to display discrete skills and isolated forms of knowledge. Rather, achievement is understood in terms of the process of acculturation of the newcomer into master participant. The developmental trajectory from inexperience to mastery, a distance that can be anywhere from a few minutes to a few months, is the measure of success for both the individual and the project. It is not a linear path, rather it is a circuitous course of spurts and dips as learners learn to master new information and skills connected to the games and activities in a natural but uneven manner. The adults—usually undergraduate students enrolled in a specially designed practicum course—and the system of artifacts, carefully guide the newcomer through a series of actions and activities that constitute the life of *La Clase Mágica*.

The transformation of an uninitiated participant into that of expert is symbolically represented by a journey through the Laberinto Mágico [The

Magical Maze] consisting of a 20-room maze. The journey literally marks the child's progress through a prearranged set of activities at the same time that it tracks the developmental trajectory of the newcomer. The learner not only practices everyday skills and language embedded in the activities, he or she also acquires the norms and expectations of an acculturated member of the system. From the very first step—when the child is asked to choose one of four possible points from which to enter the maze—the journey demands active and deliberate participation. At the end, having made hundreds of other decisions about which direction to take, what game and level to play, what language and culture to use, the child exits the maze as a transformed being; one with expert knowledge of how things work at *La Clase Mágica* (Vásquez, 1994). At that point, the first-level participant assumes the role of Wizard Assistant, the highest rank of expert in the system (apart from *El Maga*).

Thus, the metaphor of "the journey through the maze" is an ideal heuristic to examine the processes by which children accomplish the transformation of novice to expert participant (i.e., the socialization into the bilingual community of learners). It also captures the conceptual framework for viewing *La Clase Mágica* as a hybrid culture full of new possibilities and new identities. As the children move from imaginary room to imaginary room, solving problems and accomplishing tasks, we get a good look at how their learning and development is enhanced by the material and symbolic artifacts that constitute an educational activity in action. Importantly, it provides a vista for seeing how children conduct themselves in a world in which they are capable and able participants, a world in which bilingualism and biculturalism as well as intergenerationalism is the norm. Next, I elaborate on the dual nature of this constructed reality and then describe ways in which such a system of artifacts simultaneously concretizes a fantasy world for the participants and frames their behavior and social interactions. In the section following, I organize the evaluation tools in a maze format and employ a pedagogical strategy I call "collapsing the paradox" to engage the reader in a vicarious journey through the fundamental principles of *La Clase Mágica*. My goal is to provide the reader with a deeper understanding of the complex and multifarious character of both the evaluation and acculturation processes at *La Clase Mágica*. I conclude with a discussion on the projected outcome of a journey through the maze: the transformation of the participant from novice to expert.

CULTURE AND MIND IN PLAY: NAVIGATING THE FRONTIERS BETWEEN FANTASY AND REALITY

The combination of play and education strategically redefines the possibilities for what a child can accomplish at *La Clase Mágica*. It also redefines how adults can engineer learning environment that promotes optimal learning potential. Together, the adult and the child create a world between fantasy and reality that is grounded in social relations and computer technology especially designed to encourage literacy practice. As the child reads and writes at the computer, often in collaboration with more capable peers, he or she envisions another self, an adventurer through a fantasy world governed by a magical being called *El Maga* [literally, the Wizard].[2]   The order in which the children visit the rooms of the maze symbolically delineates the journey through the fantasy world of the Fifth Dimension. Play liberates the child to imagine him or herself capable of great feats at the same time that it allows the adult to circumvent constraints endemic to the educational system (Vygotsky, 1978), for example, scope and sequence, next-step progression, and a singularity in knowledge, language, authority, and place (Nocon, 1997).

Prompts from the adults and *El Maga's*, "¿En que cuarto vas?" ["In which room are you?"] repeatedly locate the children at specific junctures in time and space. To respond to the adults and *Maga*, the children must pay close attention to where they are and where they have been as well as where they are headed. The questioning holds them to the task at hand, prompts them to reflect on their accomplishments, and reminds them to set their sights on achieving Wizard Assistant status. Thus, the system of artifacts, *Maga*, and the adult participants—frequently undergraduate students trained in the theoretical and philosophical foundations of the *La Clase Mágica*—slowly craft the path of socialization for the child participants and in many ways for the adults as well.

Taking the Journey.   When a child enrolls in *La Clase Mágica*, he or she is handed a folder containing the "tools" needed for the journey through *El Laberinto Mágico*: an application, a copy of the constitution, a map of the maze, a journey log, and magical passes. The site coordinator (supervising adult typically from the community) uses these artifacts to weave an elaborate portrait of an imaginary land abounding in adventures and magical beings—*El Maga*, *La Mosca Cosmica* [The Cosmic Fly, *Maga*'s trusted companion]. The introductory instructions typically, given in Spanish, cover basic points:

> You use the maze to mark the games you have played. After each level of play, you write to *El Maga* as indicated by the task cards. You must complete 10 of the games at "good" or "expert" level so that you can become *Maga's* Assistant. As a Wizard Assistant, you will be able to join the Wizard Assistant Club and play in the Attic where you get special privileges such as cruising the Internet, trying out new games, earning money as consultants, and going on field trips.

The beginner is then shown the "Game Box," where approximately 70 "adventures" in the guise of computer and board games are organized according to the names of the rooms of the maze. Each folder contains a game-specific "Task Card" (instruction guide) that lays out the criteria for three levels of play— Beginner, Good, and Expert; "Consequence Cards" that indicate the mobility options after each level of play; and ancillary materials, such as a "Tip Sheet," free passes, and other mnemonic devices to help the traveler move through the games and the rooms.

After this brief introduction and administrative chores, the child is shown the map of the maze and is asked to make the first of many decisions:[3] "From which of the four entrances do you want to enter the maze (see Fig. 4.2)?" Not only does this question direct the little adventurer to assume control of the decision-making process, it also asks him or her to anticipate future actions. From this point onward, adults take a back-seat approach, acting as material and intellectual resources for the children as they journey through the maze. At every turn, children are called to make decisions. For example, a child who enters Cesar Chavez Room (Room 15) must decide whether to play the game "Aztlan" or the game *"El Jardín de Abuelita"* [Grandmother's Garden]. Having decided on the game, the child must then select the level at which to play: Beginner, Good, or Expert. After completing a level, other decisions arise: Should she play the same level again? Should she write to *El Maga*, as the Task Card directs? Should she play another level of the same game? Or, should she go to the next room and play a new game there? Choice and its concomitant components, awareness and engagement critical elements for learning (Stowitschek, 2000), become elemental to every action that children take in their course through the maze.

Aside from making choices, children continually practice problem posing, problem solving and self-reflection, three important elements of critical thinking. The game environments and the computer technology repeatedly impose problems that the little adventurers must face and overcome. Examples of such problems include finding the right combination of elements to grow a 100 cm plant (in the game Botanical Gardens), getting across a river (in the game Oregon Trail), or sustaining the connection to the Internet without interruptions. These and other, similar problems open zones of possibility in which the adults or more capable peers play a key role "in mediating the activities, especially helping the students [children] to be active in creating and shaping their tasks" (Moll & Greenberg, 1990, p. 330, emphasis in the original). Adults support the children's actions with their greater knowledge of the world. Taking a back-seat role, they solicit information, direct to other sources of knowledge, and often provide pertinent terminology, visuals, and other sources to help the child surmount his or her difficulties. They also provide key examples from their own personal experiences and those of the children to make strategic connections to prior knowledge.

Whereas the norms of adult–child interaction locate children in their own developmental trajectory, the system of artifacts also helps shape their mental activity. The Task Card, for example, encourages imagination, reflection, and association. One example is the Task Card for Botanical Gardens/*El Jardín de Abuelita* (see Fig. 4.3). The specially adapted Task Card asks children to imagine themselves as abuelita's helpers, a common experience among *Mexicano* populations. At the end of each level of play, the children are asked to recount their game-related activities to *El Maga*.[4] And, in the reflection section, the card asks players to assoicate their game knowledge to culturally specific ways of growing and using plants (specifically, medicinal and culinary purposes). On completion of the Good level, children are asked to create a recipe and to provide details about the process of making the food or medicine: "Would you dry it up and crush it into fine powder? Or, mix it with other things to make a healing ointment?" At the expert level, children are asked to tell *El Maga* abuelita's [grandmother's] secrets for growing 100-centimeter plants. In other words, the children are prompted to reflect upon game-related knowledge using previously acquired home experiences as a base which, according to Vygotsky's theory, build on prior history.

As the young players move through this constructed world, they change cognitively, culturally, and socially. Their growing envisionment (Langer, 1987) of self as capable and able is supported by an increasing competence across a community of learners. The children's evolution from beginner to master, marked by their advancement to Wizard Assistant, increases their status as well as their expertise: The adults begin to view them as equal partners in the problem-solving process (Litowitz, 1990). In a ritual that has come to be marked by an end-of-the quarter party, the advancement to Wizard Assistant is publicly announced and celebrated.

COLLAPSING THE PARADOX: IMAGINING OPTIMAL POSSIBILITIES

The process of enculturation to the norms of *La Clase Mágica* is gradual but deep. It is unclear exactly when or for how long the children buy into the idea of a fantasy world or accept the authority of the magical overseer. We are certain, however, that it takes a considerable amount of time before a newcomer, whether adult or child, comprehends the full extent of our proposition. Given the introduction to the magical world cited before, children eagerly take on the challenge of getting to the end of the maze. Even rank beginners seem untroubled by their utter lack of knowledge about how the conceptual system

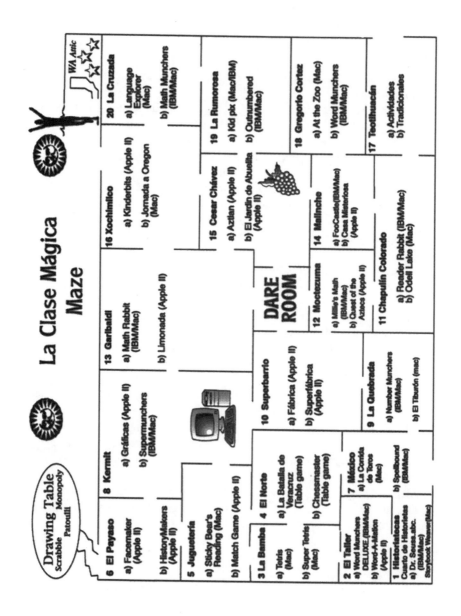

Figure 4.2. *La Clase Mágica* maze.

BOTANICAL GARDENS/ EL JARDIN E ABUELITA

You are helping your 'abuelita' (grandmother) in her garden. Your abuelita has learned through the years that changing environment elements such as water, sunlight, soil richness and heat, can affect the growth of plants. Help her find the best combination of these variables to create the tallest plant.

BEGINNER: (Use arrow key to move your hand around the screen. When your hand is on the spot you want, press RETURN.)

First, go to the SEED ROOM. Select two plants to grow.

Put Donkey-Breath in Greenhouse 1. Put a different plant of your choice in Greenhouse 2.

Leave the SEED ROOM and enter the LIBRARY to get a description of the plant.

Go to Greenhouse 1. Go to GROW and press RETURN. Very small Donkey-Breath right?

Move the hand to the ENVIRONMENT and press RETURN.

All four elements are set at 0. Try to find the amount of light that the plant grows best in by gradually changing the amount of light while leaving the other values the same. After selecting a value for light, go to DONE and then to CLEAR, then try GROW to see if the growth of the plant has increased. Go back to the ENVIRONMENT and keep changing the valuers until the plant reaches about 100cm. Be sure to only change one value at a time. Look at the GRAPH ROOM after each change to see what happened.

GOOD: Create your own plant. Does a plant grow best with little or alot of water? Does it need rich soil? What about light and heat?

Go to the main lobby of the Botanical Gardens and hold down the CONTROL (CTRL) key at the same time that you press the "T" key. (you get a new menu, right?) Now create a plant!!! Choose either A or B below:

A. Create a plant that can be used for cooking. In the LIBRARY, describe the purpose of the plant.

B. Create a plant which has a medical purpose. In the LIBRARY, describe it.

Follow the instructions the computer gives you for creating a plant, and fill in the chart to say what will happen at different settings.

Write a recipe describing how you would use your plants. For example, would you dry it up and crush it into a fine powder?, or mix it with other things to make a healing ointment?, or boil it and make tea? Who would use it?

EXPERT: This time, create a plant that will help solve a social problem, such as drought.

Read the Good Level and learn how to create a plant. Then, fill in the chart to say what will happen at different environmental settings.

Write to El Maga and describe how your plant will help solve a social problem in your area, state, or country.

(HINT: You may find it helpful to write down the values of light, soil, heat and water to help you keep track of changing the values).

After you grow Donkey-Breath to 100 cm, grow the plan in Greenhouse 2.

Tell El Maga Abuelita's secrets to growing 100 cm tall plants.

Figure 4.3. El Jardin de Abuelita task card.

works, and they are equally unfazed by the invitation to participate in a fantasy world. Adults, on the other hand, are more reluctant to commit themselves. They require justification, examples, and personal experience before they understand and accept the pedagogical rationale behind the system of artifacts.[5]

The need for a prolonged period of enculturation is problematic for the training of undergraduate Amigos/as [friends] and for adequately portraying the impact of *La Clase Mágica*. Moving a self-selected group of committed and talented students into the research sites quickly and able to assume a specific role, presents a special challenge to the professor. The prolonged period of enculturation becomes a liability for the students and the project when the course is only 10 weeks, the length of an academic quarter at UCSD. Undergraduates are sent to the site during the first week of the course, before they have a full grasp of the theoretical and practical implications of our work and their particular role in the system. As field notes strongly illustrate, students gain more from their experience when they understand what is expected of them both academically and socially. It is also beneficial to the amiguitos/as [little friends] they work with and the overall project that is invigorated by those with greater understanding and acceptance of the role they are asked to play. This understanding takes time and considerable effort.

In the past, the quarter came to an end right about the time the students had gained mastery of theoretical concepts of the course to sufficiently understand the underlying pedagogical approach. Several strategies had been built into the course to support students' understandings (e.g., site orientation, class introductions of site personnel and inclusion of site-specific research literature, videos and graphics). Still, the complexity and objectives of such a multitiered initiative proved to be too much at the beginning of the course. In the fieldnotes and in office hours, students bemoaned the 2 to 3 weeks of confusion in the early part of the course. Regrettably, this often meant a loss of almost 4 weeks (1 week was lost to the end-of-the-quarter activities) of expert participation on the part of the students.

In the winter quarter of 1996, I implemented a pedagogical strategy I call "collapsing the paradox" to remedy the extensive period of enculturation and also to facilitate a paradigm shift in the students' notions of pedagogy. As products of the educational system, the undergraduates enter the class believing in and practicing a "product-oriented" form of pedagogy. Their prior experience has taught them that grades, test scores, and mastery of discrete skills (e.g., spelling, pronunciation, recitation) are reliable indicators of children's academic ability. And, in good faith they set out to teach the children "the skills they need to make it in the real world." None of their commentary, whether in fieldnotes or class discussions, alludes to the incongruity of practicing a form of pedagogy they have very little experience with. They accept the authority of the professor or that of the written page and confidently, as they have been taught throughout their schooling. go out to put into practice a sociohistorical approach to learning and development that boggles the minds of some of its most ardent supporters.

By collapsing a framework that directly contradicts the norms of *La Clase Mágica*, I hoped to "subjectivize" the social and theoretically based practices students were expected to absorb and transmit as pure abstractions. The conventional pedagogy of the undergraduate course negated the project's fundamental principle of placing the learner in control of his or her own development. Building on Freire's (1981) work, I redesigned the course to teach through praxis and thereby expedite the philosophical and pedagogical development of adult expert participation. I focused specifically on a "continuity of experience" which Dewey (1938) suggested is critical to directing the growth of the immature. I wanted to give students first-hand experience of the many goals and objectives children were expected to achieve for themselves at site; become skilled in decision making, problem solving, and objectifying experience. By practicing in class their designated roles and responsibilities expected of them at the field site, students could better understand and therefore expect a higher quality of experience from the children. I wanted the class session to open the students' minds to new possibilities for learning. In "living" the multiple roles they were expected to play at the after school site (i.e., friends, learners, collaborators, observers, and creators of culture), I hoped they would be able to anticipate and/or create conditions that facilitate optimal performance.[6] In Dewey's terms, my goals were to render the student "more sensitive and responsive to certain conditions, and relatively immune to those things about him[/her] that would have been stimuli if he [/she] had made another choice" (p. 37).

Although the adaptation of the course was constrained by the inability to easily accommodate play and cultural relevance manifest at the field site, many of the pedagogical conditions were integrated into the curriculum. I organized the class readings in a maze format and discarded the structural arrangements that grant power to only one "authority" in the classroom, the professor (see Fig. 4.4). I conducted the class with students seated in a circle and organized the course requirements around a student-run format.[7] The seating arrangement offered numerous opportunities to deconstruct the role of collaborator for the students as I called attention to my contributions as either assuming control of the discussion or providing the scaffolding strategies the students had been asked to learn. The class "journeyed through the maze" of course readings as a collective, making group decisions about which of the two readings to do, at what level to engage the material, and which "room" to go to next. Heavy guidance from me during the first three sessions provided an excellent opportunity for introducing the course and one of its most salient theoretical constructs, the zone of proximal development. This construct posits that the amount of assistance by the "more capable peer" is inversely related to

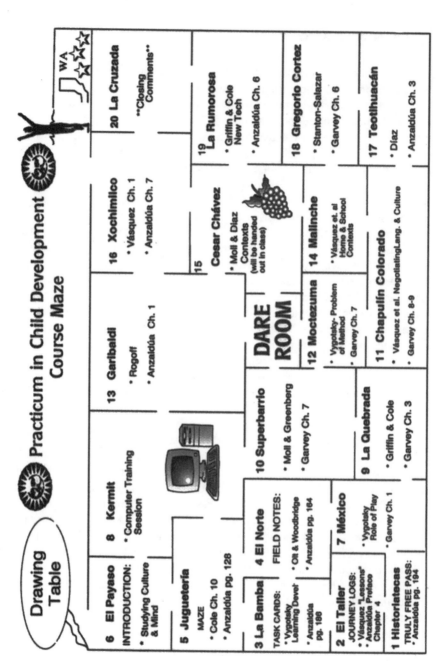

Figure 4.4. Practicum course maze.

the growing expertise of the novice (Vygotsky, 1978). As the students gained more expertise. I retreated to the role of collaborator.

The course activities provided ample opportunities for the students to engage in decision making, problem solving and self-reflection, as well as opportunities to "try out" the roles of *Amigo(a)* and *Amiguito(a)*. As *Amiguitos*, or novices, they prepared presentations of the required readings and posted a summary of the course discussion on the listserve for the class and the Mellon Consortium (in lieu of reflecting upon their experience in a letter to *El Maga*).[8] As *Amigos(as)*—more expert peers—the rest of the students supported their classmates' presentations to help them achieve a greater understanding and consequently a better presentation of the readings. They read the material in advance, focusing on specific strategies that would help the presenters give a lucid and well-informed presentation. Throughout the presentation, some helped the Amiguitos (presenters) define the main idea and key concepts of the readings. Others offered new information and personal experiences when appropriate. Others still brought visual aids and specially selected examples from the site to exemplify the theoretical concepts in the readings. At the end of the session, a couple of students were assigned to assess their *Amiguitos'* performance by filling out a Record Progress Form—analogous to the children's Journey Log— where they commented on the presenters' level of performance; noted useful strategies employed by the presenteers; and suggested ways to improve the presentation(s). These assessments were handed to the presenters to use in a fieldnote on the session—simulating the reflection exercise in the Task Cards. The format allowed students to sample first hand the multiple identities the project offers: *Amigo, Amiguito*, beginner, expert, collaborator, researcher, implementer, and authority figure—one student volunteered each week to write a comment to the class as *Maga*.

Although many of the students nevertheless experienced culture shock in the first session, overall, the course was a great success. Class discussions were dynamic, informed, and instructive. The following excerpt from a student's Self-Reflection, a final requirement asking students to track their own development across the course, is representative of the overall assessment of the student's reaction to this approach:

> What I enjoyed most about the course and visits to site was the ability to incorporate what I learned from the course readings with my experience at site. The interaction between theory presented in the readings and the practical application at site was very significant in my own learning and developmental process. I thought the readings were especially interesting and applicable to the to the environment at La Clase Mágica. The structure of the class in terms of the presentations and discussions was also a welcome change to the traditional lecture style courses at UCSD. I learned through the

continual exchange of knowledge between the participants of the class. The structure of the course allowed for a more complete understanding of the concepts introduced by the readings. [TN/Winter 1996: Self Reflection]

The Enculturation of the Reader: Journeying Through the Maze of the Project's Methodology. In real-life settings, the complexities embedded in the proposition of a possible world characterized by a new set of goals for social relations and new visions of self are negotiated in on-going social relations. But, conveying this complexity and its concomitant dynamism and potentialities in written form poses unique challenges. How best to communicate the richness of both the cultural objects and the cultural experience? This could be accomplished if only the objects and experience would hold still so that we could mount them exhibit-like on the page in the style of classic social analysis (see Rosaldo, 1989). But ours is a "garage sale," as Rosaldo called the new way of viewing social reality, and our task is the "dynamic analysis" of development that Vygotsky's (1978) theory mandates. To capture life in action, in a continual progression through multiple levels and multiple dimensions, I have to try something radically new.

At least three options for conveying a vicarious experience of life at *La Clase Mágica* are clear to me: (1) I could write a methodological treatise about how I conducted the study, (2) I could follow a child through the maze, citing the tools that were used to track his or her socialization to the culture of *La Clase Mágica* or, (3) I could collapse the paradox once again and take the reader through a maze of the methodological tools using the style of a popular genre of the 1980s where the reader participates in the construction of the narrative: "Choose Your Own Adventure Stories." In this children's literature, the reader makes a series of decisions at specified junctures in the narrative, selecting one of several options for continuing the story line.

I have chosen the third option. More than the other two, this approach offers the possibility of engaging the reader, drawing him or her to actively deconstruct the process of culture production and enculturation to a new set of norms. My goal is to go beyond the first two options in the scope and breadth of the account at the same time as I engage the reader in an imaginary journey through the theoretical and philosophical decisions that were made by *La Clase Mágica* staff in deciding the appropriate methodological tools to both create and assess the program. It is a radical departure from conventional presentation of information that builds on the first two options which I employ throughout this book. The case studies of Carlos and Rina in chapter 5 and the adaptation process in chapter 2 are examples of the first two options. Despite the absence of face-to-face interaction and the constraints imposed by a medium that necessarily objectifies experiences in order to avoid inundating the reader in the minutia of the moment, this third option grants some of the same sense of continuity that I tried to bestow upon the undergraduates when I collapsed the paradox for them. At minimum, this strategy re-enacts some of the children's experiences as they move through the maze; at best, it captures the complexity of a multilevel and multifaceted approach to learning and development.

Implored by Michael Cole to write fieldnotes on every experience we had and driven by ethnography's tradition of gathering many different kinds of data in order to increase the validity and reliability of findings (Wilcox, 1982), the staff and I treated every interaction, every text, and every artifact as method or data. When we examine these activities closely, 20 different types of tools are discernible.[9] I have organized these tools and their respective varieties in a maze format (see Fig. 4.5, System of artifacts maze).[10] In keeping with a theoretically informed and empirically based account of the learning and development that takes place at *La Clase Mágica*, I have created an imaginary account of a mythical Reader-Friend's journey through *La Clase Mágica*'s fantasy world. Modeled after Rosaldo's Lone Ethnographer, who traipses through the conceptual history of ethnography, the Reader-Friend's journeys through the world of evaluation framed in the maze of methodological tools. Although the Reader-Friend visits all of the rooms of the maze, only the visits to the first three rooms are described in full detail to avoid losing the reader in a long and winding chronicle.

Initially, our Reader-Friend, like the new Amiguitos at *La Clase Mágica* and the undergraduate Amigos(as) in the class, must decide through which of four possible entries she will begin her journey in the fantasy world of *La Clase Mágica*: *El Payaso, México, Xochimilco*, or *Teotihuacán*? Becasue the tools in *Xochimilco*, and *Teotihuacán* come late in the development of *La Clase Mágica* and will require a preliminary understanding of the project, the Reader-Friend is forced to choose between methods in historiography or ethnography. The ethnographic base of the project and prolific data that ethnographic fieldnotes have produced prompts the Reader-Friend to enter through Room 6, *El Payaso* and leave *México* for a later time. This entrance is appropriate because it symbolically represents a jumping off place from the "Drawing Table," a place where initiates, younger children, and children doing homework congregate when they "step out of the fantasy world of the maze (see Fig. 4.1)."[11]

Room 6, *El Payaso* [The Clown]

After the initial sense of intrigue produced by the opening line of the first fieldnote on file ("this project is going to make a Catholic out of me, again"— written by the project director), a feeling of awe comes over the Reader-Friend. She is overwhelmed by the volumes of notes written over the previous 22 academic quarters (7 years) by undergraduate students, research staff, site

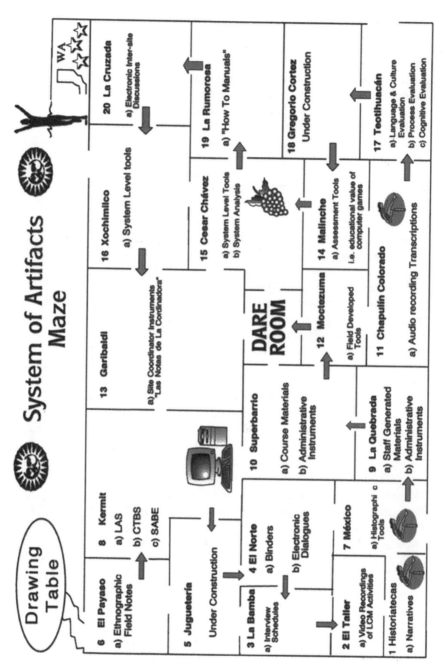

Figure 4.5. System of artifacts maze.

coordinator, project director, Wizard Assistants and parents. Each of these types of fieldnotes offers an independent opportunity to analyze aspects of the project from almost any perspective imaginable—games, children, artifacts, adults, courses, etc. Attracted to the rich data for conducting in-depth diachronic or synchronic analysis, the Reader-Friend chooses to examine the undergraduate fieldnotes, the most comprehensive and systematically collected of all the fieldnotes.

With the choice of which type of fieldnote to examine out of the way, the Reader-Friend makes a third decision about what level to engage the notes. Although she is a seasoned researcher, the fact that the notes are written by novice ethnographers and are submitted to the professor over electronic mail motivates the Reader-Friend to start as a beginner. The introductory paragraph of the Field Notes Task Card situates our traveler in the context of the fieldnote activity:

> You are a participant–observer in a faraway land between Reality and Fantasy. You have been sent there to bring back information on the language and culture of that world. You will write your observations in ethnographic fieldnotes and use them to write a final paper on a recurrent theme of your observations. Your fieldnotes are very important and will be archived for use by future generations of researchers and students.

As soon as the Reader-Friend enters the field of notes, she finds that previously accepted forms of fieldnotes such as "notes on readings or photocopied archival material" or ". . . writing on a ceramic dish for roasting sausages" (Jackson, 1990, p. 6), will not do at *La Clase Mágica*. Her notes must follow a template with three sections, entitled "Social Scene," "Focused Observation," and "Reflection" found in an electronic form on the class listserve. She comes to understand this trilevel structure: what Spradley (1980) called "changes in scope of observation" (p. 34), through the analogy of a wide-angle lens progressively closing in on one's own thinking. Social Scene captures the interrelations, seating arrangement, and dynamics among the participants from the beginning until near the end of the session. In the Focused Observation, the Reader-Friend is asked to write a "thick description" that might generate several pages of text for a 5-minute observation.[12]   In the Reflection section, the only section where personal opinion is accepted, she is instructed to elaborate on the ways that the foregoing observations relate to theoretical concepts of the class, how her own opinions about learning and development have been changed, and what she thinks should be pursued further. Having been properly introduced to the basic function of fieldnotes, the Reader-Friend is asked to write a sample fieldnote to *El Maga*, which will be used later as the baseline for tracking her development in ethnographic fieldnote writing across the quarter.

That was easy enough and our Reader-Friend is ready to continue the journey through the maze. But, she is reminded by the accompanying *Amigo* that in order to accumulate Wizard Assistant credit, she must continue to explore the undergraduate fieldnotes at Good or Expert level as specified by the Task Card. She decides on the Expert level where she faces three common criticisms of using undergraduate fieldnotes: How can notes written by untrained ethnographers be reliable? How can those participating in the creation of culture remain neutral observers?, and How can the observations of those who do not speak the language and have a mediacolored understanding of the target population be valid? All three concerns are endemic to qualitative research. The third is serious criticism often leveled against ethnographers by Paredes (1977) and other Chicano/a anthropologists (Rosaldo, 1986; Menchaca, 1997). Accepting the gravity of such concerns, the Reader-Friend is momentarily perplexed about what to do next. The *Amigo* prompts her to write to *Maga* for help. *Maga* responds with a synopsis of the staff's position on the matter:

> The lack of Spanish fluency of the undergraduate ethnographers does compromise what Spradley (1980) called the verbatim principle (i.e., recording verbatim what people say), but it also problematizes language difference. While the students cannot often understand what is being said, language becomes the object of problem solving and the subject of the fieldnotes. A focus on language is a fundamental goal of one academic quarter per year but is also covered in the other two quarters. Like other aspects of the constructed world, a putative weakness in the research design becomes a powerful tool for producing data on variables affecting language choice.

As she moves through the fieldnotes, the Reader-Friend finds that three aspects of this data source support the staff's rationale. First, she finds that idiosyncratic observations are either supported or rejected when notes written across quarters and by different students are closely examined. For example, individual students who report a child's resistance to the use of Spanish invariably assume a language shift to English. However, when the fieldnotes are examined closely for sociolinguistic data across time and across undergraduate students, the children are seen as consistently building on their bilingualism. They shift to English only when they perceive the undergraduate students to be insufficiently fluent in Spanish.

Second, the Reader-Friend finds that the comprehensiveness of the database overrides the criticism that undergraduate fieldnotes are unreliable. The database contains fieldnotes written by undergraduate students enrolled in *La Clase Mágica*-related courses offered three times a year over a period of 6 years. The great number of notes and the different types of students allow the researchers to select from the most adept fieldnote writers to capture participant and program development from many angles. For example, undergraduate fieldnotes provide endless possibilities to examine such targeted foci as enculturation, language use, and skill acquisition by topic or by individual. The fieldnote as artifact can also discern students' own development of ethnographic skills as well as the ways ethnographic methods have changed across academic quarters.

A third factor that supports the validity of student fieldnotes is that they capture fresh insights that more theoretically grounded ethnographers may overlook. Especially useful are the contributions by students whose background experiences are completely different from those of the children. A specific example is the closing remarks by Steve Melton (Andre & Melton, 1991) in his oral history of the community:

> On my last walk through Eden Gardens, I wondered why I had been shocked at the Mexican influence, with California being so close to the border, but I realized it was not the Mexican influence that I was shocked about, but the location of it. It was not until I went back through the minds of the long time residents that I was able to realize it was the Mexicanos that first settled in Eden Gardens, or La Colonia. Now, as I stroll through Eden Gardens I am not shocked but warmed. I am taken in and absorbed by a culture and family closeness that has been preserved over many years. (p. 54)

Having completed this level of engagement successfully, the Reader-Friend is immediately faced with another decision: Does she want to continue to explore other types of fieldnotes in *El Payaso*? Or, does she want to continue on her journey? If the latter, then she must consult the Reflection section on the Task Card, where she is directed to tell *El Maga* one other advantage for using undergraduate field notes and propose three new research questions she could pursue using undergraduate fieldnotes. She decides to go to *El Maga's* computer and log on for an online chat:

Reader-Friend:	Is there a lion in the house? (This is the conventional greeting when one is seeking an audience with El Maga).[13]
Maga:	SI AQUI ESTOY. ¿CON QUIEN TENGO EL PLACER? [Yes, I am here. With whom do I have the pleasure?--Maga always initiates a conversation in Spanish]
Reader-Friend:	Maga, I have just played "Undergraduate Fieldnotes" in El Payaso Room and it was great! Did you know that undergraduate field notes are also useful to triangulate with other data, such as audio-transcriptions?

Maga:	DE VERAS? YOU DON'T SAY. QUE MAS CAN YOU DO CON LAS NOTAS DE LOS ESTUDIANTES?
	[Really? You don't say. What else can you do with the notes of the students?]
Reader-Friend:	We can study many things such as gender relations, game knowledge, and how the project influences the construction of culture and mind in play?
Maga:	SI PUES, YOU CAN. ¿ PERO PORQUE QUIERES HACER ESO WHEN OTHERS ALREADY HAVE STUDIED THAT1.[14] NO TE HAGAS HOLGAZAN, THINK OF SOMETHING NEW!!
	[Of course, you can. But why do you want to do that when others already have studied that- Don't be lazy, think of something new!!]

The Reader-Friend follows Maga's advice and reviews previous student papers and the bibliography posted on the Fifth Dimension Web site. She learns that no one has studied the students' growing envisionment of Vygotksy's concept, the zone of proximal development, nor has anyone studied how gender relations and game knowledge affects adult–child interaction in the game of "Oregon Trail." She reconnects with *Maga* to share these possible research topics. Maga accepts her choices and grants her Expert status. *Maga* then directs her to the Consequence Card found in the Room folder. There she finds the mobility options available at expert level of play: (1) You may go to Room 8 or (2) You may exit and transform.[15] Since the Reader-Friend is a novice, she is unable to transform into a Wizard Assistant. She is compelled to take Option 1. She enters Room 8.

Room 8: Kermit

Here the Reader-Friend must make a decision among the three standardized tools used at *La Clase Mágica*: the Language Assessment Scale (LAS), an oral proficiency measure for speakers of languages other than English, the California Test of Basic Skills (CTBS) and the CTBS's Spanish version, the SABE (Spanish Assessment of Basic Skills). She chooses to examine the LAS test for several reasons: First, the LAS was highly recommended by consultants of the California State Department of Education and is widely used throughout the state. It is also the only measure closely related to the goals of the project.[16] And, third, the retrieval of CTBS/SABE scores from the children's cumulative folder was still in progress when the Reader-Friend began her journey.

Interested in quickly advancing to Wizard Assistant, the Reader-Friend chooses to examine the LAS test at the Expert level (see De Avila, 1981 and De Avila & Duncan, 1990 for details on the LAS). She reads the context portion of the Task Card instructing her to imagine herself as a specially trained experimental psychologist interested in measuring the program's impact on second language acquisition and language maintenance. She is asked to go back in time and join two language specialists at the nearby public elementary school who helped administer the LAS to all of the child participants at *La Clase Mágica* and organized a matched group design with nonparticipants attending the same bilingual program at two elementary schools nearby.

The Reader-Friend finds that the teachers found the endeavor was too time-consuming and requiring extra assistance from temporary help. In the second year, the school district decided to switch over to the IDEA test and *La Clase Mágica* staff was left to administer the LAS alone in 1994. Both Spanish and English versions of Level 1 were given each time and composite totals were generated using children's individual performance on the four aspects of language fluency measured by the LAS test: phonemic discrimination and production; lexical ability; oral syntax comprehension and oral syntax production. The composite scores were then used for group comparisons on oral fluency in both English and Spanish across the 3 years the test was given.

A series of quantitative analyses—ANOVA and T tests—were performed on the calculated means for factors of group (LCM vs. control), language (English vs. Spanish), and year (1991 vs. 1992 vs. 1994). The results indicated a significant difference between *La Clase Mágica* participants and their peers in the bilingual program in both English and Spanish. *La Clase Mágica* participants evidenced a significant jump in the English scores from 1991 to 1992 with an upward leveling off from 1992 to 1994, whereas the control group evidenced a steady climb and then a leveling off. The Spanish scores for the participant group also remain relatively stable across the 3 years while their peers at school experience a considerable drop in their average from 1992 to 1994. The data seem to suggest that while both groups improve their English scores over the three test points, the LCM group made bigger gains. It also suggests that the control group began to "lose" their Spanish (beginning in 1992) whereas the LCM group maintained their Spanish with a slight increase.

On reading about these results on the consortium electronic exchanges, the Reader-Friend becomes excited. Yet, she now faces one of the biggest challenges of using standardized assessment in a voluntary program. What can she conclude about program effects with such a small, self-selected sample? Although the groups were matched for background factors such as length of stay, number of years in American schools, and enrollment in the same bilingual program at school, the size of the sample and the difference in time in administering the test to both groups (it took longer for the LCM participants because of attendance patterns) precluded definite conclusions. Furthermore, the transience and programmatic schedules of nonparticipants and the voluntary participation of participants made it impossible to conduct random assignment. Additionally, scores of participants in the baseline data were lower than nonparticipants in both English and Spanish, distinguishing the two groups beyond match-comparison standards. The Reader-Friend, nevertheless, finds these findings worthwhile.

How could she not use the results when they reflect such an "exciting trend," as a staff-member indicates in the following posting on the consortium list-serve?

> an exiting trend . . . in nearly every case the children who have participated in La Clase showed a significant increase in the scores for both Spanish and English proficiency, while students who were nonparticipants showed significant decreases in their scores in both English and Spanish. [TH/02/19/1993]

The Amiga assigned to the Reader-Friend for that day echoes the concern voiced by a respected colleague on the list-serve, "How can we be excited about a finding that suggested that some kids leaped forward and others slipped backward?" A piercing question indeed. The Reader-Friend stops and reflects. True, as the staff concurred, there is no joy in learning that some children "regress," especially when the key concern that drives the efforts of *La Clase Mágica* is that so many *Mexicano* children do not "progress." Nevertheless, the need to demonstrate "credible" measures of program impact seemed so compelling that the Reader-Friend sets her mind on pursuing the expert level of experimental design against the open, context-specific philosophical framework of *La Clase Mágica*. She is willing to overlook difficulty that colleagues in the consortium had with random assignment (King, Kelly, & Edwards, 1992; Schustack, Strauss, & Worden, 1997).

But like many of the children who want to play Expert level, the Reader-Friend does not have the necessary knowledge to engage the game at that level. She must wait until she reviews the community survey to identify the factors influencing program participation. However, the survey is not completed (see later discussion) and she is anxious to move on. Not wanting to see the Reader-Friend opt out of the maze, the assisting Amiga convinces her to try the Good level of engagement. This level asks the researcher to conduct a within-group comparison with the test results and use the "most powerful kind of evidence . . . of growth . . . the narrative data in fieldnotes and in artifacts of their writing." [RC/2/19/93] to support emergent conclusions. In this way, the Reader-Friend is to conclude that children at *La Clase Mágica* make significant gains in English acquisition and Spanish maintenance over a period of 3 years.

She is also prompted to support this further by teasing out how differences in attendance, length of residence in the United States, birth order and educational background of parents affect language development as is pointed out in the case studies of Carlos and Rina in the following chapter.

At the end of her study of standardized methods, the Reader-Friend consults the LAS Task Card. She is directed to write to *El Maga* about conducting an experiment on the impact of the use of Spanish on the movement through the game of "Language Explorer." She informs *Maga* that others in the consortium are in the process of studying the effects of Spanish in that game and suggests a study of language use in "Sticky Bears" because it has a Task Card entirely in Spanish. *Maga* congratulates her and tells her to check out the wonderful intersite "scavenger hunt" the consortium projects are having on the Internet to celebrate his or her birthday on November 2, the Day of the Dead, a widely celebrated holiday throughout *Mexico*. The Reader-Friend promises to take part and goes off to find the Consequence Card that will tell her which rooms she can move to next. The two options are Room 10 or Room 5. Remembering many happy childhood memories of toy stores, the Reader-Friend decides to enter Room 5, Juguetería.

Room 5, *Juguetería* [Toy store]

The Reader-Friend is crushed when she finds that Juguetería is under construction, a ploy used by staff to update the activities in the rooms of the maze. In the case of Juguetería, the staff is working on a new tool for conducting longitudinal studies. Her *Amigo* for the day tries to cheer her up by suggesting that she could use the Magical Pass in her folder to skip over this room and go to *El Norte*. Relieved that she can move on, she decides to do just that.

Room 4, *El Norte* [The United States of America]

In this room, the Reader-Friend finds several three-ring binders and electronic forms of communication between *El Maga* and a variety of people. Some of the binders contain pictures of children's renditions of their electronic pal and others contain letters and electronic communication including email and "live-chats" (real-time conversations) between the children and *El Maga*. Much of the latter is also stored in electronic form. Collected daily, notwithstanding technical glitches, the data are so immense and so enticing that the Reader-Friend is perplexed about which aspect of it to examine. She turns to her trusted Amiga, TH, for suggestions.

> **TH:** Well, let's see. You have two options. One, you can examine the data that has already been used in published work. Or, two, you

can select data that is unexplored. For example, you can examine the ways in which language and culture in electronic correspondence affects literacy practices as Gillian McNamee's 1993 study shows how correspondence with the electronic Wizard enhances children's writing skills and the development of "a voice in written language" (p. 3). Or you can examine "live-chats," a kind of computer-mediated communication (CMC) (Herring, 1996) that is relatively unexamined and can potentially provide unique insights into development of children's language and literacy as well as their "speaking personality." (Wertsch, quoted in McNamee, 1993, p. 3)

Wanting to please *Maga* with new ways of thinking, the Reader-Friend decides to examine a developing tool in the evaluation of program impact at *La Clase Mágica*—the electronic dialogues. But, before she continues, she must decide which of the two types of CMC to examine: those between the children and Maga or those with *La Mosca Cósmica* [The Cosmic Fly], the pesty little gossip who often substitutes when Maga is away visiting other corners of the universe. Becasue there are not as many notes between *La Mosca* and the children, the Reader-Friend chooses to examine both sets of real-time electronic conversations. The Reader-Friend reads the context section of the Live-Chats Task Card:

> Bienvenida al mundo del Internet [Welcome to the Internet world].
> You are going to "listen-in" on others' conversations and try to
> imagine who is "talking" and where he or she comes from. Don't
> make any noise. The little ones will know someone will be listening
> but they have gotten used to being the object of observation.

Quietly and ever so respectfully, the Reader-Friend takes a seat next to Maribel, an 11-year-old girl who is "talking" to El Maga through the computer. *Maga* is trying to get the child to discuss her progress through the maze but the "conversation" takes a more personal tone as the child asks the proverbial question, "Are you a boy or a girl?" *Maga* answers "Neither," and pushes on to get Maribel to disclose where she is in the maze. Lasting most of the session (not unusual with older children), the conversation covers a wide range of subjects that most children are concerned about (e.g., love, marriage, school, discipline, God). Like many other conversations, this chat focuses on the topic of interest for most fall quarters, the activities of the past summer vacation and the upcoming *Maga's* Birthday. This year, 1996, *Maga* planned to celebrate its birthday with a Scavenger Hunt competition involving other after-school projects in other parts of the country. Each team of children was invited to visit the Web sites available in the Fifth Dimension Universe and retrieve special items (answers to clues on *Maga's* list). Maga promised to give a computer game to the first team to collect all of the items. Just as Maribel was about to ask *Maga* for some clues, the site coordinator announced the end of the session. The Reader-Friend watched in amazement at how difficult it was to draw the child away from the conversation and how the undergraduate student was able to gently convince her to try again the next day.

But, the next day, the Reader-Friend decides to sit in on the conversation from Maga's side (i.e., she decides to visit my office at LCHC, where the Chief Wizard Assistant is "wizarding" for *Maga's* sidekick, *La Mosca*). *La Mosca* was at the computer, buzzing around trying to speak to Esteban, a preliterate 5-year-old child. Unlike the chat between Maribel and *Maga* the day before, in this exchange the Reader-Friend has a difficult time figuring out who is writing on the "other side." Live chats, like other CMC, grow out of a collective activity visible at site, where the rich social processes in which children practice literacy are on full display. From the university side, these same processes appear murky and the dilemma of assessing individual performance in a collective process resurfaces. While several mechanisms are in place to isolate individual children's performance, they are not foolproof. *La Mosca*, who spends a lot of time at site, typically reports back to *Maga* so that the information can be logged on along with the chats. Undergraduate student-collaborators are also instructed to identify themselves as "scribes" when writing for the children but many often forget, making it especially difficult to ascertain the voice and skill level of the child. Even when students do indicate their presence, as the scribe (Norma) below does in a live-chat, the child's role in the conversation may still be obscure:

Mosca:	HOLA, AQUI HAY UNA MOSQUITA COSMICA [Hello, there's a little cosmic fly here.]
Esteban:	Hola, somos Norma (UCSD) y Esteban [Hello, we are Norma and Esteban.]
Mosca:	YO AQUI BIEN BOLADA PORQUE EL MAGA ESTA ENOJADA. [I am very flustered here because the wizard is upset.]
Esteban:	¿Porque esta enojada el maga? [Why is the wizard upset?]
Mosca:	QUE DICE QUE LOS CHIQUITINES DE LA CLASE MAGICA NEVER ANSWERED THE LETTER EL MAGA SENT. [Because the youngsters of La Clase Mágica never answered the letter El Maga sent.]

[Live Chat/2/26/92]

The Reader-Friend is perplexed about whether the "utterances" from St. Leo's were dictated by Esteban, co-authored by Norma and him, or single-authored by Norma. Convinced that live-chats illustrate participation in a literacy activity not unlike the dictation exercises in which beginning writers manage the demands of writing before they are able to do it independently (Heath, 1983; King & McNamee, 1994), the Reader-Friend decides to pursue ways in which to reveal Esteban's literacy development. She employs an analytic frame that encompasses a broader time span and additional evaluation tools. She goes back to the database and retrieves all the live-chats Esteban has had with the electronic pals. Laying this data out in chronological order, she finds a chat in which Esteban's voice is easily discernible, five quarters after the one above:

Esteban:	espero que te sientas bien por lo que te paso. (referring to Maga's literary death, see chap. 6 for details) [I hope that you are fine after what happened to you.]
Maga:	CADA VEZ QUE UNO DE USTEDES ME ESCRIBE O ME MANDA UN REGALO COMO EL QUE TU HICISTE, ME SIENTO MEJOR!!!! TODAVIA NO HE PODIDO SUBIR HASTA ARRIBA DEL VOLCAN QUE ME ENVIASTE, [a picture the child sent Maga] PERO YA SUBI Y VAJE LA MONTANA DE JUNTO O SEA QUE YA ME SIENTO MEJOR!!!! Y DIME, EN DONDE ESTAS EN EL LABERINTO???? [Every time that one of you e-mails me or sends me a gift such as the one you did, I feel much better!!!! I still haven't been able to climb to the top of the volcano you sent me. However, I did climb the mountain right next to it. In other words, I am feeling much better!!!! But tell me, where are you in the maze?]
Esteban:	ahorita vengo lo voy a traer. [I'll be right back, I am going to bring it.]
Maga:	MUY BIEN. NO TE VAYAS A PERDER EN EL. . . [Very good, don't get lost within it. . .]
Esteban:	me faltan 6 para terminar. [I need 6 to finish.]
Maga:	PUES, PUES CUANDO VAS A TERMINAR EL JUEGO QUE EMPESASTE HACE UN MES? [But, but when are you going to finish the game that you started one month ago?]

[chat 5/10/1993]

To clarify who did the writing, the Reader-Friend examines a scribe's fieldnote which triangulates our analysis and provides more information on Esteban's literacy skills. The undergraduate's note sheds light on the child's incipient reading and writing skills:

> I stayed at "*El Maga's* computer" for the remainder of the time while Lourdes worked with the Amiguitos. When I asked who wanted to talk with El Maga no one answered, but Esteban ran towards me saying "yo, yo." He sat next to me and asked me what to say. I told him to talk with *El Maga* about anything. He started to type on his own, but would ask me to type for him when he had a lot to say and he wanted to write it quickly. Esteban was concerned about *El Maga's* health since her death, and assured her that he would keep writing so that she would feel better. In reading *El Maga's* responses, he pronounced each word slowly, but if he got stuck or wanted to read it quickly he asked me for help. Throughout the conversation with *El Maga*, Esteban kept conferring with me first before writing it to *El Maga*. [CB/5/10/93]

The Reader-Friend concludes that the most recent conversation with *Maga* was written by Esteban with the help of the undergraduate Amigo almost 2 years before. Esteban had taken several steps toward literacy development: He had taken the role of reader and writer and importantly, director of his own literacy development.

At the end of this activity, the Reader-Friend consults the Expert level of the Live-Chat Task Card. It directs her to illustrate one of the following to *El Maga*: (1) Esteban's writing development or (2) the motivating strategies the electronic entity uses to prompt reading and writing through telecommunication. Playing to *Maga's* narcissism, the Reader-Friend reports some of her preliminary findings: First, even a cursory review of the live-chats indicates that one of Maga's main functions in the local activity system is to encourage children to "stay in the maze" (i.e., follow the rules). Second, *Maga* encourages language choice by beginning all interactions in Spanish and then follows the children's lead in language choice. It is clear to the Redaer-Friend that *Maga* encourages bilingualism and biliteracy in "new forms of skill and expertise in written communication and self expression," much like the Wizard does in Chicago (McNamee, 1993, p. 4). The chats also illustrate how *Maga* helps children surmount limited language ability and other sentence-level concerns by allowing children to use either language or a combination of both to make meaning. In this way, children can concentrate on conducting and maintaining the written conversation, as Colomb and Simutis(1996) pointed out. Happy with the analysis, *Maga* grants the Reader-Friend Expert level credit for such an excellent report.

Time and space constraints prevent us from following the Reader-Friend's journey through the maze in such detail. In the rest of the journey, the Reader-Friend makes brief visits to each of the remaining rooms to get a quick glimpse at the other methodological tools used to create and study *La Clase Mágica*'s innovative learning environment.

Room 3, *La Bamba* [A popular song from the Mexican state of Veracruz]

This room contains a large database of interviews (informal and formal) that were collected at different times for different purposes for almost 7 years. Although many of the interview schedules were developed to generate a demographic profile of the participants, the impetus behind this tool was to corroborate the context specificity of the cultural and linguistic resources that initially informed the adaptation process. Examples and concepts were extrapolated from work in other *Mexicano* communities (Moll, 1992; Moll & Greenberg, 1990; Vásquez, 1989; Vásquez et al. 1994), but their congruity with the *Mexicano* community of Eden Gardens had to be verified. Although community members had been included in the planning and implementation stages from the beginning, a systematic sociolinguistic profile of the research community was needed in order to evaluate the relevance of our curriculum to their lives. It was necessary to identify the "funds of knowledge" that children and parents bring to *La Clase Mágica* and to corroborate whether initial references had been accurate; this strategy would verify whether or not participants and the control group in the LAS test came from similar backgrounds. An in-depth study of the data from the community survey enabled the team to resolve issues of self-selection and allow us to more accurately determine the effects of participation.

Lisa Tripp, a graduate student in UCSD's Department of Communication with extensive ethnographic experience, helped develop and implement a survey of the *Mexicano* community of Eden Gardens. Two versions of the Community Survey protocol were designed: a long version, consisting of 46 open-ended questions targeting Spanish-speaking residents with children and long-time residents of the area who had been in Eden Gardens since before 1970. The questions in this version asked respondents about their educational and occupational background, language and literacy practices, attitudes toward the education of their children, perceptions of community life, and particular issues of concern. A separate section asked families what they thought about *La Clase Mágica* in order to assess the degree to which the project was known in the community and to learn the community's general impression of the project. A shorter version of the survey targeted the demographic characteristics of non-Latino households and short-term residents. Sixty-seven households (20% of 336 households identified as the core of the community) were randomly selected.

Due to limited resources and a staffing emergency, only 59 interviews were completed. These were later supplemented with interviews of the parents of the 12 Wizard Assistants and 12 members of the control group.

Room 2, *El Taller* [The Workshop]

This room contains video recordings of the activities at *La Clase Mágica*. A substantial number of intermittent and systematic recordings capture participants at the computers, parents at their regular meetings and end-of-the-quarter celebrations. The intermittent video-recordings done by undergraduates, children, and staff members were supplemented by systematic recording of video data collected in collaboration with the Process Evaluation Team, an outside assessment group funded by the Andrew Mellon Foundation. Together, these recordings provide a thick description of children's growth, parents' involvement in the activities, and adult–child collaboration. They have been excellent advocacy tools for *La Clase Mágica*. In 1995, Lisa Tripp produced a widely disseminated video on *La Clase Mágica*, using many of these recordings, as well as her own video shots.[17]   Here, the Reader-Friend uses another of the skip-a-room passes to jump over Room 1, *Historiatecas*, and heads to Room 7, *México*.

Room 7, *México*

In this room, the Reader-Friend finds historiographic tools for constructing the history of the *Mexicano* community of Eden Gardens: oral histories, copies of materials from the Fletcher Special Collection, and numerous news articles covering the community. Periodically, undergraduate students have conducted studies focusing on the *Mexicano* community of Eden Gardens but none was as extensive as the year-long project conducted by Tim Andre and Steve Melton. Together, Andre and Melton reconstructed the history of our research community. Andre retold the history of the area from archival material found in the Fletcher Collection at UCSD[18] and the San Dieguito Historical Society. Melton's story was compiled from interviews of long-time residents of the community. The students found that both stories were necessary to construct a cogent history of the *Mexicano* community, a history that was conspicuously absent from existing texts. Their unpublished monograph, Separate Stories of Shared Spaces (available on *La Clase Mágica*'s Website), more accurately portrays the social relations among *Mexicano*s and Anglos in the area of Solana Beach.[19]

The Reader-Friend moves quickly through three rooms, Room 9, 10, and 12 which contain field-developed administrative tools that guide the operations of the site, course and research team. These instruments provide invaluable information regarding the developmental trajectory of three different participant groups (children, students, and staff) and three different contexts (site, courses, and LCHC staff room). The contexts constitute critical points of contact between two disparate cultural systems: the university and the community. They represent sites where language, culture and identity are actively negotiated—engendering transformation of individuals as well as institutional contexts.

Room 9, *La Quebrada* [Divers' Cliff in Acapulco]

This room contains staff-generated materials—debriefing summaries, research staff minutes, monthly reports documenting individual staff member's activities. Staff members' documentation of the inspiration and implementation of particular innovations provide a historical record of the adaptation process as well as a record of the intellectual and philosophical issues that drove the adaptation.

Room 10, *Superbarrio* [Super-neighborhood, a contemporary folk hero in Mexican politics][20]

This room contains course materials, such as syllabi, student applications, quizzes and course papers. Like the tools in *La Quebrada*, these tools can provide a profile of the students' linguistic abilities; their familiarity with computers and their fields of expertise. In future studies, the Reader-Friend will be able to relate synchronic and diachronic changes in the content and focus of the course and the demographic profile of the students to their development of theoretical understandings and ethnographic skills.

Room 12, *Moctezuma* [the last reigning king of the Aztec Empire]

This room contains field-developed tools used at the site—*Amiguito* Applications, Journey Log, Map of the Maze, and Field notebook—that identify the children's movement through the maze, the strategies they use along the way and their attendance patterns. These tools are useful for constructing demographic and linguistic profiles of the children, as well as helping to document their previous familiarity with computers. The Map of the Maze, in particular, is useful in determining whether a child has met all the requirements to advance to Wizard Assistant. At this point the Reader-Friend decides to enter the DARE Room and try her luck at tossing the 20 sided die.

DARE Room

There are no games in the Dare Room, only a 20-sided die corresponding to the number of rooms in the maze. A toss of the die allows the adventurer to break the journey and restart it from another point in the maze. The Reader-Friend's toss lands on 11 but she mistakenly proceeds to Teotihuacán, Room 17, to continue the journey.

Room 17, *Teotihuacán* [The City of Pyramids]

This is one of two rooms in the maze that are specifically designed to draw upon the cultural activities of the *Mexicano* community in which *La Clase Mágica* is embedded. The context section of the Task Card asks the visitor to imagine him or herself in Aztlán, the mythical land of the Aztecs. There, he or she will find Actividades tradicionales [traditional activities] that children have brought from home or that the research staff has collected over the years. Some of these include Lotería [picture bingo], Culebras y Escaleras [Snakes and Ladders], Scrabble and chess. A special pass is given by *Maga* to any individual who suggests a traditional game that is not already found in this room.

Three Outside Evaluation Projects—the Language and Culture Evaluation, the Process Evaluation, and the Cognitive Evaluation are found in Teotihuacan: activities that connect *La Clase Mágica* evaluation activities with its broader ecological context of academia. These efforts provide evidence of the Mellon Foundation's good investment at the same time that they provide invaluable intellectual and material resources for the project directors. *La Clase Mágica* formed part of both the Language and Culture and Process Evaluation efforts and worked closely with both teams to develop data collection and analysis strategies. In return both evaluation teams made their data available to the *La Clase Mágica* research staff, as is evident in Room 2, where the Process Evaluation video recordings are stored. These evaluation perspectives provide a richly textured view of how culture and language intersect with cognitive development.

Room 18, *Gregorio Cortez* [a Texas *Mexicano* of the 1880s]

This room is under construction, its contents are being adapted to comply with changing conditions.

Room 14, *Malinche* [Fernando Cortez' interpreter]

This room contains tools for assessing the educational value of the 70 computer games and activities found at *La Clase Mágica*. While tools found in other rooms (e.g.. undergraduate fieldnotes. Maze Map. and Journey Log) are useful to track progress through individual games, they can also be used to illustrate how specific games influence the accumulation and distribution of knowledge (Nicolopoulou & Cole, 1993). Tools specifically designed to identify exactly what academic/cognitive/cultural strategies are called upon by the games were developed in collaboration with the *La Clase Mágica*-Midwest team headed by Margaret Gallego. at Michigan State University. Collaboration on the cognitive strategies project was one of many activities the two teams participated in as part of the Bilingual Partnership in the initial stages of the Andrew Mellon Consortium.

The Michigan State team focused on identifying game-related skills and their transferability to tasks performed in school (see Gallego. forthcoming, for details on La Clase Mágica-Midwest). This team spent 3 years developing a cognitive checklist for each game. Their goal was to track children's performance across games, noting the cumulative impact on procedural and conditional knowledge. Although theoretically sound, this goal proved too ambitious for the resources and time both project leaders had available as junior faculty. Two major problems arose in trying to get a clear picture of the strategies that children use in problemsolving: (1) game makers advertised different strategies than those identified by the Michigan State team; and (2) task analysis for each of the games generated cognitive strategies which were difficult to organize in a hierarchical order.

At *La Clase Mágica*, in North San Diego County. the focus was only partially on the cognitive strategies generated by the games. The children's culturally based strategies, those which formed their prior development, was the greater focus of the West Coast team. Undergraduate students recorded the children's use of culturally based strategies (e.g.. the use of Spanish. cultural references, and culturally based activities). By recognizing the origin of the strategies children employed in their collaborative activities and recording them in the journey log or in the undergraduate field notes, the team hoped to assess how children's prior knowledge facilitated the acquisition of new skills and language. Although some features are easily recognizable as based in one or the other culture, transculturation made the distinction problematic. For example. terms like Kermit, taco, Amigo, and hot dog are firmly based in both cultures. The cultural base of collaborative interaction, generally associated with a Mexican style of interaction (Delgado-Gaitán, 1994). was indistinguishable in a project that is known to foster the culture of collaborative learning (Nicolopoulou & Cole, 1993). Future analyses will provide further insights regarding the prevalence of transculturation and collaboration.

Room 15, *Cesar Chávez* [Chicano Leader of the Farmworkers' Union, 1927-1993]

Room 15 contains the method for conducting a system analysis of the ways in which a multilevel, multidimensional effort constitutes social action. This level of analysis was prompted by a study commissioned by the University of California Latino Eligibility Task Force (Stanton-Salazar et al., 1995). Interested in ways to fuel the educational ladder, the Task Force commissioned a study on the effects of participation in *La Clase Mágica* on eligibility to higher education. The research lens shifted from the micro perspective on children's uses of language and culture to a macro-level perspective of how the system of institutional relations made available social and cultural capital that could be used in the school context. The shift also highlighted how eligibility to higher education is a social practice that is learned through associations with the institutional representatives (i.e. those with intimate knowledge of how the university works).

When the broader effort of *La Clase Mágica* is viewed from this perspective, six points of contact where knowledge is exchanged between cultural systems become evident—The preschool activity for children attending Head Start, the elementary-level activity, the Wizard Assistant Club for adolescents, the Computer Class for adults, and the undergraduate course, "Practicum in Child Development." When lined up on a timeline, these points of contact reflect a life-span approach to minority representation in higher education. It also chronologically lines up important benchmarks of the educational system making clear an educational pipeline that not only funnels qualified students, but also generates new curriculum content and new goals for educational practice (see chapter 3 for details on the points of contact). This systems approach draws on extant data collected for other purposes, but re-examined from a broader perspective on how the context is changing in response to new social conditions. For example, although initially focused on language and culture, fieldnotes written by the director, the research staff, and the site coordinator are re-examined for ways in which participants are introduced to the social and cultural capital of the cultural domains of the university and *Mexicano* community. From this perspective data also illustrate the ways each of the contexts is dialectically changing in response to the theoretical and philosophical approach of *La Clase Mágica*.

The Reader-Friend ponders the success of this functional system in accomplishing its goal of ameliorating the under-representation of minorities in higher education. She is reminded by the accompanying *Amigo* that many long-term participants are about to reach college age. Once participant children reach college age a longitudinal study will be able to provide conclusive evidence that participation has affected their future options to attend higher education. When polled in 1996, all long-term participant children indicated a strong interest in pursuing their education. The promise of this approach may have been secured with the up-take of UC Links, a multidisciplinary, multi-campus consortium of university-community partnerships sponsored by the University of California.[21]

Room 19, La Rumorosa [A mountain range in Baja California]

This room contains a type of tool, the "How-to-Manuals," used to perpetuate the philosophical as well as the organizational structure of the various activities that form the points of contact discussed earlier. Initially based on the "The Official Incomplete Manual of the Fifth Dimension," *La Clase Mágica*'s How-to-Manual became a work-in progress outlining the current thinking on the multiple levels of the evolving project. Not only did the How-to Manual give a comprehensive look at *La Clase Mágica*, it also aimed at sustaining the culturally relevant theoretical and philosophical base of the project, generating separate How-to Manuals for directing Task Card development, wizarding for *El Maga* (assuming *Maga's* role), and tracking and developing all the other age-specific activities—for example, the Wizard Assistant Club, La Gran Dimensión [the Adult Computer Club] and the undergraduate course (completed by Cole's team).

Room 20, *La Cruzada* [The Crusades]

This room contains electronic intersite discussions across various participant groups in the Mellon Consortium—children, undergraduate students, and participating colleagues. The latter has been the most consistent and broad-based of all the discussions through telecommunication. This form of communication plays a vital role in engaging a lone field worker in a research collective, making real the idiom, "acting locally, thinking globally." Still, the amount and nature of the cross-fertilization of theory and practice among the participants is yet to be studied. Most of the intersite activities involving children have taken place around special occasions requiring a lot of fanfare—*Maga's* birthday, the Imagine Project, and the Pen Pal Project—short-term events that require considerable staff engagement. Undergraduate students, on the other hand, have engaged in very structured intersite telecommunication discussions as a result of co-developed courses at Michigan State and UCSD. After a brief period of apprehensive participation in which both sets of students were inhibited by each other's area of expertise, conversation flowed easily and abundantly.

This room also contains another data set which is yet to be studied. The structured telecommunication discussions among *La Clase Mágica*'s staff— otobi (acronym for Organizing Tricia, Olga, Berta and Yolanda). Otobi was used as an organizing mechanism to keep all the staff members abreast of the others' activities and the current thinking on the adaptation process. It unified what could have been a motley crew of individual research assistants focusing on isolated sections of the project.

Room 16, *Xochimilco*, [a park of floating gardens in Mexico City]

Like Room 15, which contains system-level tools, *Xochimilco* contains different kinds of methodology for conducting descriptive case studies of children's social, cultural, and linguistic development across time (Yin, 1994). This kind of tracking attempts to illustrate the child's developmental trajectory as well as his or her acculturation to the norms of the project. School records—grades, class enrollment and test scores of 12 long-term participants (those in *La Clase Mágica* for more than 4 years) supplement data that has been generated by the undergraduate students (e.g., references to these children found in fieldnotes). While still in progress, data collection, and analysis using this methodology will form part of a longitudinal study on the project's impact on children's school success and will be used in assessing specific children's college-going rates. Able to engage the activities in this room only to the Good Level, the Reader-Friend proceeds to the last room she has not visited, Room 13.

Room 13, *Garibaldi* [Plaza of Musicians in Mexico City]

Instruments used by the site coordinator for recording attendance and her overall impressions of each session are in this room. Over the years, both instruments have folded into a single measure, "las notas de la cordinadora" [the coordinator notes]. In these, the coordinator documents attendance of children, undergraduates, parents, and visitors. She also describes the beginning of the session, the important events that took place, and her thoughts about her observations. Like all other artifacts in the system, these notes provide an interesting vista into the coordinator's own development. The notes have undergone several major revisions, each time drawing increasingly longer texts from the coordinator. As I point out in chapter 6, these notes demonstrate enculturation of the coordinator, but also her language and literacy development in both English and Spanish. For example, las notas pinpoint the moment in which the coordinator makes a shift from the term *El Mago* to *El Maga*, a difficult transition for Spanish-speakers. More importantly, the notes demonstrate the attainment of one of our sustainability goals—the up-take of the project's goals and objectives by individual members of the community—at least at the level of one who is a highly respected member of the community.

At this point the Reader-Friend is ready to exit the Maze through Room 16. She sends Maga a message informing It that she is prepared to transform into a Wizard Assistant. La Mosca chimes in to tell her to send in her maze map for Maga's review. Three agonizing days later, *Maga* calls the Reader-Friend to an online chat:

Maga:	QUERDITA AMIGA LECTORA, YOU HAVE FORGOTTEN DOS CUARTOS, HISTORIATECAS AND CHAPULIN COLORADO. [Dear reader-friend, you have forgotten 2 rooms, Historiatecas and Chapulin Colorado]
Reader-Friend:	Nooooooo! No mas [no more]! I want to stop here! I want to become a Wizard Assistant. (A typical response by children about to advance to Wizard Assistant)
Maga:	ANDALE [Come on], DON'T FRET, TWO MORE ROOMS AND YOU ARE DONE AND CAN BE MY ASSISTANT. I HAVE ALL KINDS OF NEW GAMES AND TREATS SOLAMENTE PARA TI [just for you].
Reader-Friend:	Okay, if you insist. I will go do that now.

The Reader-Friend resumes play in Room 11.

Room 11, *Chapulín Colorado* [Character in children's Spanish-language television]

Reader-Friend enters Chapulin Colorado where she finds transcriptions of audio recordings collected by undergraduate students and staff members. Periodically, throughout the life of the project, staff members have audiotaped sessions with the children and parents. Interviews conducted as part of the community survey and informal interviews used in studies on identity and community relations were also recorded and form a large part of this data. In quarters 8 and 9, undergraduate students were assigned to work in observer–participant pairs in which one student was responsible for audio-recording the session and transcribing it, while the other student, standing apart, observed the interaction, and wrote a subsequent fieldnote. They alternated roles in subsequent visits to *La Clase Mágica* so that each had the opportunity to learn both research skills.

Experiencing a surge of confidence the Reader-Friend moves quickly to the expert level and begins to corroborate the mediated rendition of children's language use that is found in the fieldnotes. She is able to substantiate students' written observations of language choice and describe the social context of code-switching and fluency in either language (I provide this kind of description for *La Clase Mágica* participants Carlos and Rina in chapter 5). She communicates these findings to *Maga* and then proceeds to Historiateca.

Room 1, *Historiateca* [neologism for story room]

The Reader-Friend then enters Historiateca, which is designed to draw on children's home and community experiences. The Task Card for Historiateca asks children to contribute a story from home or school or to write one of their own for the files. Children often skip this room, and like our Reader-Friend, end up writing a story for Maga as the last step toward becoming Wizard Assistants. The Reader-Friend finds a story at the project office that she thinks Maga will enjoy: an evaluation account submitted to the Andrew Mellon Foundation by the site coordinator, Lourdes Durán. The account, included in the official report to the foundation, speaks to the integral role Durán has played in the project and instantiates the multivoiced nature of *La Clase Mágica*.[22]

Cambios que han surgido en el periodo del 1995-1996 en el
ambiente general de La Clase Mágica:

Lourdes Durán—
Apoyo y participación de los padres de familia. La
motivación de los padres de familia es la asisténcia y la participación
de sus hijos en las computadoras en las horas de La Clase
Mágica. Los padres apoyan con su presencia en juntas: Hubo
bastante apoyo por los problemas de espácio. Se preocupaban
de que hubiera un cambio que afectara al programa y que se
mantuviera en St. Leo's. Tambien estuvieron pendientes de
que no se cambiara a otro lugar. Estuvieron pendientes sobre
sus hijos. Han mostrado su interés sobre lo que iba a pasar en
la nueva etapa, en que Yolanda y Olga no iban a estar presentes
en *La Clase Mágica*. Hubo una asistencia alta de padres de
familia en esas juntas.
El esfuerzo que los papas demostraron a sus hijos
trabajando junto a ellos y apoyándolos en las actividades, todo a
cambio de hacer realidad la metas. Por ejemplo, se organizó una
venta de artículos usados en donde asistieron los niños y los papas.
Se hizo una venta de raspados el día Cinco de Mayo, después con lo
que sobró volvieron a hacer otra venta. Y con el apollo y las ganas de
seguir, se compraron una printer. El siguiente paso sera reunir fondos
para ir a un field trip y seguir comprando juegos.
Visión general: Como madre de familia miro el esfuerzo
conforme a las posibilidades de cada uno de los padres de familia por
apoyar lo que ellos creén que es beneficioso para sus hijos.
Cambios en los niños: Los niños aún colaboran más. Los
asistentes han tomado más responsabilidad y con la ayuda de ellos ha
sido más fácil darle a otros niños la atención que necesitan. Aunque
la mayoría de los asistentes son adolescentes, han trabajado con

bastante responsabilidad. Ellos planeán y buscan ser coordinados. Se precionan unos a los otros a cumplir con sus responsabilidades. Han llegado al punto en que ellos mismos con ayuda de los papás planean actividades para sacar fondos y buscan la manera de idear como hacer dinero para las necesidades de La Clase o que según ellos hace falta. Por ejemplo, se acaba de comprar una printer. Se a planeado registrar La Clase Mágica y sacar una cuenta de banco y todo esto con el apoyo de los padres de familia y con la idea de trabajar.

Se habla de ir a la Universidad: Algunos o la mayoría de nuestros niños están en el nivel de sexto para arriba. En sus conversaciones ellos hablan del colegio. Hablan de ir a la Universidad y también buscan la manera de ser informados. Se les acaba de dar una orientación sobre la Universidad, en la cual participaron la mayoría de nuestros niños con los padres de familia.

Tenemos más asistencia de niños: La asistencia de los niños ha aumentado. Aunque entran bastantes niños nuevos, siempre los que han mantenido la asistencia desde el principio son los niños que tienen más tiempo con nosotros.

Cambio en espacio de las computadoras y apoyo: Bueno este ha sido un año muy interesante en cuestión de apoyo. Después de estar con tanto relajo por el espacio de Head Start y por el mal carácter de las directoras, este año recibimos el apoyo y reconocimiento del beneficio que trae a la comunidad *La Clase Mágica*. Head Start ha incluído este programa como parte de la enseñanza de los niños de Head Start. Head Start a manifestado su apoyo haciendose parte del grupo de coalición que fue formado por un equipo de varios programas que trabajan en relación con UCSD. La meta de este equipo es crear una entrada de dinero que ayude a *La Clase Mágica*. El plan es trabajar y buscar donaciones para una misma meta de crear programas de probecho para nuestros niños. La Coalición es el grupo que ha logrado reunirse y en el cual unidos podramos salir adelante; el Boys & Girls Club, Sky Line Elementary, Head Start y los padres de *La Clase Mágica*. Creo que estamos en el puntos máximo en el cual se podría decir que se ha alcanzado la meta.

[Edited version of copy submitted as part of the Annual Report to Mellon]

[Translation]

Changes that took place in the general environment during 1995-1996
Lourdes Durán—

Support and participation of the parents. The parent's motivation is the children's attendance and their involvement with their children on the computers during the time of *La Clase Magica*. They support the program through their presence in meetings: There was ample support regarding the problem of space. They worried about a change that would affect the program and they wanted the program to remain at St. Leo's. They were worried that the program would be relocated to another place. They had accompanied their children. They demonstrated interest in the new phase in which Yolanda and Olga would not be present at La Clase Magica. There was a high turn out of parents at the meetings.

The parents demonstrated effort in working with their children, supporting them in the activities, and helping them meet their goals. For example, they organized a yard sale in which both the children and parents were present. There also had an ice-cone sale on Cinco de Mayo and later held another sale with the money that was left over. With all the support and desire to continue they purchased a printer. The next step will be to raise funds for a field trip and the purchasing of more games.

General vision: As a parent, I see the effort that has been demonstrated within the capability of each parent in supporting what they think is beneficial for their children.

Changes in the children. There has been more collaboration by the children. The Wizard Assistants have taken more responsibility and with their help it has been possible to provide attention to those children who needed it. Even though many of the Wizard Assistants are in the adolescent years, they have worked very responsibly. They make plans and want to be organized. They pressure each other to fulfill their responsibilities. They have reached a point with the help of their parents have planned activities to raise funds; and they have looked for ways to raise money to meet the needs of La Clase Magica or what they consider to be the needs. For example, just recently a printer was purchased. Plans have been made to register *La Clase Mágica* [as nonprofit organization] and to open a bank account with the help of the parents and with the idea of working together.

Talk of going to the university. Some or many of our children are in sixth grade level or higher. They talk about going to college. They talk about going to the university and look for ways to be informed. They have just received an orientation on admissions to a university in which the majority of the children and their parents attended.

We have an increase in children's attendance. The attendance of children has increased. Even though many new children have enrolled, those who have maintained a consistent attendance have been those children who have been with us the longest.

Change in space of the computers and support. This has been a very interesting year in terms of support. Despite the commotion of the space situation with Head Start and the bad disposition of the directors, this year we received the support of the community and the recognition of the benefits that La Clase Mágica brings to the community. Head Start has included a version of our program as part of the learning that their children acquire. Headstart has demonstrated its support by becoming part of the Coalition team that was formed by a group of different agencies that have worked with UCSD. The goal of this group is to raise funds to help La Clase Mágica to continue. The plan is to work together to secure donations for programs that benefit our children. The Coalition team has been the group which has managed to unify us and together we will be able to forge forward. The Boys and Girls Club, Skyline Elementary, Head Start, and the parents of La Clase Mágica children). I believe we are at the maximum level at which we could say that we have met our goals.

Impressed with this story that the Reader-Friend sent to it, *Maga* asks to "speak" with her about her advancement to Wizard Assistant.

Maga:	SI READER-FRIEND, SI TODOS LOS PAPELES ESTAN EN ORDEN, Y SI QUIERES TENER LA RESPONSIBILIDAD DE SER WIZARD ASSISTANT ENTONCES TE DARE ESTE PAPEL. COMO SIENTES? [Yes reader-friend, if all the papers are in order and you want the responsibility of being a wizard assistant, then I will give you this role. How do you feel?]
Reader-Friend:	Yes, yes, yes.
Maga:	VAMOS A CELEBRAR! TAL VEZ TENEMOS UNA FIESTA EN EL DIA DE LOS MUERTOS PARA CELEBRAR MI DIA DE CUMPLEANOS Y TU "GRAUDATION" A SER WA. COMO TE PARECE? [Let's celebrate! Maybe we'll have a party on the day of the dead to celebrate my birthday and your graduation to wizard assistant level. What do you think?]

[actual conversation between Maga and another WA, 10/14/94]

THE TRANSFORMATION OF THE READER-FRIEND

Generally, it takes a first-level participant 2 or 3 years to advance to Wizard Assistant. In that time, the children encounter 6 to 9 different cohorts of undergraduates, establish friendships with 48 to 72 undergraduates, and attend approximately 180 to 270 sessions of *La Clase Mágica*. If children communicate with El Maga as often as once a week (as is expected of them), we can estimate that they had 60 to 90 interactions with their electronic pal by the time they become Wizard Assistants. Their age, language fluency, motivation, and previous experiences—and their interactions with their Amigos(as) and Maga individually sculpts the journey they have taken through the maze. By the end of the journey they become expert participants of *La Clase Mágica* and more often than not outperformed their older "peers" (Amigos/as) in applying their knowledge to keep the system and the technology active. They assume the role of master, assistant, and representative of many of the activities of *La Clase Mágica*.

But what has the Reader-Friend learned? How has she been transformed? What is she expected to do now? In the possible world that the maze of the methodology represents, the Reader-Friend transforms into an expert participant of *La Clase Mágica*. She is very well versed in the history of the project, its philosophical and theoretical foundations. She can now advance from initiate to researcher–implementer, able to create her own design experiment. She not only understands the multiplicity and philosophical basis of the project but is also able to take on the responsibility of setting up a new site corresponding to the resources and constraints of the partner institutions. She is poised to use the knowledge gained from this journey to culturally and linguistically adapt the methodology of *La Clase Mágica* as well as to develop new tools, research questions, and new methodologies reflective of a new target population.

My attempt to "collapse the paradox" for the readers has, I would hope, accomplished at least one other goal—that of adequately portraying the complexity and multiplicity of the systems of artifacts that constitute the broad-based effort of *La Clase Mágica*. Integral to the adaptation process, these methodological tools, "grown" in situ, project a living, breathing quality as they continuously change and evolve in response to the changing needs of the children and the context. They create life in the crowded quarters of *La Clase Mágica* and their extraction for objective and individual analysis of them or any aspect of *La Clase Mágica* would stultify the rich texture that together they help create. The imaginary journey of the Reader-Friends through the methodology maze re-situates the analysis at the intersection of a micro–macro perspective and at the juncture between the social science and humanities by providing a vicarious experience for the distant reader. The subjective knowledge that the

Reader-Friend's journey accords, re-infuses in the evaluation an abundance and dynamism of life at the borderlands of *La Clase Mágica*.

NOTES

[1] This problem is not unique to *La Clase Mágica*, it is one that other Fifth Dimension programs have struggled with as well.

[2] "*EL Maga*" engenders both feminine and masculine qualities. "*El*" is a masculine noun in Spanish while "*Maga*" is feminine. The term was deliberately constructed to eliminate the ascription of gender qualities to an entity in a position of power. Throughout the text "*El Maga*" will be referred to as "it".

[3] Usually accompanied by a parent, the child completes the application and signs the consent form to be included in the research activities at *La Clase Mágica*. At this time, parents are also adviced of their responsibilities to attend the parent group meetings, help with fund raising and help sponsor the community-run session of *La Clase Mágica* one day a week.

[4] At Fifth Dimension sites, Task Cards are called Adventure Guides. Both are designed according to 3 levels of difficulty--beginner, good or expert; and both have the same theoretical purpose--to promote self-reflection, imagination, and remembering.

[5] For example, in 1991, during a round-table discussion honoring Soviet visitors to LCHC, one of the first community members to work at *La Clase Mágica* informed the group that when she first heard me, talking about a fantasy world and educational activities, she thought I was crazy. Two years later, she was convinced she was crazy, too.

[6] I am indebted to Michael Gebeau for labeling the practice of practicing what you preach, "collapsing the paradox."

[7] I did retain some control over the presentations by asking the students to meet with me ahead of time. This policy was challenged at around the seventh week by students who thought they had gained enough expertise. I allowed students to present without prior consultation with me for several sessions but curtailed this independence when the quality of the presentations began to slide.

[8] Several of these postings generated very interesting discussions in the Mellon Consortium with participating scholars from all over the world.

[9] In our database these tools are organized primarily by type and participant group--e.g., Field notes—student, staff, coordinator, WA's. Several rounds of analysis as re-organized these data by theme—adaptation, language and culture, *Maga*, institutional relations—participant group—Wizard Assistant, coordinator, undergraduate student—and, by variations of artifact—Maze, Task Cards, new artifacts. *El Maga* has its own data base consisting of letters to and from children, electronic "conversations" with the children, and "debriefings" by *Maga's* assistant.

[10] I use the children's maze instead of constructing a new one more relevant to the reader's reality in order to convey the cultural and linguistic context in which children participate.

[11] Homework takes precedence at *La Clase Mágica*. The Drawing Table allows children a space to engage extra-curricular activities schiuch as playing Monoploy and Scrabble but it also provides the first stage of the enculturation process. At the Drawing Table, little ones (5 years old and younger) and new recruits, begin to acquire the fine motor skills, attention span, and collaborative engagement required to participate in the games of the maze.

[12] Students are repeatedly reminded to include details on how children use language and cultural strategies in their meaning-making. Another inevitable discussion that takes place repeatedly

throughout the quarters is the interpretation of observation from a perspective of deficit. "Children do not know how to read, therefore something is wrong with their family."

[13] To communicate with *Maga* we use the "write program" an e-mail program for kids, which at one time had several Wizards chatting with the different Fifth Dimension sites in the area. To alert *Maga* that *La Clase Mágica* wanted an audience, we used the code, "Hay un leon en casa?" ("Is there a lion in the house?").

[14] Graduate and undergraduate students have written course papers on gender at the Fifth Dimension and *La Clase Mágica*. Ageliki Nicolopoulou and Micheal Cole have written about Mystery House and Olga Vásquez and Antonella Cortese are preparing a paper on the role of the electronic enitity in the development of culture and play.

[15] Consequence Cards accompany each room of the maze, regardless of the games inside (see Cole, 1996 for details on the theoretical rationale of the Consequence Cards). The mobility options in this section are taken from the 1996 version of the Consequence Cards. These artifacts repeatedly change in response to current conditions at *La Clase Mágica* and are continuously updated in the materials that are available on the Web site.

[16] The *La Clase Mágica* team was not completely convinced that the LAS was the most appropriate tool to measure language proficiency but was restricted by the lack of comparable measures. The decision to use the LAS test was accompanied by the resolve to support the findings with informal measures of language fluency—e.g., with field notes.

[17] The video, entitled *La Clase Mágica* is available through *La Clase Mágica's* research office at LCHC, UCSD, 9500 Gilman Drive, La Jolla, CA. 92093-0092.

[18] Other sources in the Fletcher Special Collection, such as the Chancellor's files, have informed sections of this book as well. In particular, the historical sketch of UCSD in chapter 3 relies on Special Collection sources.

[19] Separate Stories of Shared Spaces can be found on *La Clase Mágica's* Web site: HTTP://communication.ucsd.edu/LCM/index.html.

[20] Superbarrio is the closest to Superhero that Mexican culture acknowledges. However, this hero is far from being the model of invincibility typical of American superheroes.

[21] For more information regarding these efforts, visit the UC Links Web site.

[22] In support of community members' literacy practices, and as Mrs. Durán aptly points out, "to honor the difference in access to opportunities," *La Clase Mágica* has had a policy of not changing texts contributed by community members. Mrs. Durán's text has been edited, however, to include diacritical marks not possible in the original electronic text. Surface level revisions have also been made to add to legibility of the text—e.g., punctuation and capitalization. Spelling and grammar changes have not been made.

5

Language and Identity
in a Bilingual Learning Environment

In adapting La Clase Mágica to the needs of bilingual children, we reshaped the Fifth Dimension's conceptual and linguistic structures to accommodate the resources found in the children's homes, schools, and communities. In according children with intellectual support drawn from multiple knowledge sources, we complemented the Fifth Dimension's research interest in language as a tool in cognitive development (Griffin & Cole, 1984). We readjusted the research lens and strategies for practice to focus on the role of bilingualism and biculturalism in meaning-making and problem solving. Specifically, we became interested in the ways children's prior knowledge was brought to bear on the learners' social, cognitive, and linguistic development. In essence, we made multiplicity and affirmation of cultural and linguistic background fundamental to our research and pedagogical objectives. Although identity was not an initial concern of our initial research or program design, it emerged as a recurrent theme in the recorded observations of language use among the children, especially among the long-term participants known as Wizard Assistants. We supported, children claims of "soy Mexicano," "I am a Wizard Assistant," "I am a teenager," "I am a student," and "I am American" equally and felicitously.

The data on children who remained in the program for long periods of time pointed to key connections between language and identity. These data were persuasive: A bilingual environment where either English or Spanish are used interchangeably to optimize a learner's potential has a decisive impact on long-term participants' language choice, engagement, and sense of self. Interestingly, these findings provided a contrast to the inhibited role of minority learners reported in other research. For example, research on teacher–student interactions (Heath, 1983; Mehan, 1991, 1992), literacy practices (Gee, 1990; Michaels, 1981; Scollon & Scollon, 1981) and participant structures (Philips, 1983) illustrates the detrimental effects of privileging Standard English and mainstream codes of interaction in conventional classrooms. The voices and identities of learners whose backgrounds are discontinuous with those of the teachers and the school are silenced, overlooked, or undermined by these same practices. As a result, if non-mainstream students do participate in classroom activities, they do so unevenly and oftentimes unsuccessfully.

Given a culturally supportive curriculum and environment, however, was shown to be insufficient in counteracting the effects of English dominance and conventional norms of student comportment. The ideologies surrounding the dominance of English flowed freely into the daily life of *La Clase Mágica*, even though children were continually given the opportunities to negotiate and re-negotiate their bilingualism and their identities according to the sociolinguistic character of the activity. In the early stages of the project, children were often heard parroting the ideologies of significant others outside the project. Repeatedly, they admonished their peers with "We speak English here!" They also called the staff by the title of "Maestra" [Teacher] and outside of the lure of the computer games they subjected their will to the adults. It took many quarters and much encouragement by the adults before children assumed "control of their own development" as had been inscribed in the system of artifacts of the program. The struggle with the common assumption that speaking a language other than English is a source of embarrassment, a public branding of inferiority, however, continued throughout. As Carlos, a long-term participant of *La Clase Mágica*, explained:

> Yo pienso que es porque a veces los Americanos asi dicen cosas de los Mexicanos, que no sirven para nada y todo eso. Y a veces uno tiene miedo de que sepan que es uno Mexicano. [AV/05/95]

> [I think it is because sometimes the Americans, they say things about Mexicans, that they are not good for anything. And, sometimes you are afraid that they will find out that you are Mexican.]

To "pass," and more importantly, to succeed, children like Carlos have to adopt the sanctioned linguistic norms and expectations often to the detriment of their home language and culture as Wong-Filmore (1991) pointed out in her research among the Chinese American community. The alternative, of course, is failure, which according to McDermott (1998), is a viable option that children "achieve" with the full support of the educational system.

The development of *La Clase Mágica's* bilingual–bicultural learning environment centered on counteracting the norm of attaching a higher status to the language of the society's dominant group (Kalantzis, Cope, & Slade, 1989). Rather than promoting an assimilative or oppositional culture, *La Clase Mágica* developed a "third space," where discourses from multiple learning domains merge to replicate the everyday experiences of bilingual children Gutierrez et al., 1995). We incorporated normative practice of learning and teaching into a melange of forms of interaction, language use, and collaborative activity. Using the expanded notions of third space developed by Gutierrez , Baquerano-López, and Tejeda (1999), *La Clase Mágica* became a hybrid activity merging the codes of behaviors, texts, and practices found in official and unofficial space into a covenant of collaborative action. By preserving the everyday sociolinguistic reality of bilingual children while complementing it with formal educational activities and materials, learners are not limited to one language or to one identity. The bilingual design of the program gives participants the option to draw freely on the resources of either *Mexicano* or mainstream culture that flank each side of *La Clase Mágica*. Numerous identities and language practices are at their disposal. Over time, free access to language choice maps on to a positive and multiple sense of self. As evidenced in the undergraduate fieldnotes, long-term participants displayed a particular preference for the identity of "Wizard Assistant" otherwise recognized as the highest status member of the community whose expertise and participation is repeatedly valued and publicly rewarded.

In this chapter, I approach the connection between language and identity from a constructivist position that views language choice and identity as socially constructed in the interactions among members of a group or community. This analysis contributes to a small but emergent literature that theorizes the social and psychological effects of learning settings that draw on multiple knowledge sources to achieve new understandings (González, 1995; Gutierrez et al., 1995; Gutierrez et al., 1995 Moll & Greenberg, 1990; Vásquez, 1989; Vásquez et al., 1994). I show how ideology and social structures linguistically encode success and failure, and by extension inscribe a sense of self. I begin by sketching out a framework from which to conceptualize the origins of identity in social relations. Next, I focus on three artifacts in *La Clase Mágica's* assemblage of artifacts that mediate children's progress and use of language: the Wizard Assistant Club; *El Maga* (the electronic pal); and the undergraduate Amigos/as. Then, I present a case study of two long-term participants (a boy and a girl) who advanced to Wizard Assistant status to show the ways this system of mediation affects language choice and identity. I conclude with a discussion of the multiple identities that *La Clase Mágica* supports and I argue that encouraging access to language and identity might be a useful strategy for educational practice and an essential skill for members of the global society of the 21st century.

THE SOCIAL CONSTRUCTION OF IDENTITY

The notion that identity takes shape in the interaction between the social and psychological realms of individual action is informed by the work of two prominent psychologists: Erik Erikson, who popularized the concept of identity, and Lev Vygotsky, whose work on the role of language in development offers important conceptual tools for studying identity formation. Together, these theorists lay out the parameters from which to theorize the emergence of identity in social interaction. They situate identity formation at the nexus of sociocultural processes and psychological functioning. It is at this center point, that Erikson claims, the individual is accorded the choices for "being" in two separate but interrelated realms of human functioning—the individual as an independent entity and the individual as part of a collective. Although Vygotsky did not explicitly address the topic of identity in his work, we can infer, however, that he would have credited social relations as mediating the possibilities for "being."

Erikson believed that identity is "a process 'located' at the core of the individual as well as at the core of his communal culture" (Gleason, 1983, p. 914). In the face of maturity and the ensuing progressively changing views of self, these processes present the individual with a perpetual dilemma of maintaining a stable relation between the two. Each subsequent developmental stage, with its corresponding cultural contexts and role relations, presents the individual with an "ever expanding circle of individuals and ideas, the self must commit to" (Cole & Cole, 1993, p. 358). The individual changes across time in relation to others, as he or she meets the challenges of social expectations that support or reject the developing conceptions of a social self. Granted the support for a positive growing sense of self at the subjective level "provides the ability to experience oneself as something that has continuity and sameness" (Erikson, 1963, p. 43). Importantly, it signals support for the "acts and feelings" an individual displays in a given social setting (Ochs, 1993, p. 298). Continuity wards off disintegration and pathology. Alongside this stabilizing current is the ever present threat of an "identity crisis," that ensues when a person finds him or herself unable to meet social expectations, whether intentionally or because of some inadequacy. Unnourished or rejected by the objective world, the personality suffers disintegration or pathology, and thus becomes a likely candidate for the ever willing recipient, the prison system.

Vygotsky's formulation of development provides the conceptual and methodological tools for examining how sociocultural processes shape identity formation (Penuel & Wertsch, 1995). Vygotsky's most well-known theoretical construct, the zone of proximal development, is useful for conceptualizing the process through which the individual comes to acquire a sense of self in the midst of social relations. According to Penuel and Wertsch, the zone of proximal development incorporates three core themes in Vygotsky's work: (1) development as the framework for studying individual functioning; (2) social relations as the genesis of mental functioning; and (3) tools and signs, such as language and literacy, as mediators of human activity. The "zoped" (a widely used contraction of the "zone of proximal development") marks off the distance between two points of development in which the learner accomplishes, in collaboration with a more expert assistant, what he or she eventually will be able to accomplish unassisted (Vygotsky, 1978). In the process of moving between actual and future development, the individual appropriates into his or her repertoire the nuances, skills, and language—as well as the goals and objectives—of collective activity. Identity thus emerges at the moment in which the individual stands back from the collective process and acts upon it in a new and transformed way. This process may be represented visually by an elongated loop indicating the individual's progressive and intermittent regressive movements in the process of achieving the next stage of independent performance (see Fig. 5.1).

Zone of Proximal Development

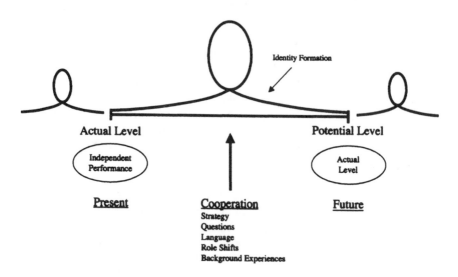

Figure 5.1. Zone of proximal development.

At *La Clase Mágica* learners move from one stage of development to the next through a series of activities designed to draw on the their previous experiences as critical intellectual tools for meaning-making. Collective activity is co-constructed through the theoretically informed scaffolding of the adults collaborators and the material and symbolic system of artifacts such as instructional guides known as "task cards" and the organizing maze. Collective activity privileges nonhierarchical relations, a dialogic process of collaboration and a link between old and new knowledge in a deliberate attempt to move the learner to his or her future potential. For example, the "context" segment of the task card for the commercially designed game, "Facemaker" labeled "Haciendo Caras" [Making Faces] the learners' first language and culture are used to locate a familiar event in children's lives—disagreements with adults that lead to a long face (see Figure 5.2). Children are roused to action with the prompt. "Hoy nadie te va decir nada [Today no one will scold you] . . . this is your opportunity to make as many faces as you want!!!"

FACEMAKER/ HACIENDO CARAS   #6a

Stop making faces! "¡Te vas a quedar asi!" Es lo que tus papás te dicen cuando te enojas. Hoy nadie te va a decir nada. This is your opportunity to make as many faces as you want!! ¡Pero cuidado! Antes de comenzar con tus carotas ¡PRECIONA LA TECLA PARA LAS MAYUSCULAS! MAKE SURE THE CAPS LOCK KEY IS ON!

Figure 5.2. Facemaker context.

This portion of the task card inscribes a bilingual bicultural temper onto the activity according the children freedom to draw on multiple cultures, languages, and contexts to accomplish the object of the game: to make faces. The child is given choices for action and identification.

A segment of a longer fieldnote written in 1995 by CM, an undergraduate enrolled in the practicum class, illustrates the attention to the child's needs in the collective activity of *La Clase Mágica*. It also illustrates the effects of prior knowledge on "on-task" behavior. Noting the disengagement, CM attempts to divert the learner to a more collaborative and "more academically challenging" game and away from Tetris, a game stressing fine motor skills and independent play. CM tries to entice Javier to numerous games but to each suggestion, he shoots off the object of the game, indicating his familiarity with all the games, all except the "map game." Finally, CM captures the child's attention through the use of personal knowledge:

> Javier started to scroll through the names and I thought I should try to turn this into a more interesting game for him so that he wouldn't lose interest. I asked him to point to three countries from the list where people spoke Spanish. First, he highlighted Brazil. I told him that he was close because Brazil is a South American country, but that people there did not speak Spanish. I told him they spoke

Portuguese which is the language of Portugal, a country that shares a border with Spain. Then he tried again and highlighted Argentina. I congratulated him and asked him what he knew about Argentina. He told me about the soccer team and pointed to the country on the map. He then tried to pick another Spanish speaking country from the list. He scrolled to Mexico and selected it. I congratulated him again and asked him about Mexico. He told me that his family was from there, from a city near Mexico City. He told me a little about his family. Then he went back to the list and chose another country, the USA. I laughed and told him once again that he was correct. He said that he chose it because many people speak Spanish here.

Both these examples situate the learner on familiar ground as a basis for securing a smooth transition to new understandings. The adult and the especially designed materials not only reaffirms the individual's sense of self but also opens the possibility for internalizing the nuances, skills, and language—as well as the goals and objectives—of collective activity. The moment at which the individual realizes that he or she can perform the new task independently is the exact moment that personal identity is formed. Having appropriated selected norms and actions as his or her own, the individual separates from collective activity. This point is what Penuel and Wertsch, call, "rhetorical action" (p. 85), the individual uses language to define and support the choices he or she has made. Language, then, becomes a crucial conduit by which identity, both at the collective and the individual levels is formed.

Erikson and Vygotsky provide the terminology and analytic space to examine a sense of self at the nexus of social and psychological functioning, they offer, however, little insight into the formation of identity in situations where a multiplicity of viewpoints and codes exist. Mead's (1939) work, for example, depicted the sense of self as predictable, continuous, and uncomplicated in homogeneous communities where life is bound to tradition and a common existence. What, however, is the sense of self portrayed by members of such diverse communities as those Sellers and Weis (1997) described in the anthology *Beyond Black and White?* Specifically, how does an individual member of a "democratic multicultural community"—as large sectors of the United States are increasingly defined today—view him or herself (Carlson, 1997)? What is the concept of self in activities embedded within intersecting cultural and linguistic practices that are related to diversity in class, language, race, ethnicity, sexuality, and gender? In particular, what are the ways in which multilingualism inscribes a relation between the individual and the world? Following, I sketch a framework from which to examine the role of language and culture in the formation of a sense of self.

A BILINGUAL–BICULTURAL SYSTEM OF MEDIATION

The system of artifacts that inform everyday life within *La Clase Mágica* privileges multiple funds of knowledge drawn from English and Spanish and Mexicano and Anglo mainstream culture as viable intellectual tools. Together, the material, symbolic, and electronic components of the program form a bilingual–bicultural community of lateral relations, multiple knowledge sources, and active participation on the part of all. Activities are organized to stimulate the imagination of a possible multicultural world where they are capable and able learners. Children use their unique resources to "create meaning, negotiate tasks, and solve problems" therefore engendering a social and cognitive development that allows them access to and mastery of multiple cultural contexts (Vásquez et al., 1994, p. 14). Participants learn not only to draw on but also value the formal and informal knowledge sources of the home, school, and community.

Thus, when the 15 to 25 children who regularly attend the program imagine themselves taking a "journey through the maze," they conjure up a multicultural world of multiple possibilities.[1] Their decisions are respected and supported whether they are engaged in game playing or socializing. The children are given the freedom to decide which language to use, with whom, and for what purpose (Vásquez, 1992). They also have the choice of which culture to use: their home culture; the culture of mainstream society; or the culture of *La Clase Mágica*. The bilingual–bicultural design of the accompanying resource materials at once serves as a platform of actual development and as a basis for accomplishing new understandings and new ways to use language introduced by the games and the university students. For example, in written and verbal interactions, we often ask the children in Spanish to talk about games they played entirely in English. Conversely, we ask them in English to discuss games they played entirely in Spanish.

The material and symbolic artifacts of *La Clase Mágica* constitute a bilingual–bicultural system of mediation. They shape cognition and action at the intersection of multiple worlds. No specific culture or language defines either the questions or the answers to the many problems that emerge in daily life at the site. There are no "set rules" other than those imposed by the technology or the fantasy worlds of the games. Used within conventional forms of politeness in *Mexicano* culture, the use of colloquial, regional, or "nonstandard," forms of language are deemed acceptable in face-to-face communication and written text. Thus, the merit of such variants as "chante," "canton," "casa," "vivencia," or "hows," "house," and "pad" to refer to an individual's place of residence, is subordinate to the more important goal of meaning making. Attention to the misspelling of "hows," (house) for example, frequently used by a Spanish dominant, community staff member when writing in English, diverts the focus away from the point of the missive. In time, and through reading written responses from the university-trained staff, community learners are expected to learn appropriate more formal forms of language use.

This operating principle, developed in collaboration with representatives of the community, has been particularly useful in encouraging parent participation in written tasks. Unfortunately, it has also generated repeated and widespread criticism from scholars who find our acceptance of nonstandard Spanish a form of denigration of the project's Spanish-speakers. Rather than rewording or editing our participants' written language to make it grammatically correct, we have repeatedly chosen to accept it in its "raw" form. This open policy has given "voice" to our collaborators. It has also generated rich discussions about resources and "linguicism"—the domination of one language at the expense of others— (Skutnabb-Kangas, 1988, p. 10), in our staff meetings and other venues in which participants of *La Clase Mágica* have played a part.

One example of the debate engendered by our acceptance of nonstandard language use involves a letter posted on the program's Web page by Mrs. Durán, a staff member from the community, on behalf of "Los padres de Familia" [the parent group] of *La Clase Mágica*. Some members of the listserve felt that the misspellings and improper grammar in Mrs. Durán's letter should have been corrected before the letter was posted. The sensitive but tense discussion that ensued was exactly the kind of exchange that the consortium needed in order to address the variability of resources and languages among the populations we served. An unintended and unfortunate outcome of the debate, however, was the silencing of Mrs. Durán. In the end, rather than "speaking" for herself on the consortium listserve, a research assistant "ventriloquated" her words:

> It has been brought to my attention that the form of Lourdes' letter, representing the thoughts and feelings of *La Clase Mágica* parents, was distracting in its use of grammar and it may make some feel uncomfortable about putting it in on LCM's Web page.I brought this concern up to Lourdes and she said that it is important to understand the parents' capabilities and limitations. She said that she and other parents didn't have the resources and opportunities accorded to those working within the University framework. It's important to move beyond the form, and try to capture the meaning of the message, from the parents' perspective. This is not to say that editing will not take place. It has and will continue, but always trying to carefully preserve the parents' language and their voice.[2] [JY/01/04/97]

The community's voice, regardless of its form, has been critical to the philosophy and practice of *La Clase Mágica*. It has generated an organic character to the adaptation process. Most of the program activities and materials evolved naturally from the resources that were available in the immediate working environment--and these were drawn from the parents and the research staff themselves. The preferences of the community representatives were integrated into the design of the program from the onset. The childhood experiences and acquired knowledge of members of the research team (Anglo and multigenerational Mexican origin undergraduates) also became rich resources for adaptation (Henry, 1993). Not only was the community knowledge integrated symbolically into the intellectual fabric of *La Clase Mágica*, the community assumed control of the process. Mrs. Durán, with a junior high school education, began to single-handedly conduct the adaptation of the task cards from the third round of adaptation on. These strategies accorded respect and parity to community members and staff and thus encouraged active and committed participation at the same time that creativity, self-reliance, and leadership were encouraged. Effectively, the approach supported a bilingual community of learners that was not lost to the child participants as was amply reflected in the familial character of the site noted by one and all who visit the site. These positive effects are evident in the community members' decision to take over the responsibility of running one of the sessions of *La Clase Mágica* given throughout the week. From 1996 on the parents and the Wizard Assistants took over the operations of the Friday session without university support.

THREE CULTURAL ARTIFACTS IN ACTION

Although all artifacts are bilingually adapted to promote the use of either language or culture, three in particular—the electronic entity, the undergraduate *amigos/as*, and the Wizard Assistant Club—reflect the organic, on-going, and enabling nature of *La Clase Mágica*'s activities and materials. The notion of "culture-as-mediating-artifact" by Holland and Cole (1995) is a useful rationale for the selection of these three interactional activities as promoting children's choice of language. These artifacts truly embody a "collectively remembered use" (p. 476) of the norms and expectations of behavior and language use at *La Clase Mágica*. Like the activity of "setting the table," discussed by these scholars, the activities involving *El Maga*, los amigos/as, and the Wizard Assistants Club, actualize a "theory of the task" and a "theory of the person." Each has distinct participants and particular roles they perform in the daily life of *La Clase Mágica*. Each contributes a distinctive role in the construction of the bilinguality and biculturalism of the *La Clase Mágica*.

   El Maga, the Electronic Pal. At the level of objective reality, *El Maga* or Wizard, as it is more commonly known throughout the Fifth Dimension universe, is an electronic entity to whom child participants report their progress through the prearranged set of activities at the site. Children read and write electronic messages and other correspondence from and to their electronic pal. Their progress through the levels of difficulty in game play is marked by their correspondence to *El Maga*. Thus, when a child completes the beginner, good, or expert level of play, they are directed to communicate with *Maga* by the instructional sheets that accompany each activity. When children fail to stay in touch, *Maga* "calls" them individually to the computer from her perch in cyberspace for real-time written conversations, commonly called online "chats." Just as frequently, children call on *Maga* to share news, secrets, or to simply ask for advice from someone outside their immediate circle of friends or family.

Theoretically, *El Maga* is a language construction. It exists only through communication with participants of the program both local and distal. In communicating with it, participants collude in substantiating his or her existence and as such acquiesce to its authority. In and through language, participants grant Maga power to oversee their progress, making it the only source of power in the local system. In this capacity, *Maga* corroborates with other artifacts in the Fifth Dimension model to inscribe a nonhierarchical structure in the social relations of the site. Rather, than answer to the dictates of any one person at the site, child learners and on occasions, the adults too, must defer to the authority outside the local activity system. In the following segment of a longer conversation, *Maga* asserts her authority as overseer of the children's progress through the maze during a live-chat session on April 12, 1993:

Maga:	HOLA ISIDERO. QUE BUENO QUE ANDAS POR ACA. DIME, EN QUE JUEGO ESTAS DEL LABERINTO? [HELLO ISIDERO. SO GOOD THAT YOU ARE HERE. TELL ME, WHAT ROOM ARE ARE YOU IN THE MAZE?]
Isidero:	No se. [Don't know.]
Maga:	NO?? WELL, IT IS TIME FOR YOU TO TALK TO ONE OF MY ASISTENTES Y QUIERO QUE LES PREGUNTES QUE ES LO QUE TIENES QUE HACER PARA EL MIERCOLES, OK? [. . . ASSISTANTS AND I WANT YOU TO ASK THEM WHAT YOU NEED TO DO ON WEDNESDAY, OK?]
Isidero:	No.
Maga:	NO QUE? [NO, WHAT?]
Isidero:	Si. [Yes.]
Maga:	BUENO, NO TE AGAS. . .

YA LEISTE LA CONSTITUCION DE LA
CLASE MAGICA?
[GOOD THEN . . . HAVE YOU ALREADY
READ LA CLASE MAGICA'S
CONSTITUTION?]

Isidero: Que es esa cosa?
               [What is that?]

Maga: PUES POR AHI VAS A EMPEZAR MIJITO!
               LLAMALE A NORA.
               [WELL THEN, YOU WILL START THERE!
               CALL NORA.]

Nora: Hola Maga, yo soy Nora.
               [Hello Maga, I am Nora.]

Maga: QUERIDISMA NORA, WELCOME, ME
               DAMUCHO GUSTO QUE ESTE AHI
               CUMPLIENDO RESPONSABLEMENTE,
               GRACIAS. OYE, QUIERO QUE TE
               ENCARGUES DE MOSTRARLE AL NINO
               ESTE, QUE ESTA UN POCO ALTANERO,LA
               CONSTITUCION DE LA CLASE MAGICA
               POR FAVOR!!! SIRVE QUE TE SIRVA DE
               REPASO A TI TAMBIEN. OK?
               [DEAREST NORA, WELCOME, I AM VERY
               HAPPY TO KNOW THAT YOU ARE THERE.
               THANK YOU. HEY, I WANT YOU TO TAKE
               IT UPON YOURSELF TO SHOW THIS
               KID,WHO IS BEING A BIT HAUGHTY, LA
               CLASE MAGICA'S CONSTITUTION
               PLEASE!!! IT WILL BE GOOD FOR YOU TO
               REVIEW IT TOO, OK?]

The affordances of the technology allow *Maga* to assert her authority from outside of the local system. In her directives *Maga* not only moves the participants to action—"LLAME A NORA POR FAVOR" ["CALL NORA FOR ME"] and "QUIERO QUE TE ENCARGUES DE MOSTRARLE . . ." ["I WANT YOU TO TAKE IT UPON YOURSELF TO SHOW . . ."], she also orchestrates the use of the artifacts of the site, in this case the Constitution, and the supervisorial role of the Wizard Assistants, to reinforce her power. Strategically, she uses these mediating artifacts to reinforce the culture of the site, reminding both Isdero, a first level participant to follow the expected rules of behavior—"DIME, EN QUE JUEGOS ESTAS DEL LABERINTO?" ["TELL ME, IN WHICH ROOM YOU ARE IN THE MAZE?"], and then Nora, a Wizard Assistant—"SIRVE QUE TE SIRVA DE REPASO A TI TAMBIEN" ["IT WILL BE GOOD FOR YOU TO REVIEW IT TOO"].

Fluent in a variety of languages, dialects, and vernaculars, *Maga* also privileges the bilingual and bicultural quality of life at *La Clase Mágica*. On many occasions, *Maga* has communicated with the children in Russian, French, and Portuguese and in other language varieties such as Calo (vernacular of Mexican origin youth) and California cool such as "Valley Talk." This flexibility reinforces language choice as a standard practice. So, too, does the policy of initiating the "conversation" in the children's native language, and then allowing the correspondent to pursue his or her language of choice. For example, in the clip provided earlier, *Maga* begins the conversation in Spanish as customary but later gives the child an opportunity to shift to English. When there is no indication that the child will follow suit, *Maga* returns back to Spanish. *El Maga's* apparent lack of vested interest in one language or the other frees the children to communicate in their first or second language, or to mix the two. To reinforce the maintenance of a language that succumbs to the dominance of English beginning as early as the first generation, *Maga* gently reverts back to Spanish and opens the opportunity for children to continue in their native language when the appropriate space becomes available. However, *Maga* does not always take the opportunity to shift as is demonstrated in the following conversation with Carlos on February 28, 1994 where *Maga* continues in English through the entire 41-turn conversation about the Wizard Assistant fieldtrip and Carlos' school experiences:

> **Maga:** HOLA CARLOS! HOY ME ESTABA RECORDANDO
> QUE CUANDO ERAS CHICO YO TE DECIA
> CARLOSIN TIN TIN! PERO YA NO TE PUEDO
> DECIR ASI PORQUE YEA ESTAS MAS GRANDE.
> COMO HAS ESTADO?
> [HELLO CARLOS! TODAY I REMEMBERED THAT
> WHEN YOU WERE YOUNGER I CALLED YOU
> CARLOSIN TIN TIN! BUT I CAN'T CALL YOU THAT
> ANYMORE BECASUE YOU ARE OLDER NOW. HOW
> HAVE YOU BEEN?]
> **Carlos:** Hi!
> **Maga:** HOW'S MY OLD BUDDY DOING? GEE, IT SURE
> IS GREAT HEARING FROM YOU! I MISSED TALKING
> TO YOU. BUT I UNDERSTAND THAT YOU HAVE A
> LOT OF HOMEWORK. SO WHAT YOU BEEN
> UP TO LATELY?

Los Amigos y Amigas [the Friends or Children's Buddies]. Another key artifact that supports the children's language choice and their sense of importance as problem solvers is the hierarchically balanced interactions they have with the adults in the program—mostly undergraduate students enrolled in the practicum course attached to the program. The students' role as *Amigos/as* is designed to promote children's independence and command of their development. The students function as participant-observers, creators of culture, and collaborators. Importantly, they serve as proponents of children's active participation. They provide learners with numerous supporting strategies that include eliciting their little partners' understanding and plans for action in the problem-solving process. They encourage rather than direct the children's development. They use their greater knowledge of the world and more sophisticated analytical skills as scaffolding strategies to help children pose and solve problems. They question, provide examples, and offer explanations for difficult concepts posed by the games and activities, all the while leaving control in the children's hands. More importantly, they support children's choice of language by continuing in the chosen language if they are fluent in Spanish and, if not, by enlisting the children's assistance in understanding the text. So, when an undergraduate is reading a task card and comes to the word, "tiendita," he has only to ask the child, "Oh, what is that?" and the child can promptly respond, "store!" Data sources are replete with examples such as this where undergraduates and children negotiate the bilingualism inscribed in the artifacts and the conversations of peers and other adults.

The nonhierarchical relations between children and adults make this give and take possible. The power structure embodied in the age difference and social distance between undergraduates and children is offset by the following factors: The students' formal title as Amigos/as; their novice status in the culture of *La Clase Mágica*; and (for many) their command of only one language. These three factors solidify the students' role as collaborators both in terms of their knowledge base and their position in the problem solving process. The undergraduates are a part of *La Clase Mágica* for only 10 weeks (the length of the academic quarter) and have only a limited knowledge of the games and the culture of the program. These factors place them in the awkward position of novice–experts at the same time that they elevate the children's status. The children's knowledge of the workings of *La Clase Mágica*, on the other hand, places them in the status of expert. Their accumulated knowledge allows them to solve technical glitches and obstacles to game progress that often perplex the staff and other adults (Nicolopoulou & Cole, 1993).

The delicate balancing act required of the *Amigos/as*, however, is not easy to achieve without language and culture of the child, as the segment of the following fieldnote documents—especially with long-term participants of the project. The limitations of her English monolingualism and lack of cultural knowledge is not lost on KG, one of the first undergraduates assigned to develop an activity for the Wizard Assistants based on the philosophical foundation of *La Clase Mágica*. Her lack of Spanish weakens her authority over the children's attention and she is unable to hand over the control of the problem-solving process:

> I don't really know how to keep the club organized. I do not want to assume a position of authority and yell for them to sit down and do the task, since this is supposed to be a voluntary enjoyable experience for them. It seems as though when orders need to be given, CB, YJ and LD [staff members] use Spanish. Also, when they went to talk to the kids (for example when YJ went to get Julian off the computer) they tend to use Spanish. Indirectly, this results in the assumption by the children to take the adults that speak Spanish as the ones to listen to, and the non-Spanish speakers, they don't need to pay attention to, unless they feel like it. So without YJ or CB telling the kids to come and sit at the Wizard Assistants' table, the kids won't do it. DR, EV and I wanted to create a habitual thing of the 6 kids meeting there the first five minutes of each class, but this is a hard thing to do. I don't want to have to bribe them with candy to sit down, and I don't want to force them. Any suggestions are helpful, but how much emphasis should we put on the club? They want a pizza party or something fun, but we can't do that unless we all discuss with them and have them work hard for it. Norma and Nina agreed to work with me on their task cards and I think EV has Julian and Carlos. The club is coming along, but its going to take lots of motivation and work. [KG/2/8/93]

This incident clearly implicates bilingualism in the construction of thought and action at *La Clase Mágica*. Bilingualism had taken root and was the operating mechanism by which interrelations were organized. Problem solving, the setting of goals, and states of mind were communicated bilingually. Importantly, KG's fieldnote makes clear that learning takes place on both sides of the partnership, although the stated goal is to promote the children's optimal potential. It is collaborative activity that is mutually beneficial. While the children hone their respective skills, the undergraduates gain a more positive understanding of ethnic minority children and of their educational possibilities (Gallego, 1995). They learn to negotiate differences in languages and cultural contexts. Several quarters after this fieldnote, the Wizard Assistant Club became one of the most successful activities that grew out of *La Clase Mágica*'s adaptation process.

The Wizard Assistant Club: Redefining Expertise. The Wizard Assistant Club is one of the most important and unique aspects of *La Clase Mágica*, one that sets it apart from its predecessor, the Fifth Dimension. In late fall 1993, the need to modify the organizational structure of *La Clase Mágica* for long-term participants who completed a preset number of games was observed. Once children achieved this expert status, they were no longer structurally integrated into the system. They had no defined role and no games left to master.

Our concern over how to retain these children led to the design of an activity that would not only reify the norms and expectations of a bilingual–bicultural learning environment, but would also capture the children's attention. Over a period of several quarters, good-natured and extremely patient undergraduates worked diligently to carve out an activity that would maintain the interest of children who by that time had learned to be fiercely independent, expressive, and assertive (Vásquez, 1994). As KG makes clear earlier, the process was uncharted, time-consuming, and quite frustrating.

To help reduce the problems and frustrations of both the children and the undergraduates, *El Maga* began consulting directly with each. Th followign segment responds to KG's plea for help with moral support, direction, and transference of power. Ever vigilant of the uses of language, she instructs the student "manager" (title given to the undergraduates leading the construction of the activity) to note the ways in which bilingualism organizes the interrelations at site. She also nudges KG to use what ever Spanish she does know, well aware that non-Mexican individuals who are not native speakers of Spanish are given a lot of leeway in the Mexicano community. Not only will her misuse be overlooked, she will be rewarded in-kind for her effort.

Hi KG,

Nice notes, give a specific example of an interaction between two people that occurred in English-only and then changed language, etc. This would be great to reflect upon later. Set up what your expectations are for the students in the club. Tell them you expect what you say to be done. Do not settle for less or the children will have control over you. For example, tell them that they are to get together at the beginning of EVERY class and their not doing it is NOT an option. Before they do anything else they must do this. Enforce this the next time there is a session. Once they know you mean business, they should respect you more. It is interesting to be in a bilingual setting. Keep taking notes on how language is used and when it switches. Usually once someone asks me a question in one language (English or Spanish), I answer in that language and often continue conversation in it even though they may be able to speak the second language as well. The bilingual children should respect that your Spanish skills are not as good as theirs, but you are trying and want to interact with them. Hang in there!! MAGA [quoted in KG/2/8/93]

It took three academic quarters before El Maga, the children, and the students were able to carve out a set of activities and norms of behavior that were amenable to the goals of the project and also attractive to the child participants.

Membership in the Wizard Assistant Club positions the children as integral to the workings of *La Clase Mágica*. The WAs, as they are more commonly called, put into practice much more than the game-playing skills they have learned in collaborative activities with the undergraduate students (Stanton-Salazar et al., 1995). They enact and re-enact the norms and expectations of enculturated members of *La Clase Mágica*. They are active, cognizant, and valuable members of the problem-solving process, much like their much-admired *Amigos/as*. They exercise choice of language, culture, or activity as a right and wield it nonchalantly, occasionally to the chagrin of the adults. Not infrequently, we hear them say, "I am a Wizard Assistant. I can do that." They present themselves as independent thinkers and doers in either language.

The role of expert, helper, and ambassador is defined in a written agreement the Wizard Assistants sign soon after the end-of-the-quarter celebration where they receive a certificate of achievement. In the agreement, they promise *Maga* they will assist first-level children, create new artifacts, test new games, and regularly report their activities through telecommunication. They also agree to complete their school homework before they carry out their responsibilities or take part in any of the high-tech activities especially designed for them (such as cruising the Internet). One of the most prestigious functions the Wizard Assistants perform is the role of program ambassador. Throughout the year, these children are asked to represent *La Clase Mágica*, speaking at university courses, project meetings, conferences, and at the site itself. For example, each academic quarter the Wizard Assistants, along with the site coordinator and research staff, introduce the new set of undergraduates to *La Clase Mágica* in a formal orientation session. One day per week, they also perform the duties of the Amigos/as at the session of *La Clase Mágica* the parent-participants run without assistance from the university students or staff. In all of these activities, children collaborate, share knowledge, and perpetuate the material and symbolic culture of *La Clase Mágica*.

In 1996, 12 adolescents were enrolled in the Wizard Assistant Club—5 girls and 7 boys. Their ages ranged from 9 to 16 years; 10 of these children had participated in *La Clase Mágica* for an average of 5 1/2 years. Although some of them had entered with little English fluency or with a preference for Spanish, by 1996 all were increasingly choosing English as the language of choice. The results of the Language Assessment Scale (LAS) indicated that these children were able to stave off the loss of Spanish for 3 years longer than members of the control group at the local elementary school. Yet, by the fifth year, they too were showing a dip in their native language oral fluency. It is possible that *La Clase Mágica*'s bilingual environment affected the children's retention of their first language for the first 3 years. However, the cumulative effects of their families' length of stay in this country, their years of schooling in an English-only system, and their integration into American pop culture eventually resulted in the inevitable shift from Spanish to English that has been noted as early as the first generation (Veltman, 1988). Even if a shift was not occurring as the LAS indicated, the children's language of choice certainly was changing to English (Pease-Alvarez, Hakuta, & Bayley, 1998).

We might ask ourselves what the gains and losses might be if the context were one in which both languages and cultures held equal status? What sense of self would develop in this "third space," where opposing discourses merge in a transformative dialogue? (Gutierrez et al., 1995). Does the need for a unified self compel individuals to maintain a "native," "dominant" identity, or does a fusion occur, so that the self represents neither one nor the other but something new and transformed? A careful review of the data on two long-term participants of *La Clase Mágica* helps us to understand the way learners might see themselves if their learning contexts were engineered to draw and build on their background experiences rather than to reject them.

A CASE STUDY OF TWO WIZARD ASSISTANTS

I focus on two long-term participants of *La Clase Mágica*—a boy and a girl— whose popularity and reliability are characteristic of the "ideal" Wizard Assistant. As older siblings of other participants, Carlos and Rina received adulation and respect, but it was their status as Wizard Assistant that commanded deference and recognition from adults and peers. Both children entered and left the program at around the same time. Carlos was 11 when he joined *La Clase Mágica* and Rina was 7. Five years later, Carlos left *La Clase Mágica* to take a job after school and Rina transferred (for a short period) to a nearby Fifth Dimension because of a disagreement with the site coordinator. The discussion that follows is based on 22 academic quarters' worth of data, including fieldnotes collected by undergraduate participant-observers, structured and unstructured interviews, and audio transcriptions. The data indicate that *La Clase Mágica* nourished these children's bilingualism against mounting pressure to shift language and identity. It confirms that they held a positive regard for their Spanish language skills[3] and had affirmative attitudes toward their ability to use both languages. For example, when asked how he felt about his bilingualism, Carlos exclaimed, "O sea me siento, o se siente great." ("Well, I feel, or it feels great"). Years of using either language to promote understanding and solving problems at *La Clase Mágica* underlie his comments about the value of bilingualism:

> puedo ayudar a personas que no hablan íngles o español. Puedo hacer
> nuevos amigos o como a veces que hay unos que no saben de un

idioma y tu vas y les ayudas y sí los dos hablan dos idiomas se pueden
ayudar y resolver los problemas hací rapido.

[I can help people who don't speak [either] English or Spanish. I can
make new friends or like sometimes there are those who don't know
a language and you go and help them and if they both speak the two
languages, they can help themselves and resolve problems much
faster.]

Carlos: A Tenuous Thread Between Success and Failure. Carlos
presents an interesting case study of the ways in which bilingual children
develop socially and intellectually at *La Clase Mágica*. Like the other
participants, Carlos was socialized to "achieve his optimal potential," using
bilingualism as an intellectual tool to create new understandings. *La Clase
Mágica*'s organizational structure made strategic use of Carlos' home language
and culture to support his acquisition of skills in English, game playing, and
computer literacy. Over time, he learned to communicate, problem solve, and
negotiate tasks using either Spanish or English. Carlos straddled both cultures.
For a while, he took up the music and style of dress of his peers in his adopted
country: the distinctive dress of "Cholos," a youth group known for their baggy
clothes and bandannas. Later, his attire came to pattern the youthful style of the
undergraduates—"California casual."

Carlos joined *La Clase Mágica* almost immediately after arriving from
Mexico City in the fall of 1991. He spoke only Spanish at the time but chose
either silence or pigeon English to communicate with the undergraduate students.
As described in the following extract from a fieldnote, in a spontaneous form of
apprenticeship (Rogoff, 1995) Carlos lost his reluctance to use Spanish.

> Throughout our session we were all good humored about the fact that
> Carlos didn't understand English and that I was trying to explain
> things to him in horrible Spanish. I tried to explain that we were
> trying to make the plant grow by doing impromptu sign language for
> "grow," once Carlos told me that "plant" was "planta." After
> struggling with that, I asked Nina, "Como se dice, 'grow?'" She
> replied but I couldn't understand and I repeated, "neser." They both
> laughed and simultaneously repeated, "creser" and this time, I heard,
> "hereser." This became progressively funnier until Nina grabbed my
> pen and spelled, "creser" and double checked with Carlos to make
> sure she had spelled it correctly. [GF/11/11/91]

In this exchange, use of the Spanish word for "grow" illustrates the use of the
home language as a tool for meaning making for both the adult and the children.
Even more so, it speaks for the bidirectional benefits of adult–child
interactions—both the child's and adult's zone of proximal development is

enhanced through this interaction. Both learn something in the second language. The child learns the English word "grow" and its meaning and the adult learns its equivalent in Spanish, "crecer."

Barely a month into the program, Carlos claimed to know only "jack-o-lantern," "pumpkin," "goodmorning," "candy," and similar Halloween-related words in English. Yet, he was able to maneuver through an English-based game using Spanish as a base. Six months later, still using mostly Spanish, Carlos began to integrate into his utterances more English or "pelinguish," as he jokingly remarked. Words such as "røng" (wrong), "IBM," "A multiple," "shark," "play," and "thank you" are heard throughout an audiotaped session recorded at the time. Carlos' use of his prior knowledge is also repeatedly documented in the fieldnotes of the undergraduate students. Next, a segment of transcribed interaction between Carlos and a Spanish-speaking female undergraduate demonstrates his knowledge of Spanish. He teaches the undergraduate (A), who purposely plays ignorant, basic concepts called upon by "Kinder Bits" and "Piñata," two computer games focusing on readiness skills. [AP/4/15/92]

[6] A: No le entiendo
[7] C: A pues, tenemos que . . .
[8] A: Una estrella?
[9] C: Esa, porque me la gane!
[10] Ira, tenemos que buscar, eh, como, de que . . .
[11] ¿Cual es? Como del triangulo este . . .

[6] A: I don't understand it.
[7] C: Oh well, we have to . . .
[8] A: A star?
[9] C: That, (pointing to the screen) because I won it.
[10] Look, we have to look (searching with the cursor)
[11] Which one is it? Like this triangle here . . .

The computers and warm ambiance of *La Clase Mágica* appeared to have a strong pull for Carlos. The site coordinator noted in the first months of his participation in 1991, " . . . No se aburre para nada, ni se cansa de estar en la computadora" (. . . He doesn't get bored nor gets tired of being on the computer) [MN:10/15/91]. He learned to use computers for game-play as well as for searching the Internet for relevant information. A few months later, an undergraduate student related that Carlos was "clearly in charge" of game playing at *La Clase Mágica*, having "come from being what everybody thought was quiet and shy, to being the virtual 'ring leader' and initiator of jokes" [TF/05/22/92]. Carlos was well respected by both children and adults throughout

his time at *La Clase Mágica*. The next segment, taken from an undergraduate
student's written observation in 1995, illustrates the high status Carlos held:

> Surprisingly, Carlos was not present, and his absence was felt. He is
> a very influential figure at LCM. He helps the children, the students
> and the adults. He is a great asset to LCM. [TQ:11/20/95]

By 1995, Carlos was drawn away from *La Clase Mágica* by work and
other extracurricular activities, including having a girlfriend. When he did
attend, he functioned independently in English—and when speaking with his
peers, favored English over Spanish. His scores on the English oral fluency
measure of the Language Assessment Scale had shown large leaps over 3 years,
moving from 31% in 1991 to 88% in 1994. The fieldnote extract reproduced
next illustrates the facility Carlos had achieved in English by 1995. The note
also indicates the persistence of the collaborative nature of interactions at *La
Clase Mágica*, even when the language choice changes to English. Here, Carlos
and a couple of other Wizard Assistants are trying to solve a list of riddles El
Maga sent to the children at all the Fifth Dimension sites to commemorate her
birthday:

> Carlos and some other boy[s] were all working on a game called
> Scavenger Hunt. They had a piece of paper in front of them and they
> would read the questions and have to find the answers in some
> literature found in the computer. When I sat down they were reading
> something titled, "William E. Blanton." The question is, "What does
> the Wizard call his home?" Juan was using the mouse, reached across
> the other boy to do it. Carlos was standing next to boys sitting down.
> They all discuss where to go to find the answer. When they agreed,
> they'd go there and all read independently to themselves. Carlos
> shouts out, "He calls the whole world my home" as he read directly
> from the article they all were reading.

Although outward appearances might suggest that Carlos was losing his Spanish,
this was not the case. His Spanish scores on the Language Assessment
Scale indicate that he had not only maintained his first language but had topped
the scale by the third administration of the test. This is noteworthy because
the comparison group at the school was showing a precipitous drop in
Spanish scores by the third year. Also, close observation revealed that in
most cases Carlos continued to use Spanish at *La Clase Mágica* when
he was conversing with native Spanish-speaking adults. An hour-long
interview conducted by a native Spanish-speaking undergraduate in May of
1995 documented Carlos' fluidity in Spanish. Remarkably, the transcription
reveals not a single incident of code-switching. This is in contrast to

the intermittent code-switching in an audio recording from 4 years earlier when Carlos spoke only Spanish. The recurrent concern voiced by colleagues at conferences and other forums, that the norm of code-switching at *La Clase Mágica* is detrimental to children's language development, is not supported by Carlos' case. Further analysis of the language use of the other Wizard Assistants should shed light on the generalizability of this outcome.

Carlos emerges from the interview as a young man who is well aware of the societal pressures on him and his compatriots to use English only. He acknowledges the instrumental value of speaking English in this country—"es más fácil agarrar trabajo, de aprender más, es estar estudiando, y así también puedes hacer amigos que no son Mexicanos" ["it is easier to find work, to learn more, to continue studying, and also to make friends who are not Mexican"]. In the context of *La Clase Mágica*, he feels free to emphatically claim to be "Mexicano!" When probed—why *Mexicano* and not Mexican American, Chicano, cholo, or Americano?—his allegiance to his natal country is definite: "Porque yo nací allí, y yo nunca me voy a olvidar de mí raza" ["Because I was born there and I will never forget my, my people."]

Carlos' apparent success masked a deeper fragility, however. Like many other first-generation *Mexicano* students enrolled in American public schools, Carlos was constrained by a lack of cultural knowledge and information, English-only instruction and an absence of advocacy by institutional agents (Stanton-Salazar, 1997). For example, in the second semester of the 1994-1995 school year, Carlos' grades took a sharp dive, yet his parents were not contacted by the school administration. The report card issued at the end of the school year was the first sign that something was amiss. A year later, this young man's once-bright future was only a memory. Carlos was suspended for fighting and weapon possession. He was transferred to a continuation school where his chances for success grew ever more precarious.[4] Fieldnotes written by *La Clase Mágica*'s coordinator reveal Carlos' remorse. He learned that "He had lost his place in school and enrolled in a program where he was more advanced than the other students, completing 8 times as much as his peers [translation, LD/5/96]." The project staff had hoped that the individual attention Carlos received at the alternative school might offset the lack of academic challenge. In the end, though, Carlos dropped out before he graduated.

Rina: To Be or Not to Be. At 7 years old, Rina wielded Spanish and English with the confidence of a bullfighter. Standing firm and vigilant, she struck verbally with elegance and finesse in either language. Her use of humor, her candor, and her inner softness were unmatched among the program participants. Her verbal antics regularly surprised and amused adults, provoking bursts of laughter. Passages from two fieldnotes written by a female undergraduate illustrate the verbal ability this little girl commanded throughout her stay in the project:

> On the way to the room, she [Rina] saw Lisa [undergraduate female] and yelled hello. Then she said, "There's Lisa. Lisa, Lisa, hello! Lisa is a very nice person. She can be my friend. Yes, she can be my best friend." I asked if I could be her best friend someday and she answered, "Oh, no, you're much too TALL" (I nearly fell over laughing). [AC/1/28/91]

> At the beginning of the game, a pitcher of lemonade appearson the screen and Rina said that we had to wait for 'something tohappen.' Then several ice cubes dropped into the pitcher and Rina said, "ice, look ice" "Yeah, ice cubes," I said. "Ice. . . Ice . . . Ice, ICE BABY!" I laughed SO loudly when she said this. Ice Ice Baby is this annoying rap song. I just couldn't believe she had just said this. I turned to TH [staff member] who was writing up her notes next to me and said "did you hear her? She just said ICE ICE BABY! [AC/2//11/91]

As happens with such forthright individuals, especially girls, Rina was often shunned by her peers. Even undergraduates occasionally recorded in their notes that she was "pushy and demanding of her own way." Periodically, she quibbled with the children and the site coordinator and complained that others were receiving preferential treatment. Several times, Rina's mother also lodged the same complaint. Although there may have been a reason for the special treatment of some of the children (four of them belonged to the site coordinator), the ecological context of *La Clase Mágica* was also a contributing factor. Church politics at the time engendered invidious relations that placed the parents in opposing camps. Rina was caught in the middle and her strong no-nonsense nature aggravated matters. In the fall of 1997, she quit the program because "she did not like it anymore."

In spite of these tensions, the data strongly suggest that *La Clase Mágica* did nourish Rina's intellect and strong-nature. It also was able to retain her for 5 1/2 years in spite of her apparent discomfort. At *La Clase Mágica* she was able to excel, and even to bask in the limelight of her accomplishments. She could and did rightfully demand and receive the kind of individual attention from the adults that girls typically do not get from teachers (Thorne, 1993). She also received the intellectual challenges accorded boys in the schooling system (Corson, 1986). Within the environment of *La Clase Mágica*, Rina was accepted and rewarded for her independence, initiative, and creativity. This is evident in the following conversation Rina and her peer Julie conducted with *El Maga*. Instead of censuring Rina's sarcasm, *Maga* patiently and lovingly argues for her ingenuity and for the logic of Its existence.

Rina:	Have a party.
Julie:	Go on field trips.
Rina:	Better games, make people come when we tell them to . . . I'd rather go to school than come here.
Maga:	ORGANIZE AND MAKE PLANS--THE WORLD IS YOURS! WRITE YOUR OWN NEWSPAPER, INVITE IMPORTANT PEOPLE, PHOTO CLUB . . .
Julie:	Grrrgh! I don't want to write stupid newspapers. (She gestures as if she's shooting the screen of the computer. Then she types"NEVER" (She expresses satisfaction)
Maga:	IT'S ONLY BORING IF YOU MAKE IT BORING.
Rina:	Ya write [right]. I think I know why people don't believe in you.
Maga:	WHY?
Rina:	I won't tell because we need to see you. Who would like a boss that we don't know?
Maga:	HAVE YOU EVER BEEN TO HAWAII?
Rina:	Ya, but what does this have to do with this?
Maga:	HAVE YOU EVER BEEN TO RUSSIA OR JAPAN? NO, BUT YOU KNOW THAT THEY EXIST RIGHT?
Rina:	I've seen God!
Maga:	HAVE FAITH AND TRUST!

The nature of the attention Rina received at *La Clase Mágica* was shown to be overwhelmingly friendly, mentoring, and supportive in a study conducted by an undergraduate research scholar (Quirante, 1996). Many accounts related direct praise for her work and none reported disciplinary action or teasing from the undergraduates. Numerous undergraduate fieldnotes reported Rina's assistance-seeking behavior, a concern for completing her homework and a concern for the well-being of others and the program. Rina used the resources available at *La Clase Mágica* to her benefit. As one undergraduate so aptly stated when Rina asked her for help on her math homework, "she lucked out because I am good at math." Rina completed more than half the games required for advancing to Wizard Assistant within a year after joining *La Clase Mágica*. Inexplicably, though, it took her 3 years to achieve the status of expert. The delay did not affect the seriousness with which she took up the responsibility of being a Wizard Assistant, however. Repeatedly, undergraduates noted her quick and positive response to new and exciting activities with "complete control of the situation." When others didn't follow, she continued, undeterred. Although she was often too controlling for other Wizard Assistants, Rina's organizing skills were nevertheless exceptional. Practically alone, she designed an activity room called "Lenguas" for the Wizard Assistant Attic. She also interviewed several people on video and email about their views on the electronic entity producing two noteworthy projects on *El Maga*. The video was so finely crafted that I have screened it several times at conferences. The electronic interview Rina conducted with me regarding my thoughts about *Maga* while I was on leave at the University of California at Santa Barbara was written up in the Wizard Assistant Chronicle.[5]

La Clase Mágica did more than support Rina's intellectual development. It also provided her with the kinds of experiences in math and science that girls do not typically get in school (American Association of University Women, 1991). Like Carlos, she was drawn to computers. She became proficient in using the technology to play games and to do homework assignments and everyday tasks—printing cards, drawing, and writing letters. She also became familiar with electronic mail and cruising the Internet. She loved Nintendo and she was the only Wizard Assistant to design a computer game. "Zordon" has its own elaborately decorated task card, on which Rina proudly inscribed:

> This is a really excellent game that was created by the magnificent, extraordinary, great . . . Rina Amable
>
> If you're asking where I got this idea of making the game of **Zordon**, then you should know that I did this for the kids that want to know more about what might happen in their lives or even the world after them.

The earlier dialogue with Julie and *Maga* is symbolic of the fine line children like Rina must walk between involvement and resistance. Caught between the peer culture and the emergent academic challenge placed before her as a Wizard Assistant, Rina teetered, sometimes being cooperative and sometimes resistant. She was eager to comply and help build a Wizard Assistant Club but she was easily swayed by Julie's insolence. Challenging Maga quickly took precedence over helping with the Club. With Julie's departure, however, Rina's serious, helpful nature reasserted itself, prompting her to express her allegiance to her electronic pal.

> **Julie:**   Tell him I'm leaving. This is boring.
> **Maga:**   HATE TO GO—I STILL LOVE YOU ALL.
> **Rina:**   Please don't go. I still believe in you.

Rina also walked a fine line between expressing pride in her bilingualism and denying that she spoke Spanish well. An audio transcription of a conversation in 1991 between then 7-year-old Rina and an undergraduate attests to Rina's proficiency in both languages. She reads off such phrases as "juegos selectos," "bienvenidos," "Sí puedes jugar un juego actual?" with ease, correcting the undergraduate's pronunciation of "cámpeon" with "campeón." As was common throughout her stay at *La Clase Mágica*, in the video Rina spoke English to the undergraduates and Spanish to the Mexican-origin staff and her peers. However, on the video she vacillated between saying that Spanish was "importante, . . . no voy a olvidarlo," and saying that she "doesn't understand nor speak Spanish well." She is correct in her own assessment of her relative strength in the two languages. Her Language Assessment Scale scores across three tests administrations indicate that her oral fluency in English is only a point or two different from her oral fluency in Spanish, but both scores were in the native-like range from the beginning. Like Carlos, Rina was well aware that Spanish is the low-status language. She attributed her inability to "speak her native tongue well enough because she grew up around White people" [ME/5/4/94]. But Rina's reluctance to use Spanish is also related to possible perceptions of incompetence, as she explained during an interview on language choice conducted by another undergraduate:

> I explained to her that a big portion of my paper is dedicated to language choice. I asked her for her opinions on why some kids refuse to speak Spanish. "Some reasons are." she told me, "It's too confusing. When I start speaking in Spanish and then I can't think of a word, I switch to English and then I just keep speaking in English." She explained that one of her reasons is her vocabulary in English is much more sophisticated. "And, some are embarrassed even through they are Spanish because they may not know a lot and someone might say, "Oh my gosh, that's a Mexican and she doesn't even know how to speak Spanish or some words in Spanish." [DS/03/09/94]

Interestingly, in an earlier interview, Rina had noted the value of bilingualism for achieving self expression (Vásquez, 1993).

"To be or not to be" bilingual or studious is the dilemma that Rina faces in intercultural communication. At times, observers noted a "tone of pride in [Rina's] voice and it seemed that she thought that it [being bilingual] made it better than the other children." On closer examination, however, these discussions are embedded in a context that is supportive of bilingualism. Rina confidently acknowledged the value of bilingualism whenever she observed the use of the native language and the positive regard others attributed to it. Otherwise, she was careful to conform to the dominance of the second language. At the end of the third grade, she asked to withdraw from her bilingual education program. This action may have been related to her desire to avoid a conflictual position, a desire also displayed during her earlier dialogue with *El Maga*.

At the end of the academic year of 1996, a cursory review of her Cumulative Folder at school showed Rina to be "making excellent progress." Although the number of skills that she performed at the 70th percentile or higher in the national norms on the Stanford Benet progressively decreased between the second and sixth grade, her academic grades indicate an opposite trend. Her grades in reading and written expression slowly creep from satisfactory to above average ("B's") but they are not exceptional, in contrast to what her determination and strict adherence to home-work assignments would suggest. When questioned about Rina's progress in the seventh grade, her teacher had very few specifics to share, except to comment on Rina's ability to use computers.

Culturally and linguistically, Rina and Carlos stand at the crossroads of home and school. Their proficiency in and their attitudes toward bilingualism waver, depending on the social context. Yet, their case studies underscore an underlying commitment to their native language and culture. Sadly, *La Clase Mágica* is one of only a very few places outside the intimate circle of friends and family where the maintenance of Spanish and *Mexicano* culture is a priority. We anticipate that the longetivity of the children's participation in *La Clase Mágica* will reduce the pace of language shift, but this is an expectation only a long-term study can confirm.

MULTIPLE IDENTITIES IN A BILINGUAL CONTEXT

La Clase Mágica helps shape several competing identities at the same time that it nurtures participants' core identity as members of a Mexicano community. Regardless of which identity they choose, the children develop a uniquely bilingual consciousness. They learn to see language as a strategic tool that allows them to move in and out of different cultural personae. Although it is still a marker of difference, their bilingualism is not an impediment to communication. They also became aware that the learning environment is continuously adapting to their needs and that they do not have to face an inflexible context that demands a specific identity. In sum, they learn to value who they are as human beings. Fieldnotes are replete with statements about the value of speaking two languages—remarks that arise directly from the note-takers' observations on site. Although there are also many instances in which children refuse to speak either language,[6] when we follow these children on video and audiotape, we find that they are consistently constructing a bilingual identity—using one language or the other in specific contexts, for specific purposes. Their language choices do not appear to exact an emotional toll; they seem to be made simply, without artifice, and for immediate purposes—communication, amusement, or personal connection (Vásquez, 1993).

Fieldnotes also document the presence of social and intellectual support for the development of particular identities, such as teenager, jokester, or introvert. In an extraordinary case, one child's quiet demeanor was strongly validated as a result of an undergraduate student's research paper. By tracking the child's behavior through several quarters of fieldnotes, the student found that the boy was an able learner. This discovery freed the child of the "learning disabled" label undergraduates and teachers had attributed to him (O'Dwyer, 1994).[7] In another case, a child who was generally recognized as a storyteller and comedian was asked to compose jokes for the project's newsletter. *El Maga*, ever unintrusive and always accessible, also helped ease adolescent ambivalence over such issues as age-related social roles and rights, morality, and sex (Cole & Cole, 1993). In *Maga*, the older children found an attentive listener who is invested in them and is always available. Moreover, the anonymity of their electronic pal frees the children to ask questions and raise issues that they might be reluctant to share in face-to-face interaction with undergraduates.

Although *La Clase Mágica* was designed to provide the optimal learning environment for children's cognitive and linguistic development, it also supports a strong Mexicano identity. This sense of self is evident in the responses the Wizard Assistants have periodically provided to interviewers' questions about daily life in their homes and in their community. *La Clase Mágica's* affirmative environment validates a core identity that is threatened in every other context of American life. Sharing their experiences of quinceañeras, trips to visit family in Mexico, or the new rave in dances and bands in the context of educational activities inscribes value to experiences centered in Mexican culture.

References to a *Mexicano* social identity are found throughout our data. It was not, however, until we conducted unstructured interviews and asked about *Mexicano* culture and Spanish language use in the home, school, and community that we found that *"Mexicano"* was the underlying theme unifying the self across all contexts. Certainly, we were not surprised to find the children identifying as *Mexicanos*. We expected that, and we tailored *La Clase Mágica* accordingly, giving a foundational role to the Spanish language and *Mexicano* culture in the program's material and intellectual resources. What did surprise us was the discovery that the children occasionally used language choice as an explicit identity marker. We repeatedly heard the response "Porque soy Mexicano" ["Because I am Mexican"] as an answer to questions such as "Why did you choose to play that game in Spanish," or "Why do you use Spanish with your friends?" This answer exemplifies how fully language and identity seem to overlap for these children. At the same time, it suggests a closer sociolinguistic relation between language and identity than some scholars may be willing to accept (Ochs, 1993).

La Clase Mágica also validates other social identities, such as amiguito/a (little friends—the name given to first-level participants), cholo, teenager, American, and Wizard Assistant. The last is perhaps the most important. Certainly it is the most frequently noted by the undergraduates in their fieldnotes. How highly the children value their identity as a Wizard Assistant is captured in such comments as "I am a Wizard Assistant; not a child;

You have to be a Wizard Assistant to be allowed in here;" and "Wizard Assistants always have more fun." Wizard Assistant status is a public recognition of a child's mastery of the workings of *La Clase Mágica*. The role reflects knowledge of and accords access to advanced computer technology. It signifies possession of linguistic and cultural knowledge that spans multiple learning contexts. Finally, being a Wizard Assistant means being seen as a valuable member of the problem-solving process. This in turn means being eligible for an invitation to represent the project at public events. For example, most of the Wizard Assistants have had at least one opportunity to talk about *La Clase Mágica* at conferences and university courses. They also frequently chat with the many visitors who come to observe at the site every year. Periodically, since 1996, the Wizard Assistants have been paid as consultants. For example, when a new site was established in an adjacent community several WAs helped in the effort.

Growth in the children's self-esteem and self-concept are important by-products of our efforts to provide access to the full range of the learners' own rich and varied funds of knowledge. Our experiences confirm the wisdom of accepting children as whole beings. Rather than asking them to shed their ethnic identity at the door, we invite them in and acknowledge the value of their previous experiences by making their backgrounds a key element in their current and future development. Thus, by validating children's bicultural–bilingual identities, we are helping to create the rhetorical moment in which they can step back from the intersection of the social and psychological realms and confidently affirm the popular Mexican saying, "Yo soy quien soy y no me paresco a nadie" ["I am who I am and I am like no one else"].

EDUCATIONAL IMPLICATIONS FOR SCHOOLING IN THE 21ST CENTURY

As our research is complemented by similar efforts undertaken at new sites, we hope to learn how an activity system like *La Clase Mágica* can be translated into a medium for promoting children's success in the formal context of school (Vásquez, 1996). In the meantime, our suggestions about how the insights we have gained may apply to schooling must be tempered with an acknowledgment that *La Clase Mágica* was engineered without the constraints and accountability that characterizes the typical classroom. Nevertheless, the personal and academic success that children such as Rina and Carlos experienced at *La Clase Mágica* raises important questions about the use of a pedagogy that does not consider the cultural and linguistic resources of learners. Given the opportunity, children in *La Clase Mágica*, like those in the Spanish language arts class Moll and Díaz (1987) studied, use their background experiences as tools for achieving greater levels of meaning-making.

The children's demonstrated ability to adequately and appropriately use either language or a combination of both deflects repeated concerns that dual language use results in confusion. Children in our program are very clear about their language choices: "I speak only English in school because everybody speaks it"; "I speak only Spanish at home because my parents speak Spanish"; and "I speak both languages here and with my friends."

The concern voiced by parents, community members, and educators regarding the need for stimulating and supporting greater educational achievement among minority students must be addressed by the educational system. Presently, Latinos have one of the highest drop-out rates in the country, and those who do graduate do so with minimal skills. A dismally low percentage of this population enter high-ranking universities; and, once in college, these students are greatly under-represented in many of the sciences. Numerous studies, including our own, indicate that parents of minority students want a better education for their children. However, few of these parents have the resources to provide their children with the kinds of institutional support and technological expertise required in most classrooms.

La Clase Mágica offers a real-life preview of what a classroom in this country could look like in the 21st century if policymakers were committed to the value of a highly educated minority–majority population. Children's minds and languages are "national resources," as distinguished scholar Kenji Hakuta (1986) reminded us. As we move ever deeper into an information-based global society, the ability to participate effectively in multiple cultural contexts will be an even greater asset. A command of the English language and a sense of ease with mainstream culture will continue to be valued commodities, but they will be only a part of a much larger constellation of possibilities open to the citizens of the 21st century.

NOTES

[1] Journeying through the maze is a conceptual metaphor for the preorganized series of up to 70 computer and board games adapted to reflect the participants' background experiences.

[2] The immediate concern is to encourage a dialogue among participants, especially with parents. Given the time and resources as well as the opportunity to discuss changes, editing takes place.

[3] Although the project is on-going, I draw on 22 academic quarters of fieldnotes written by the research staff and undergraduate students enrolled in 10-week courses offered through the Departments of Psychology and Communication at the University of California, San Diego. The students are trained to use electronic mail and in ethnographic methods of observation and to write fieldnotes. They submit the latter via telecommunication to the professor. The possible criticism of the students' untrained eye as unreliable can be countered with the freshnesses that it provides, uncluttered with a particular paradigm or ideology.

[4]Although, there is quite a bit of anecdotal information on performance outcomes of alternative schools, a review of the literature yielded no extended research on the topic.

[5]This interview can be viewed on the *La Clase Mágica* Chronicle on the World Wide Web at http://communication.ucsd.edu/LCM/lcmchronicle.

[6]Most often, children who remain silent do so because they decline to speak Spanish with the undergraduates.

[7]The undergraduate found that "Jake" (a pseudonym) worked well with undergraduates who were firm yet accepting of him and poorly with students who were overly strict or uncaring.

6

The Politics of Participation: Navigating Cultural Borders

Whether *La Clase Mágica* participants drive the 7 miles from the university to the after-school site or step across the street from their home to the mission yard, they cross illusive as well as more defined borders of thought and action. Not only do they move in and out of the cultural contexts of the home, school, and community, they also move in and out of the secular into the domains of the imagination and often the divine, each with its own forms of relations, epistemologies, and knowledge base. Repeatedly participants step across that which is known and accepted into that which is new and emergent. At home and at school children follow prescribed sets of norms for word and action. At *La Clase Mágica*, they must negotiate new paths of understanding and development. In essence, this means that members of the staff, parents, undergraduates, and even the electronic entity, too, navigate multiple cultural borders through language, culture, and activity. The deeply rooted and inflexible normative structures within and outside this cultural domain are confronted, problematized, and re-shaped in the daily conceptualization of what is and what is not possible.

For the most part, these discordinations are inherent to cultural contact. Understanding their dimensions, although often illusive and ephemeral, was crucial to understanding the modifications that have to be made to accommodate cultural differences. The staff pursued these deliberately and aggressively in order to fold them into the adaptation process. As Yrgo Engeström said repeatedly in the LCHC seminars, "discordinations are a way to understand the processes of culture." Much was to be learned in negotiating cultural borders. The staff learned very early on, for example, that carving a new path required respect, patience, and time to understand the nuances of collaboration. Tensions and ambiguities invariably emerged from their own cultural differences and the emergent cultural dimensions of the new project. Making time to nurture trust and a solid understanding of the personal and group histories that informed each others' individual stance on issues, required time and openness. Although at times, this approach did not eliminate the pain of challenging one's own inertia, it did provide for a supportive environment that fostered exploration and development.

Other discordinations were anticipated and plans were made accordingly. We involved parents in all of our activities, anticipating that access to new resources and epistemologies might affect parent–child interactions, as Delgado-Gaitan (1994) and others (Wong-Filmore, 1991) have found in relation to schooling practices. Yet, the references to the Wizard Assistants as "unruly," "chaotic," or "boisterous" in the fieldnotes written by the undergraduate students raised concerns that other adults (e.g., teachers) would interpret the children's attempts to "speak their mind with adults," as a challenge to their authority. We were able to incorporate ways to enculturate the undergraduates and parents to the norms of participation. These strategies, however, did not include changing teacher expectations because it was beyond the scope of the project.

These conditions have the potential to support multiple ways of seeing self, as I point out in chapter 5, but they also raise questions about the role participants play in constructing self and their ecology. How *do* participants negotiate competing cultural values and concomitant ambiguities? And, more importantly, how do they envision their role in the making of and the impact it has had on their own personal lives? In this chapter I address these queries by using a multivocal approach to construct a participant perspective on *La Clase Mágica*. I include the accounts of select participants who were either instrumental in the development of the project or whose story captures the essence of the experience of a particular participant group. Written specifically for this chapter or drawn from our data pool, these accounts articulate the concerns and the triumphs of moving in and out of emergent and fixed sets of norms. Although many other individuals could have been included, the selected individuals have left an indelible mark on the social and intellectual development of *La Clase Mágica* and, by extension, have inscribed their mark on the thought and action of future participants.

Next, I begin with the cultural fabric that forms the backdrop of social relations at *La Clase Mágica*. I then use a combination of objective and subjective accounts to sketch out various participant groups that constitute a community of learners located at the intersection of multiple borders. I introduce each participant group with a developmental sketch based on a variety of extant data—fieldnotes, transcriptions of video and audio recordings, and formal and informal interviews—and then I turn the discussion over to a representative of the group who shares his or her reflections on *La Clase Mágica*, his or her role in the project's development, and the impact participation has had on his or her own development and future options.[1] I conclude with a discussion on the lessons we learn from the voices of these individuals.

LIVING A BORDER REALITY
IN SOCIAL RELATIONS

A visitor to the after-school site will invariably refer to the sense of "family" or "community" when recounting his or her impressions of *La Clase Mágica*. The actual locality and social relations readily attest to these sensibilities; the site is in *the* community and many of its participants *are* literally members of the same family. However, these descriptors capture much more than the location of the physical site and genealogy of the participants. Family and community are interchangeable values in the moral make-up of *Mexicanos*, enduring longer than language as defining characteristics of later generations of Mexican origin individuals (Keefe & Padilla, 1987). Ties to "la familia" [family] and "la communidad" [community] feature prominently in important career decisions. According to Hurtado and Gonzalez (1994), it is not uncommon for adult children to make career choices that keeps them close to the family. Even those who leave the area nevertheless remain actively involved in the financial and emotional life of the family.

These cultural values are foundational to the intense commitment demonstrated by many participants of *La Clase Mágica*. Parents, for example, run the Friday session, attend meetings and help raise funds as part of their commitment to their children and to the well-being of the community. Mrs. Durán, the site coordinator, was a salaried employee of *La Clase Mágica* but volunteered many more hours than she was paid for. "Es por el bien de mis hijos y la comunidad" ["It is for the good of my children and the community"], she repeatedly tells the other parents. She saw no difference between her service to the Church and her work with *La Clase Mágica*. "The difference is that I get paid here" as she told the audience of the National Association for Chicano Studies (NACS) in March 1993. Other participants, in particular Mexican descent students and staff members, often generously share their talents and resources as a way to "give something back to the community." Others still, invest their time and energies for the personal reward they received for participating in an activity that promises meaningful social change.

It is not surprising then, that family and community define the participation structure of all the activities at *La Clase Mágica*. Children and adults alike, from the director to the youngest child, are bound to social norms of politeness common in *Mexicano* homes and communities. The most salient of these, "respeto" [respect] and "confianza" [trust], add an affective layer to the ways in which children and adults interact with each other. Rules of formality also dictate a deference to authority figures in the position of church officials, teachers, and elders. To do otherwise casts the offender as a miscreant or an outsider, two roles most of the participants avoided and assumed only when there was no other recourse. The imminent closure of *La Clase Mágica* was one such occasion in which I was compelled to act in a manner unbecoming my status and gender. When Head Start served *La Clase Mágica* an eviction notice, I refused the Deacon's offer to relocate *La Clase Mágica* to the main church in a strongly worded position: "We stay where we are or I take the program to the Presbyterian church down the street!" The facial expressions and inaudible gasps of the father who had accompanied me clearly signaled a breech of conduct. Although he admired my brazenness, he would never have assumed a non-negotiable stance with such an eminent individual.

The contradiction between *Mexicano* cultural values and those of mainstream society (Delgado-Gaitan, 1994) is repeatedly played out at *La Clase Mágica*. For example, in spite of being intensely unhappy about specific arrangements, it was a rare child who disrespected an adult. Instead of challenging an adult directly, children tended to lend a deaf ear, direct their aggression toward objects, or refuse to participate in the activities. Even long-term participants who had been socialized to aggressively engage adults in problem solving, nevertheless, experienced great difficulty in challenging adult authority. This was particularly true when the Wizard Assistants were annoyed by the way the coordinator allocated responsibilities. They complained among themselves for many months before they were able to charge this highly regarded member of the community with favoritism. Unable to achieve satisfaction, one of the most vocal dissenters, Rina (see chapter 5), transferred to a nearby Fifth Dimension, rather than verbally challenge or subvert her authority.

Rina's departure could have been influenced by the life forces of adolescence—sports and other extra-curricular activities—yet, her decision clearly signaled a strong adherence to a seemingly discordant mix of values that had developed at *La Clase Mágica*. On the one hand, self-determination, exploration and decisiveness are strongly encouraged. On the other, deference to authority and adherence to the rules of the project is expected. In leaving, Rina followed both sets of norms: She asserted the right to make her own decisions and managed to maintain the relationship with the coordinator, a strategy that also left the door open for her when and if she were to return. Participants literally pick and choose the paths of activity, language, and culture moment by moment as they interact with those around them. Not only do they create their own path through these dimensions but they also recreate *La Clase Mágica*. Thus, both the individual and the context are transformed through participation.

A COMMUNITY OF LEARNERS AT THE BORDER(S)

The multitiered effort of *La Clase Mágica* incorporates six participant groups with varying membership. Two groups whose membership extend out into the broader Distributed Literacy Consortium, the group of similar projects distributed throughout the U.S. and Mexicó, have consisted of only one member within the local context—the electronic entity and the project director, *El Maga* and I. The other four groups—children, students, parents, staff (in order of size of membership)—have a greater number of members each quarter and accumulative across the life of the project. The selection of individuals was arbitrary, although it was guided by the representativeness of their experiences or the clarity of program impact their accounts made evident. For example, the majority of students report the significance of their experience in their Reflection Essays, but Yolanda Alvarez poignantly illustrates the immediate and direct affects the program had that may not have been as apparent in other accounts. Lourdes Durán's account, too, speaks to the optimal possibilities that parent involvement and parent empowerment can have on participating adults. The other individuals were selected because of the singularity of their contributions: Berta Jotar Penezuela was the Chief Wizard Assistant who wrote the first draft of the *Maga's* manual, inscribing a critical analysis on the role of the electronic entity and the project's direction; Yolanda Santiago Venegas, known at the time as Yolanda James, helped lead the research team to new heights during the 5-year period she was with the project; and Juan Gómez was the first child participant to attend college.

Following, I include essays written by each of these individuals. Yolanda Alvarez and Lourdes Durán's essays are the only two that were written for other purposes. All other essays were written at my request. These were edited and returned to the authors for approval. Editing participants' contributions has been a practice we have avoided for two reasons: We did not have the funds or the expertise, and editing contradicts the project's philosophical stance on accepting the natural language of the participants. I deviated from this principle here because I wanted the participants' contributions to receive the attentive revision I have given to the rest of the book. I did, however, only correct the spelling, punctuation, and grammar, careful not to change the intended meaning. In the translation provided, I interpreted rather than literally translate the Spanish portion.

El Maga: From a Figure Head to a Fictive Kin. The electronic entity, the most prominent figure in the Fifth Dimension organizational structure was initially conceptualized as an omniscient figure whose panoptic gaze tracked the progress of all of its child subjects. Over time, this figurehead loses its authoritarian character at *La Clase Mágica* and takes on the gentler kinder demeanor of a fictive member of the family—a madrina (godmother) to be specific. Its omniscience becomes less prominent as it assumes a more social role in the making of community at the local site and in the broader Fifth Dimension universe. Locally, its primary responsibility turns to shaping a culture of exploration and multiplicity for the children. At the broader level, its role becomes that of galvanizing cross-site communication through a series of activities and events.

One event in *Maga's* early stages of development depicts the strong hand it played out in the beginning of the broader project. It flexed its power in the consortium listserve by calling for a discussion on violence. When its plea for communication was disregarded, it excommunicated itself. It was an act of acquiescence to an effigy depicting its death in a faraway site, an opportunity *Maga* saw to connect the "literacies" of its many subjects in the Fifth Dimension universe. It was a defining moment where the fine line between fantasy and reality became even more obscure. In proclaiming its death, *El Maga* relinquished all of its power only to assume a more commanding role in the life of *La Clase Mágica* and the wider project. Its gesture to promote commentary on a story depicting the violent death of a little girl was received by more symbolic violence, its literary murder. Through *La Mosca, El Maga* ventriliquated its aversion to violence and refusal to come online until "SOMEBODY EXPLAINS THIS VIOLENT TYPE OF BEHAVIOR." Rather than dialogue, *El Maga* was killed graphically in a picture of a drive-by shooting at the offending site. The Wizard, too, violated *Maga's* voice by announcing on the listserve that she or he "love(s) the Fifth Dimensioneers too much to tell them I'm dead."

The director at the faraway site had been willing to share the story with scholars around the world but saw no need for the imposition of an ecological framework on "educationally relevant cognitive skills." *El Maga* thought otherwise, "human activity is never outside politics and social context." Rather than repress children's imaginations, *Maga* called for dialogically exposing the story's underlying assumptions of women as objects of violence. As the distant director pointed out, it was a difference in how each of the research staffs perceived the Fifth Dimension. One saw learning as locally defined, the other saw it as a part of larger sociopolitical context. *El Maga's* futile attempt to incite a critical analysis on minority community issues and the role that the teleconference could play in connecting local experiences with global processes was not lost to our research staff. The staff recognized the foundational value of both aspects; however, they did not agree that the local children should suffer the loss of their magical pal because of ideological differences with individuals in far away places. They noted the children's genuine sadness and pleaded with *Mosca* to help them get *El Maga* back.

The *Amiguitos* and members of the staff wrote countless letters and engaged in extended live-chats with *La Mosca* trying to find a way to resuscitate *El Maga*. "If words were its food," they reasoned, as *Maga* had previously informed them, "then letters would bring it back to life." Language as a life source was a successful strategy but instead of bringing back the "good *Maga*," it stirred the dark side of *Maga's* consciousness and gave birth to a surly, mean-spirited Terminator Two who spewed sarcasm and indignities. Children had grown accustomed to the gentle prodding of good *Maga* and rejected the sarcasm and indignities of the new *Maga*. It was only when language was emblematic of *Mexicano* culture that the children were able to will *Maga* back. "I cannot respect you when you act that way," were the magic words that brought *Maga* back to the center of the social and cultural life of *La Clase Mágica*. From that day on, *El Maga* has been a gentler kinder guide who helps children in their journey through the maze. At times, it assumes the role of an indulgent permissive "madrina." At other times, according to the children's needs, it serves as a wise counselor or expert advisor. "Good *Maga*," was one who would use more persuasive tactics to compel them to adhere to the linguistic and cultural norms of the site.

This event also secured *El Maga's* prominence as a powerful tool in the cultural production of the broader project as well as that of the local system. *El Maga's* birthday, fittingly celebrated on the 2nd of November, *El Día de Los Muertos* [The Day of Dead], is one of the most successful intersite activities in the entire Fifth Dimension universe. Each year, *El Maga* plans an elaborate celebration in which gifts and letters are exchanged across sites and children scour the Internet looking for clues to the games that the electronic entity concocts over the year. In the preparations much is communicated about Mexican culture and history. Participants learn the symbolism of a Mexican holiday increasingly gaining popularity in this country. *El Maga's* bilingual messages also introduces children and adults to Spanish language terminology.

In conversation with Berta Jotar Penezuela who served as its Chief Wizard Assistant during a critical period of development, *Maga* articulates below some of the most foundational ideas that shaped its role as a mediator of language, culture, and critical reasoning. The conversation reflects the synergism that grows out of a close working relationship between an assistant who acts in behalf of the system's authority figure and a boss who exists only in communication. Although, other Chief Wizard Assistants have stamped their own personal touch to *Maga's* character, Berta's contributions were seminal. Not only were her ideas incredibly creative and grounded in critical theory, they were also reified in the *Maga's* manual, which other Chief Wizard Assistants since read as a part of the training for the position.

> ***Berta Jotar Penezuela: Across the Years: EL MAGA. Jan.***
> ***11 '98.*** As mentioned elsewhere, *El Maga* is the cultural adaptation
> of the Fifth Dimension's Wizard. My participation in this research
> took place during a time in which the Wizard was transformed from a
> monolingual English-speaking electronic entity to a bilingual
> Spanish-speaking entity. As *El Maga's* Chief Wizard Assistant from
> 1991 to 1994, my responsibility was to support *El Maga's* mediation
> of children's spontaneous bilingualism and biculturalism in play and

learning. When I think of *El Maga* , I think of a constellation of different knowledges from site-specific geopolitical ones pertinent to North San Diego County and the border with Mexico, to the conceptual and epistemological ones related to learning and cognition, and finally, to the cultural and national ones embodied in community, memory, and history. But in this brief attempt to articulate *El Maga's* contribution to *La Clase Mágica*, I decided to engage *El Maga* in a live-chat and let it speak for itself.

Berta: Maga, one of the challenges for *La Clase Mágica's* site coordinators and student assistants has been to make the children believe you are real and not just a person behind the computer screen.

Maga: Yes, children always want to identify me or make me into a person. When they draw a picture of me, I appear to be mostly a male. Sometimes they might think I am Santa Claus. Others think I am the Wizard of Oz and others still might think I am la bruja maldita [the wicked witch] or any T.V. character popular at the time. But, beyond [these popular images,] I am real. My presence is this text in front of your very eyes where you can read me and even possibly hear me now, in the present time. Each sign is conjugated in meaning. So, I am as real as the amount of meaning you give to this text. I am, as long as the children want me to be.

Berta: Yes, but for the purpose of this book, lets make something clear for the reader. Even though this text is written, frozen in the pages of this book and in time will survive as an object of knowledge, it is also speech. It is a recording of a conversation with you via computer technology called a "live-chat."

Maga: Certainly, although I am what the children and you read on this surface, I am also speech recorded in writing. If the reader sees me as purely a written sign, he or she looses the performativity of speech, the moments of improvisation, interruption and spontaneity only possible during a live-chat, a virtual conversation. Virtual speech without sound. Whatever you call it, the reader loses me on the surface of the page because I am presence via speech and writing, improvisation and interruption.

Berta: Yes, but you write a lot! Children also receive letters and instructions from you. You even have a special collaborator responsible for your personal mail.

Maga: Simon, of course my horse. In *La Clase Mágica* I have to be constantly generating information. I have to produce various levels of communication between the children and I. I talk to them, I write to them, I draw for them. I send them prizes for their efforts. Every effort they make has results, as well as every effort I make requires particular technologies. forms and structures: and remember, each type of technology produces particular ways of knowing. However, *La Mosca Cósmica* is my connection to your material world, and it is responsible for taking my mail from here to there. but as you know *La Mosca* is very chismosa and you can't count on her truth. So, yes, I write un bonche [a lot] but it is not purely writing but story telling, drawings, montage. In another words, I say things to them in different ways even though it gets reduced to writing for practical reasons. The Cosmic Fly delivers the written instructions: letters, drawings. and material envíos. But, computer technology allows me to speak with the children live, in real time in spite of our constant technical problems. I don't want to privilege writing over speech. For me, both serve important functions in learning for and about the children.

Berta: Well, you might be a virtual consolidation of speech and writing, you might be presence via written speech but so far. our conversation is sound-less.

Berta: Well. could we say that you are cognitive activity?

Maga: We could say that my speech/writing is performative, and that it is via the children's performance of writing, reading, communicating and learning through which I become present. and alive.

Berta: Yes, you are read. and I would add constructed and imagined within the intersection of two particular communities: the children's immigrant Mexican community of Solana Beach and the diverse cultural and class backgrounds of UCSD students and staff members helping at *La Clase Mágica* who are monolingual and for the most part from non-latino backgrounds . . .

Maga: Yes, the majority of the children and the site coordinators are of Mexican descent and the students and staff aren't part of the *Mexicano* community of Eden Gardens. This is not a problem. It is just an example of the larger context of San Diego and California. But, I can't ignore the specificity of the children's cultural background which is by no means homogeneous. The children come from different regions of Mexico and many are first generation. Although I have to be multi-culti; there are certain national narratives in Mexico common to most children who remember, visit or travel back and forth to Tijuana or the interior of Mexico. I know and talk to the children about popular TV characters like Chapulín Colorado or popular culture figures like wrestlers *El Santo*, Blue Demon, *Mil Mascaras* and so forth. Children are very hip in terms of who is popular in US TV, sports, etc. and I must be too! [I am using what they already know to open doors]

Berta: Going back to the fact that your presence is constituted via various forms (speech, language) and structures (script and computer technology) what is your take on what is proper language? And what is the impact of your bilingualism and your "espanglishism"? How does your use of slang and popular culture affect language acquisition at site?

Maga: Let the academics answer that question. In fact, you are trying to trick me. You know that *La Clase Mágica* is located in a highly conservative area, a region where Proposition 187 passed, where demonstrations like Light Up The Border are thinkable and do-able, where English is the official language, where Affirmative Action is vanishing and bilingual education is a target. You must answer your question in this context. Listen, what is important is to make the children comfortable with both languages in a playful manner. *La Clase Mágica* is a learning site but is not a school. I am strategically used as an experimental and experiential language tool. Children direct these live-chats more often than me; they choose the language they want to speak, and I tell stories to them based on their onda while I integrate new vocabulary in both, English and Spanish. I believe that I am *La Clase Mágica*'s attempt to reconstruct and promote more effective bilingual and bicultural cognitive sites. I am the mediator through which bilingualism and biculturalism become skills rather than marks of "otherness" and difference (I am getting too politically correct here). I am the result of a need to renegotiate the convergences and clashes of various knowledges (and the prejudices they generate) articulated via speech, writing, legislations, and culture.

Berta: Maga, I didn't know you knew about all these troubles in the land. I thought you belonged to a magic realm or cyber space.

Maga: Umh, well, I have to be aware of my children, where they come from and the type of society they live in. I have to know the rules of your power games, your legislations, your borders, what is to be considered "proper" in your society. Asi, the children have to know the rules of my Laberinto Mágico, the Maze is not a random thing, it is like a city and I am the traffic coordinator in the highways of La Clase Mágica. Believe me, I get crashed very often!!!

Berta: Are you a political project?

Maga: Mira esa, let's say that as long as second citizenship is a
common experience for lower class immigrants and their
children; as long as undocumented immigrants or
undocumented children are simultaneously criminals and
outside of the legislative system (different than political
exiles for instance who do get job permits); and as long as
Latinos are stereotyped as illegal aliens—unless they open
their mouth talking perfect English—we have to create
alternative educational sites and *La Clase Mágica* is my
canton [home]. My house is your house, and I don't
have a backyard.

Berta: Well Maga, we have ran out of space in these pages and I
want to conclude by saying that even though your presence
in real time is only possible via computer technology, El
Maga lives through the reiteration, research and efforts to
produce alternative cognitive sites. El Maga is a necessary
language construct that continues to develop and transform
in the articulation of bilingual and bicultural speech and
writing activity.

Wizard Assistants: Encaminado Hacia la Madurez [sending off to maturity].[2]   Although child participants include preschool children and high school students, the target group of the Fifth Dimension iniative and subsequently *La Clase Mágica*, has always been children in middle childhood. Typically, children enroll in *La Clase Mágica* age 5 or 7 and continue on into their first few years of adolescence—between 12 and 15 years of age. Thus, the time they spend in the program is a period of great change in their physical and social development. Their social relations and social contexts widen and, in effect, they enter into a new kind of life (Cole & Cole, 1993). They separate from their parents and leave the security of the home for an extended period of the day. They learn to read and write and do basic math, and for the first time, establish close social relationships with individuals outside the family. They develop a sense of self that changes from a focus on personal features— "I'm 6 years old"—to how one compares with others— "I'm bigger than most kids"— and, finally, to how one fits within the social context— "I'm an honest person, so people trust me" (Cole & Cole, 1993, p. 555).

For children from the Mexicano community of Eden Gardens, middle childhood is a period of dramatic and often frightful change. Not only do children leave their homes and families to enter into the activities of the broader society (i.e., school), they are also leaving their understandings of how the world works and the tools for interacting with it. Typically Spanish dominant, with relatively little English speaking ability, and preliterate in both languages, these children enter school with a lot of apprehension. They are not only entering a new kind of life but are entering a new kind of world. In situations where transition mechanisms are not in place to integrate the children into the new learning community, they are relegated to silence, misbehavior, absence or separation.

The cultural and physical location of *La Clase Mágica* situates it in a perfect position to serve as a transition mechanism for the move from the Spanish-speaking home to the English-medium school. The system of artifacts, the adults and *El Maga* gently guide children through potentially one of the roughest parts of their life journey from the home to the outside community. The bilingual–bicultural character of life at *La Clase Mágica* "encamina," or walks the children part way to a monolingual, English-medium context. This "walk along" represents one of the most critical periods of social development in which this age group learns the ways of a second culture in a relatively less stressful environment (Padilla & Durán, 1995). The children receive the social support and attention that have been reported to "buffer life event stressors" and enhance "a positive school experience" for immigrant children in other contexts (p. 152). For the most part, it is the parents who facilitate the transition for children who are not fully prepared to separate from them. But, as many immigrant parents acknowledge, they know little about the culture and language outside the home to effectively intervene for their children.

Although *La Clase Mágica* does help children transition into mainstream contexts, it nevertheless, engenders cultural tensions and discordinations. As Juan points out below, he knows the value of *La Clase Mágica* intimately but he also knows that it is not "cool" to talk about it to nonparticipants. With time and growing expertise, the children learn to negotiate this culture clash in the same way that Heller's (1987) French–English bilinguals learn to navigate cultural conflicts. Participants become confident in their accomplishments and the numerous interrelations with adults from dissimilar backgrounds helps them ease into a new stage of life. The change in perspective from novice to one of "being capable" (Litowitz, 1990) is particularly striking among the Wizard Assistants. Although they assume responsibility, children are also aware of the positive status bestowed upon them with the title of Wizard Assistant. Their sense of entitlement is evident in their expression of their opinions, in the choice of activities, and in their sense of responsibility to others less knowledgeable. They are fully aware of why they have access to the newest games, the latest technology, and extracurricular activities such as fieldtrips: They are Wizard Assistants. They readily and skillfully assume the role of ambassadors of *La Clase Mágica*, achieving what one Manager related in her course paper as the ability to construct a balance between privileges and duties and self-discipline and responsibility. They become expert negotiators and socially conscious of their responsibility to others. They learn to express a self-confidence and parity with adults that is at once refreshing and impressive.

The comfort that these young people achieve in cross-cultural communication is evident in the discursive tag, "Are there any questions?" Juan Gómez added to all his comments in a videotaped session with school district officials interested in the activities at *La Clase Mágica*. In his own words, Juan, points out further how he has changed as a result of his participation in the project.

Juan Gómez, From Wizard Assistant to College Freshman. Juan is the first long-term participant to reach college-going status. He was born in San Diego and his family has been in Eden Gardens since 1988. His school records indicate that Juan was initially unmotivated in the classroom and for the first few years of his participation in *La Clase Mágica*, did not aspire to become a Wizard Assistant, "like those kids who think they know it all" (J. O. Gomez, personal communication, April 3, 1993). But, a Wizard Assistant he did become and also a low "B" average student who set his sights on going to college only too late to qualify for a 4-year college. Today, he is highly admired by his peers, his family, and his community for his accomplishments.

> *La Clase Mágica by Juan Gómez:* About 5 years ago. I didn't know what a computer was. I thought they were small, black and white TVs. I also didn't think that computers would play such a prominent role in my or anyone else's future. Learning about computers at *La Clase Mágica* has helped me and other kids who were in the same situation as me. if not worse. By the end of my high school year, I had mastered the computer. I knew how to get into the Internet but also could type faster and easier without having to look at the keyboard. I learned how to surf the Internet and to use the computer more effectively.
>
> From one perspective, *La Clase Mágica* has been like a mother to me in terms of teaching me about computers from the very beginning. For instance, it taught me the simplest things from learning to turn the computer on and off, to type, to play the computer games as well as to have fun. And. I learned all of this stuff on machines such as the Apple IIe computers which are now considered to be in the stone age in the field of computer technology. Imagine playing games in floppy disks such as "Conan" and "Old Frogger?" This stuff was old-school: Computers with old green screens and tan color keyboards using arrows to do the work that the mouse of today does.
>
> LCM not only helped me a lot, it affected my life dramatically. Who would have thought that I would stay there for as long as 5 years? I not only stayed but I traveled through the entire maze and became a Wizard Assistant. Then I began helping other kids and was able to work on projects for school and those for LCM. We also helped the college students who were new to the program and often did not have a clue of what was expected of them. Our job as

Wizard Assistants was to make them feel at home and to deal with different situations. We helped the kids when there weren't any college students available such as during the Friday session of LCM. But, it wasn't about working like any other regular job. It was about taking a kid and thinking of him as your brother who needed care and love. It was about taking them under your wing and protecting themand teaching new things, like other Wizard Assistants had taken me under their wing.

I remember when a UCSD graduate student asked me to help him find students or some of my friends that would be interested in learning about computers. A new branch of LCM was being suggested for the high school if we could only have more students who would want to learn about computers and be able to stay after school. It wasn't that easy because most of them didn't have the time to stay because of their jobs or other things. But, most of the time, they made excuses such as. "I can't because I don't have a ride," and then I would see them after school talking to their friends and playing around. It wasn't easy also to talk about or stay after school because I didn't want to be the only one in the class to do that. I thought it wouldn't be cool to talk about it.

It wasn't like that at all when it came to talking about LCM. I would talk about LCM and how it worked. Some were interested in going to LCM but once I told them what days we meet and who went they'd back down and they would never say anything again. By asking who went. they meant to ask if there were any young pretty girls attending. I would tell them that it wasn't about how many fine girls were at LCM but about becoming more skilled in computer technology so that in the future they would not stay behind other people. After a while, I decided not talk about LCM because I felt stupid when they would say that they didn't have to learn because I told them to. But, it ended up that I was the only one who knew more about computers than any of my friends. They were actually surprised that I had told them the truth.

LCM has really been good for not only me. but also for my little sister who is still involved. I really would like to thank the person who started to organize this program because it has helped a lot of kids and grown-ups around the St. Leo's community. Many other children would have been involved in mischief but because of LCM. that has not been the case. And, those who actually did the work, such as Yolanda Venegas. Olga, and Lourdes, if it had not been for their hard work, I wouldn't be talking about LCM or know much about my own future. I wanted to go to a 4-year university or college but that's not going to be possible right now. Unfortunately. I learned through the admissions counselor who visited LCM that I did not qualify and would have to go to a JC first. She helped me select the classes I would need as a freshman, then I'll see if I can transfer to a 4-year college or maybe join the Navy.

The Undergraduate Amigos/as, Achieving a New Perspective on Learning. The undergraduate students, like the Wizard Assistants, are also in a critical period of their life when they take part in the project. The majority of them are about to complete their studies and enter the workforce. Although they come from a variety of backgrounds and interests, their academic training has been quite similar. Except for a small percentage, most come from privileged backgrounds in which a second language was learned in school. They are well-trained academically and have had ample resources throughout their educational career. They major primarily in Human Development, Psychology or Communication, highly theoretical fields of study and in the early 1990s, all but a few students were well-versed in computer and telecommunication technology. They are the top 12% of the students in the state and attend one of the most prestigious public universities in the state of California. They are the best and the brightest. They are truly the leaders of the not-so distant future.

It is not difficult to locate the pedagogical or ideological orientation of most of these students. They were part of the Generation-X who had been raised with television as a major source of knowledge. At the time many had had little meaningful and sustained interaction with individuals from minority communities other than through mass media and folk culture. Mostly were non-Latino and monolingual in English. If bilingual, they spoke English and one of the many Asian languages. They believed in the system of meritocracy and that effort and perseverance guarantees success. They also believed that grades and test scores define the capabilities and future options of individuals. And, most importantly, they believed in the power of education.

There is no better time to reconsider one's past and one's future than in the moment one is going to step into the world of work and power. In the 10 weeks students go through our course—longer if they stay on to join the staff or continue their research in independent study—the students confront long-held views on pedagogy and intercultural communication. They find the course and their site experience a rarity in their college careers. They tackle a rigorous curriculum in the context of a meaningful application, internalizing difficult and divergent theoretical concepts. They also explore a deeper understanding of themselves and others—re-examining their own and others' assumptions and generalizations about minority group members and their communities (Gallego, 1995). On several occasions, students have publicly confronted their own narrow and previously unexamined perceptions about *Mexicanos*/Latinos as "self" and "other" and have asked themselves tough questions about aspects of their own identities and religious beliefs. They also recognize the boundaries they create to separate themselves from others and begin to work toward dismantling these barriers, frequently describing their experiences during the quarter as constituting an especially valuable form of education. Some openly acknowledge the children's contribution to their growth as NR points out in the segment of a fieldnote:

> I have also realized that the kids are jus t as capable of helping me as I am of helping them. I realize now that I learned something each time I visit LCM. For example, I now know that our skin is the largest organ of our body. I also got free lessons in Spanish. [NR, 10/27/93]

Students learn about "children, cultures, and education" and realize that language is an important tool of cultural understanding. A comment in a student's fieldnotes capture this sense of discovery vividly: "If I was bilingual, I am sure I would have so much more insight on what is really going on! I feel like I am missing half the information but even half is still TONS." [AL, 05/22/92]

The overall importance of the course to its undergraduate enrollees is evident in their reflections in required essays at the end of the quarter. Many stress the importance of having had an opportunity to apply theory to everyday practice, to understand the role of language and culture in their own lives, and to contribute to a meaningful experience for children. The following essay was written as part of the requirement for the course in which students are asked to use their fieldnotes to track their own development across the 10 weeks of the quarter. Outside the experience of motherhood, Yolanda Alvarez', "Reflection Essay," captures the experience most students have in the class. They learn the prominent theoretical concepts (e.g., the zone of proximal development, social scaffolding, cultural relevance, comprehensible input, mutual relations of exchange), not to pass a test but to apply them at site and to their own life. Many students could have been selected for this section, their essays cover many of the same points Yolanda does. But Yolanda's life situation makes it possible to capture the immediate benefit that such an experience engenders, a depiction that would not have been so obvious or possible in other students' essays. At the time of the course, Yolanda was balancing motherhood and student life. On occasions, to align both responsibilities she took her 3-year-old boy to the site and exposed him to the computer world of *La Clase Mágica*, an experience both the child and the *Amiguitos* enjoyed.

> *Yolanda Alvarez, Engagement Versus Presence.* It is amazing how much a child can progress in an hour and a half. It is amazing how much a child can progress in a few weeks. However, what is even more amazing is how much I, along with the children have developed in the last 10 weeks. I was very hesitant to take this class after the first day because I was so unsure of what was truly required of me. Structure, after all has seemed to be the basis of all classes at UCSD. Suddenly, a professor like Olga comes along and throws all that off

base and all I can think of is chaos. Now after all that, I can mark this experience as a stepping stone toward my zoped [zone of proximal development] by taking a risk. Yes, a risk. It is indeed a risk to take a course in which you start off with an 'A' rather than being told exactly what to do in order to achieve an 'A'.

One of the areas in which I saw my biggest development was in the area of social scaffolding. First, I had to learn how instructional tasks are engineered to produce the zones of proximal development. Understanding the concept of the zoped took several on-site visits to learn. Briefly, it means helping a child accomplish with the help of others what he or she will be able to accomplish alone tomorrow. For example, at first I began giving children the answer every time they did not know it. This included saying words that they were having difficulty pronouncing or giving them the answer when they could not solve a math problem. Eventually, I began taking into account scaffolding and zopeds when working with children at site. Rather than reading a word for a child I would have them try to pronounce it by sounding out parts of the world and then connecting those sounds. Eventually, the children would come to a difficult word and would start on their own free will to sound out the word without my having to tell them. I also took from my own "funds of knowledge" to teach math problem-solving techniques rather than just relating the answer. It is very common for a child to get stuck and look up to an adult counterpart to relay the answer. By giving the answer I am in no way helping that child to accomplish his or her zone of proximal development because instead I am teaching them to always depend on others rather than on themselves.

The best thing about my experiences with the children from *La Clase Mágica* is that they have helped my relationship with my son. In the last 10 weeks I have grown very fond of the children at site. I've noticed that they also have their preferences in terms of the undergrads. I see that many of them have used that time to develop trust between themselves and the undergrads. For some children the time they spend at site has been extremely important and beneficial. I myself felt a very special bond developing. For many of the children I was not only the expert participant but also a special friend with whom they were able to share dreams and goals.

After having this experience, I thought about my relationship with my son and realized that it was not as strong as I would have liked it to be or thought it was. Everyday, while I am away from him I try to think of a way in which I can come home earlier to spend more time with him. I thought that spending time with him was me being in the house doing chores while he followed me around. Then it hit me. Every time my son was following me around, he was trying to tell me that I was not giving him enough attention. I realized that what he needed was for me to sit down and read him a book, or wrestle with him, or simply sit down and watch cartoons together. Supervising the kids at site would not be the same as engaging with them and scaffolding them through a computer game. Likewise with my son. Being with him in the house was not special quality time.

Overall this is one of the best classes I have taken at UCSD. Not only was I given hands-on experience but I was also introduced to a new form of instruction which broke away from the traditional lecture given by a professor. I learned more than I had ever learned in any of my other classes. With all the 29 students in that class, I feel like I know most of them very well. This was the one class where I got to know people's true feelings and ideas in terms of many of the issues which were covered in the class. I felt that this class never intimidated anyone or scarred us out of our opinions. This was truly an experience because often enough we tend to go a whole quarter without ever talking to another person or speaking up in class. This has been a most enjoyable class and I hope that in this type of instructions is continued here and elsewhere.

Community Representative. Community involvement has been integral to the life of the Mission and *La Clase Mágica*. Many mission-sponsored activities are directed at and by its Mexicano laity--mass, catechism, religious celebrations—and by the broader Spanish-speaking community— EGAD (Eden Gardens Against Drugs), immigration and voter registration, and a variety of social and educational activities. such as the youth group, after school tutoring. Head Start, and adult-education classes. Although some of this work is performed by salaried employees, much is performed gratis. When I walked onto the thick of community activity with a proposition for establishing a computer program for Spanish-speaking children. people listened. even those without children. From the priest on downward, people were readily available to talk to me and to attend group meetings.

Two women, at the center of much of the mission activity, María Nieves. the mission receptionist and María Lourdes Durán, the catechism director. both highly respected members of the community and long-time residents of Eden Gardens were particularly attracted to my proposal. Neither had used computers before nor spoke English beyond a basic level but were immediately attracted by the proposed computer program. My gender. age, cultural background. and Spanish-speaking ability most likely influenced their interest in the project but so did their social consciousness. Both women recognized the possibilities that the program offered for helping the community keep the children off the streets at the same time that it brought much need educational resources. These women were instrumental in recruiting children and their parents for the weekly planning sessions during the fall of 1989 and for the overall success of *La Clase Mágica*.

Although both women exhibited natural leadership qualities and a general working knowledge of the world, their involvement in *La Clase Mágica* expanded their expertise into other realms. My general impression at the time—cited in my fieldnotes—was that while they had notable experience in organizing groups and speaking in front of audiences, they nevertheless ceded the authority to Church officials—the priest and the deacon who oversaw the social and funding activities of the mission. Repeatedly, they organized the social situation so that I would do the talking even when they were more familiar with the topics at hand. Many of my fieldnotes recount Lourdes' fits of laughter and María's shyness when having to speak to either the priest or the deacon in those early sessions. Within their own group, these women were notable leaders and shakers, however, in front of outsiders they experienced, an uneasiness both would lose over time. Welcoming students, visitors, and conference audiences who came from all over the world, repeatedly gave them the opportunity to practice cross-culture communication. When María left the program after the ninth quarter, Lourdes skillfully and confidently took over the coordination of the program, an accomplishment that took me by surprise given that I had put more stock in María because she was single, spoke English, and had at least a high school education in Mexico.

In 1996, when I pulled away to write this manuscript, Lourdes followed suit. Slowly she began to withdraw from the center of activities. She was doing this not only because she had moved to a city 30 minutes away but because she felt strongly that *La Clase Mágica* remain steadfastly in community control. She had observed how the staff and I had gradually and deliberately turned over to her the control of all operations of *La Clase Mágica*. She proceeded along the same tact. She continued the in-service of parents and regularly paid individuals, out of her own salary, to take over the running of site. Later, she officially stepped out of the site-coordinator role and "meta-coordinated" or oversaw the other activities in the other contexts that constitute the broad-based effort of *La Clase Mágica*. Fully versed in the philosophical and pedagogical goals of the program, she continued to train others through a socialization process by integrally involving them in the activities and then guiding their participation. She directed the third round of the adaptation of the curriculum materials and trained students and parents alike in developing culturally relevant curriculum.

In sum, Lourdes has been a major contributor to the success of *La Clase Mágica*, drawing children and parents to its activities. Initially a monolingual Spanish-speaker with a junior high school-level education, Lourdes learned to use computers and telecommunication technology for the purpose of site activities and later incorporated their use into her own personal life. She regularly uses the computer to write letters, keep records, and create information flyers and certificates. Over the last several years of the project, her fluency in English has improved dramatically, as has her sophistication in supporting and advancing her own personal development as well as her children's schooling. Today, she is not only comfortable in her life but is also actively advocating for her children and *La Clase Mágica* outside her own community group. Although it is hard to say how much impact *La Clase Mágica* has had on her involvement in her children's schooling, it is clear that she has learned much about her children's abilities, both from observing them interact with the undergraduates and from engaging students in extended conversations about her children's learning. The following is taken from a talk Lourdes and other members of *La Clase Mágica* gave at the National Association for Chicano/a Studies Conference in San Jose, California.

Lourdes Durán, Site Coordinator, Parent, and Community Representative. Voy a dar un breve resumen de mi relación con el programa de computadoras, o sea con La Clase Mágica. Yo he estado involucrada en la comunidad de San Leo's desde que llegué de Jalisco en 1982. La mayor parte de este tiempo, he tenido un acercamiento a las familias por medio de mi experiencia con la iglesia. Mi participación continua en la comunidad me convierte en su representate dentro de La Clase Mágica. Mi prioridad ha sido de trabajar con la comunidad a tráves de mi trabajo con los jovenes, coordinando el programa de computadoras y el de la catequesis. Para mí este compromiso nunca ha sido muy difícil porque es algo que me encanta.

He estado comprometida con el programa de catequesis desde el principio. Todos los domingos dabamos clase de catecismo a mas o menos de 220 niños. Eramos un equipo de 30 catequistas y a mí me toco ser la directora por 13 años. Todas nosotras como catequistas hemos tratado a la mayoria de niños y jovenes de esta comunidad. La relación es con niños, los jovenes, y con las familias, con las cuales me identífico mucho porque la mayoría de ellas son como yo que se emigraron a este país y ahora sus hijos son nacidos aquí. También hay familias que tienen poco tiempo de haber llegado, así que viendo la necesidad espiritual, cultural, económica y educativa que ellos tienen, yo he tratado de poner mi granito de arena conforme a mis posibilidades. He hecho lo que he podido. Quiero enfatizar, que no existe espacio entre mí trabajo en el catecismo y mi trabajo en La Clase Mágica, ya que por medio de los dos trabajos hago las mismas conecciones. Como parte del trabajo que he hecho en conexión con el programa de computadoras, he logrado dar una parte significante en acuerdo con las metas de La Clase Mágica, cuales son de desarrollar un programa bilingüe bicultural basado en las características de la comunidad local.

Al comienzo de esta connección entre la universidad y la iglesía, se presentó Olga presisamente en el momento en el que yo me encontraba en la clase de catecismo. Conversamos sobre diferentes aspectos de esta comunidad y despúes ella me hablo sobre un proyecto para los niños que se trataba de un programa de computadoras. Al mismo momento me iba dando la idea de que quería que yo me involucrara en este programa. En mi mente solamente cabía la idea de ayudarle en darle publicidad con los niños de catecismo. En primer lugar, en ese tiempo yo no manejaba la computadora porque era algo que yo nunca había tenido la oportunidad ni de tocarla menos de usarla. Y en segundo lugar, nunca había pensado que yo necesitara una computadora en el futuro.

Para mí sus ideas me manifestaban muchas barreras. La idea de participar en ese programa estaba fuera de mi alcanze—pues yo no hablaba inglés y apenas había terminado 3 años de secundaria en México. Para este tiempo yo ya tenía mis 4 niños y la mas chiquita tenía 2 meses de nacida. Así que pensando en todo esto, hice el comentario que me sentía incapacitada para lo que ella pedía de mi. Para Olga fue lo mas fácil del mundo. Me sugerio que podía traer los niños conmigo al programa o cuando fuera a UCSD a tomar mi entrenamiento. También había una posibilidad que la secretaría del padre, María, támbien fuera a involucrarse. Hací que ella podía manejar a la univarsidad porque en ese tiempo yo no manejaba. Ella me aseguró que mi corto inglés no sería un problema porque ella iba a asistir cuando tuviéramos el entranamiento. Támbién me aseguro que los estudiantes que iban a venir de UCSD iban a ser bilingües, y que los niños de esta comunidad todos hablaban inglés y español. Animándome comento que podría ser una buena oportunidad para que aprendiera más inglés. Despúes de todo esto, Olga se puso en contacto con el padre de San Leo's y consiguío el permiso para poner el programa.

Aunque no había espacio apropiado en ese tiempo, el padre dió su apoyo para que se iniciara el programa aunque por ese momento hibamos a estar adentro de la iglesia enfrente del altar. En octubre de 1989, empesamos María y yo por ir a UCSD a recíbir entrenamiento donde empezaron por enseñarnos desde como se prende la computadora hasta lo mas bácico para poder iniciar el programa de La Clase Mágica. Dos meses transcurrieron para todo esto y en 1990 iniciamos. Aunque fue un poco incomodo por el espacio y problemillas que se nos presentaron. Por ejemplo, teníamos solamente 4 computadoras y eran al rededor de 15 niños. Teníamos que estar turnando a los niños y a la vez mantenerlos activos. A veces nos encontrábamos con una computadora que no pasaba la imagen y mirábamos que el problema era un cable que faltaba. En ocaciones se les tenía que llamar la atención a los niños porque se les ocurría subirse hasta arriba del altar y jugar con el microfono. Otro problema que hemos tenido desde que empezamos es mantener la connección de telecomunicación con la universidad—para hablar con El Maga. Pero bueno todo esto fue algo breve que de cualquier modo era normal porque se trabaja con niños de 5 a 12 años.

Otro detalle que María y yo estubimos tratando de balansear era de vigilar que el estudiante no forzará al niño al estar usando solamente el inglés. Tratamos de que se le hablara a los niños conforme su capacidad ya sea el inglés o el español. Hasta ese momento tratamos de seguir la idea de Olga de que el programa de computadoras fuera una ayuda especial para los niños que no tuvieran la oportunidad de tener una computadora en casa o en la escuela. En La Clase Mágica hay varios beneficios que reciben los niños por ser miembros de la comunidad como yo.

Podría decir que, existen varias formas en las que las familia y los niños salen beneficiados. Por ejemplo, en lugar de que los niños se queden solos en sus casas, o pierdan el tiempo pegados en la televición pueden estar aprendiendo un variedad de cosas en las actividades de La Clase Mágica. El programa les da la oportunidad de desarrollar otras habilidades. Los niños tienen la libertad de elegir algún juego: colorear, usar rompecabezas, escribir cartas o notas al Maga, avanzar en el laberinto, comunicarse con otros sitios como el de Chicago através de la correspondencia por telecomunicación.

La Clase Mágica ayuda a los niños a relacionarse con otros y desarrollar más su aprendizaje. Aprenden a usar sus reflejos en los juegos y tambien su imaginación y fantasía, con la idea de un mago y la quinta dimensión dentro La Clase Mágica. Tienen oportunidad de desarollar diferentes actividades, asimismo los ayuda y motiva en el lenguaje español e inglés. Hasta sierto punto yo me atrevería a decir que el niño adquiere seguridad en si mismo. No podría decir hasta que grado, pero si tengo la seguridad que algún efecto positivo surja en su comportamiento personal. Yo tengo mis cuatro niños en el programa y veo como el programa les ha ayudado a desenvolverse de tal manera que les ha dado seguridad personal, en el caso de mi hijo veo que lo introvertido con el paso del tiempo esta mejorando y se desenvuelve más activamente con los estudianates, usando el inglés o español. Los beneficios recibidos en dicha clase, son variados aparte de aprender en diferentes formas, estan envueltos en un ambiente sano.

El estar relacionada en un ambiente bilingüe me ha dado la oportunitdad de practicar y aprender inglés con los estudiantes y con los niños. Esta relación con La Clase Mágica me ayudo a tener una visión mas amplia con todo lo que va relacionado con la universidad y la importancia de prepararse. Todo esta información hacido de gran importancia porque la he podido poner en práctica con mis hijos. Me he dado cuenta del valor de estar bien informados y las consequencias de no tener la informción apropiada para seguir motivando y orientando a los niños.

Translation

***Lourdes Durán, site coordinator, parent, and community
representative.*** I am going to give a brief summary of my
involvement with the computer program, or I should say with *La
Clase Mágica.* I have been involved in the St. Leo's community since
I arrived from Jalisco [state in central Mexico] in 1982. For much of
that time, I have had a close relationship with the families as a part of
my involvement in the Church. My continuous participation in the
community makes me its representative within the structure of *La
Clase Mágica.* The youth are my priority in the work I do in the
community and I accomplish this by coordinating the computer and
catechism programs. For me this commitment has never been very
difficult because it is something that I love to do.

I have been committed to the catechism program since the
beginning. Every Sunday we used to offer catechism classes to more
or less 220 children. We were a team of 30 catechism teachers and
for 13 years, I served as the director. All of us women as catechism
teachers have interacted with a majority of the children and young
people of this community. My commitment is with children, the
young people, and also the families with whom I identify very much
because most of them are like me who immigrated to this country and
now their children are born here. Some of these families have only
recently arrived and seeing the spiritual, cultural, economic and
educational need that they have, I have tried to do what little I can to
help according to my ability. What I want to emphasize that there is
no difference between my work in catechism and my work in *La
Clase Mágica.* I accomplish the same thing through both jobs. As far
for working with the computer program, I have managed to contribute
significantly to the goals of *La Clase Mágica* which are to develop a
bilingual bicultural program based on the characteristics of the local
community.

At the beginning of the partnership between the University
and the Church, Olga showed up at my catechism class. After talking
about different aspects of the community, she spoke about a project
for the children that consisted of a computer program. At the same
time she was proposing that I get involved in the program. In my
mind, I thought that I would help only with publicizing it among the
catechism children. In the first place, I didn't even know how to use
a computer. Computers were something that I had never had the
opportunity either touch, or much less use. In the second place, I had
never thought that I would ever need a computer in the future.

Her ideas raised many barriers for me. The idea of
participating in that program was out of my reach—I did not speak
English and I only completed 3 years of junior high school in Mexico.
By this time I had my four children and the youngest was only 2
months old. Considering all of this, I commented that I did not feel

capable of doing what was being asked of me. For Olga it seemed the easiest thing in the world. She suggested that I could bring the children with me to the program or to UCSD for my training. There was also the possibility that the priest's secretary, María, would also get involved. She would be able to drive to the university because at the time, I did not know how to drive. Olga assured me that my limited English would not be a problem because she would be at the training sessions. She also assured me that the students that from UCSD would be bilingual, and that all the children from this community spoke both English and Spanish. Trying to encourage me, she suggested that it would be a good opportunity for me to learn more English. Later, Olga contacted the St. Leo's priest and secured permission to install the program.

Even though there was not enough space at that time, the priest gave his support to open the site inside the church in front of the altar. In October of 1989, María and I began going to UCSD for training. They began by teaching us how to turn on a computer and the most basic things about initiating *La Clase Mágica* program. This all took place over 2 months and we opened in 1990. It was somewhat uncomfortable at the beginning because of the space and small problems that presented themselves. For example, we had only four computers and there were about 15 children. We had to give each child a turn and at the same time keep them active. Sometimes we found ourselves with a computer that did not project an image and we discovered that the problem was a missing cable. Other times, we would have to call the children's attention because they would climb onto the altar and play with the microphone. Another problem that we have faced from the beginning has been maintaining the telecommunication connection with the university to talk with El Maga. But, all of this is normal when you are working with children from 5 to 12 years of age.

Another detail that María and I tried to keep on top of was that the students not force the child to use only English. We tried to have them speak to the children according to their ability to use either English or Spanish. Until that time we tried to follow Olga's idea that the computer program was special help for the children who do not have the opportunity to have a computer at home or in school. There are many benefits that the children receive at *La Clase Mágica* by being members of the community like me.

I could say that, there are various ways in which the families and the children are benefited. For example, instead of the children being alone at home, or waste their time glued to the television, they can be learning a variety of things in the activities of *La Clase Mágica*. The program gives them the opportunity to develop other abilities. The children have the liberty to choose a game, color, solve puzzles, write letters or notes to *El Maga*, advance in the maze and, communicate with other sites like the on in Chicago through telecommunication.

La Clase Mágica helps the children to get along with others and to increase their learning. They learn to reflect on their game play and to use their imagination and fantasy with the idea of a Wizard and a fifth dimension within the structure of *La Clase Mágica*. They have the opportunity to develop different activities that help them and motivates them to develop both Spanish and English languages. To a certain extent, I would go as far as to say that the child acquires self-confidence. I would not be able to say to what degree, but I do have the confidence that the program has a positive effect on the child's personal behavior. I have my four children in the program and I can see how the program has helped them to develop in such a way that are they more sure of themselves, as in the case of my son, I see how his introversion has lessened and he has become more involved with the students, using either English or Spanish. There are many benefits that the children have received at *La Clase Mágica*; aside from learning in different ways, they are immersed in a healthy environment.

Being involved in a bilingual environment has given me the opportunity to practice English with the students and the children. My involvement with *La Clase Mágica* has helped me develop a greater vision of all that is related to the university and the importance of being educated. All of this information has been of great value because I have put it to practice with my children. I have learned the value of being well informed and of the consequences of not having adequate information to encourage or guide the children.

The Research Staff. Harvesting the fruit of the vine. Although the research staff included several community representatives such as the site coordinators, it is the undergraduate student staff who I address in this section. With the exception of a few graduate students who joined the staff, the research staff consisted of upper division students or students who stayed on after they completed their Bachelors' training. Although trained at this level, they took on graduate level work. They practiced every step of the research process. They collected, archived, and analyzed data, wrote end of the year reports and gave presentations at regional and national conferences as part of their responsibilities. A few, took on the charge of project director, as I removed myself to write up the results of the various studies we were conducting. They were my fledgling colleagues. With few exceptions, most went on to complete higher degrees. At this writing, three are about to finish their doctoral studies.

This participant group was key to navigating the new cultural borders that *La Clase Mágica* was traversing. Their social consciousness and their idealism served as a buoy for imagining optimal possibilities. They provided the project with ideas of what was possible if only all things were equal. The institution on the other hand, tampered those dreams with tradition, rules, and lack of support from same-minded colleagues. My task was to masterfully maneuver between these two extremes; least I hit upon obstacles and old hurts that caused immeasurable emotional or symbolic pain. I had to guide them and the project through insurmountable barriers—lack of funding, what Michelle Fine calls, institutional fetishisms, and an immense problem that no matter how much or how hard we tried could not be surpassed. To accomplish this successfully, I used their strength and their interest in the particular part of the project where they and the project could benefit most.

La Clase Mágica, was this group's last opportunity to put into practice what they learned in their previous years at UCSD and unleash their drive to make a difference in the world before they faced the reality of graduate school or adulthood. Many were hard-core activists who had given much thought to the inequities in their communities and the institution. In many of their courses, they had been the ones that professors had leaned on as the voice of diversity. Others were barely beginning to realize that there was another world besides the picture-perfect world painted by the curriculum and middle-class backgrounds. They were just now coming to grips with the different perspective on theory and practice that minority-oriented research offered. Whether they were seasoned activists, theorists, or just talented individuals completing their undergraduate training, many, if not all, were drawn by the lure of doing action research. *La Clase Mágica* offered them an opportunity to serve society and the common good. They felt empowered by being able "to give back to the community." In all, they were the fruit of a union between the community and the university.

Yolanda Santiago Venegas stands out as one of the most powerful voices of the early research staff. A seasoned researcher and hard-core activist, she appeared at my office as if she had just stepped out of the Lacandone jungle. Her army surplus backpack, heavy with "theory" and her experience in the field—both in the literacy project she was heading among farm workers and in Suarez-Orozco's research team, gave her an edge over the other students who I had specially trained through a number of courses I taught through the Department of Communication. Her passion to help "nuestra gente" [our people] by intervening in the most transformative way had already been demonstrated in her efforts to single-handedly institute an adult literacy program for *Mexicano* farm workers living in the hills and canyons of North San Diego County. In her Masters thesis, she had condemned the media for portraying these communities as "migrant camps," cliff dwellings inhabited by semisavage peoples living in squalor and desperation. She was disillusioned at the time and thought that it was not worth the price to affect change through the institution.

Throughout the course of her service, I asked Yolanda for her unbridled opinion, although at times it painted me as a "passive Chicana activist" willing to compromise the integrity of our efforts. She was my most audible buoy. Although often times painful, I treasured her conclusions and made every effort to not only encourage them but to also protect from outside intervention. I never censored her nor permitted others to do so. It was a difficult role she played, one that was not only singular but painful as well. It took several years for her to agree to write the following piece. It brought up too much pain. But, I insisted as I had done so many times before. And, as I had also had to do so many times before, I had to accept them without tempering to suit those who are implicated in her words. I offer her conclusions about the experience she had drawn from the project in the raw as I have had to accept them.

Yolanda Santiago Venegas, From Jungle Activitist to a Full-Fledge Scholar. I offer my story in the spirit of Angie Chabram whose call for oppositional institutional ethnographies has yielded interesting insights into the conditions of Chicano intellectual production and the ways we are complicitious with the forces that promote the very inequities we diligently scrutinize and attempt to eradicate.[3] My participation in *La Clase Mágica* did, in fact, convince me to go on to graduate school. After all, I was already hooked on research and my "concientizacion" within a Chicano *Movimiento* ethos required that I add a second shift to my academic work, " to do my part for the revolution." Yet, my brief involvement in the establishment of UC Links, the system-wide consortium that grew out of our efforts at UCSD and the simultaneous dismantling of affirmative action policies led me to understand my experience not as a success, but rather as irony, a paradox and a contradiction.

When I came to *La Clase Mágica* I was still split between the need to give back to my community and my engagement with theory which I then characterized as an indulgence. What I found most compelling about *La Clase Mágica* was the possibility to reconcile both my love for theory and my need for social action. From the beginning I saw in *La Clase Mágica* the many possibilities for one to be an academic and an activist at the same time. I was able to heal my intellectual schizophrenia and flourish. With time I not only became critical of the split between "community work," and "academic work," but I also began to understand the ways it was reinforced by the Chicano nationalism so integral to my intellectual formation.

If my participation in *La Clase Mágica* taught me to be critical of Chicano nationalism and introduced new possibilities for critical intervention, I also became keenly aware of the costs involved in doing community-based research. That there is a stigma involved with this type of research is nothing new, however what I learned from LCM is the way this stigma affects scholars of color. We pay a different price for our commitment and this price is set by both the

inferior position of community-based research within the academy
and the scholar's particular sociohistorical history. In California, a
scholar of Mexican descent engaged in this type of research must also
contend with a nineteenth-century intellectual landscape that assigns
"all that pertains to the proper discipline and enlightenment of the
intellect, the Californians, as deficient.[4] A Chicana academic doing
community-based research faces the double burden of the stigma
universities place on community-based projects, on the one hand, and
the fact that 500 years of colonization make any woman of color's
intellectual rigor suspect until proven "smart enough." The specter of
inequity, she is "good for nothing except to shell beans," looming over
the conference table as the tenure debate slips from her valuable
contributions to the community and superb teaching skills to the real
crux of the matter; the intellectual rigor of her work.[5]

     While the university, fully supports programs such as *La
Clase Mágica* at the macro level and may even offer special
"community service," awards to primary investigators, the
institutional aporia I zero in on here results from the way community-
based research is received by individual university departments,
review committees and other levels within the system. Within the
department a scholar may find herself continually justifying her work,
reasserting its intellectual soundness and carefully concealing just
how much "community work," her project requires. At some point,
her wisest and most caring mentor is likely to pull her aside and
suggest she cut back from the community and get to the real work
required by her department. I highlight this basic contradiction within
the institution because there seems to be a trend within the UC system
to replace affirmative action with programs such as *La Clase Mágica*.
To put it most succinctly, if affirmative action policies are going to be
replaced by long-term solutions such as the one offered by *La Clase
Mágica*, the intellectual elitism of the dominant discourses will
automatically foreclose the participation of scholars of color in these
efforts. In social science terms, the subordinate position of
community-based research within academia is something that needs
to be reckoned with, if in fact, the UC system as a whole intends to
deal with diversity and outreach by shifting their emphasis from
affirmative action to community-based long-term solutions targeting
K–12 education.

     Having brown bodies not only as participants but actually
developing and leading diversity models is not only an ethical issue
but in fact the only way the system will succeed in its effort to
adequately represent our state's population. A wholehearted effort to
deal with diversity needs to be lead by minority scholars not because
of "something in our blood" or because life of the margins is a
required experience for tackling diversity issues, but quite simply
because we do in fact speak and think of these things from a different
space.[6]

I know this from my experience with *La Clase Mágica* as our program was institutionalized on a system-wide level. In 1996, while the votes for 209 legislature were being counted, Olga Vásquez put together the final touches on a proposal which requested initial funding for the institutionalization of the *La Clase Mágica* model at the UC system level. In this proposal we were asking Richard Atkinson, the newly appointed president of the University of California, to show his commitment to diversity by funding the establishment of sites modeled after *La Clase Mágica* on all nine UC campuses. The proposal was turned in a day after 209 passed, in the heat of the moment, and was instantly funded. Thus began what is now UC Links. Initially I was ecstatic about the possibility of a *La Clase Mágica* site on each UC campus. I had witnessed the effect our program had on all levels of the educational pipeline from grade school to my own experience as a soon-to-be graduate student. I attended the first meetings at Berkeley and UC Davis, seeking to recruit minority scholars as primary investigators. During my Berkeley visit, I spent two days shuttling between UC Links planning meetings and visits to professors in the Ethnic Studies graduate program where I was applying.

While I was excited about the possibility of expanding *La Clase Mágica* on a UC-wide level, I soon became ambivalent and began to vigilantly watch the process unfold. In a fieldnote written after a visit to UC Davis, I wrote that I was struck by the fact that Olga Vásquez, who developed the proposal in the first place, was not the person spearheading these presentations. "Olga did stand up and talk for about five minutes," I noted angrily.[7] As our "successful model for dealing with diversity," moved system-wide our role shifted from leadership to something not unlike classic anthropology's native informant—who was left out after he told his story. In an e-mail message to the UC links consortium list I wrote, "I guess the main concern for me is that in setting up, or inviting others to set-up sites in minority settings we have neglected to adapt the setting up process, in other words the process of setting up a 5thD in a minority setting needs to be adapted both at the university end and at the community end."[8] The most salient question for me at the time was, "how is the university group put together? How is it decided who will be invited to open up a Clase Mágica site?"[9] When I sent this e-mail I was still under the naïve impression that I could critically intervene in the formation of UC Links as I had done for *La Clase Mágica*. I did not yet understand my role had shifted. On a system-wide level, I represented the successful site and was asked to speak when the need to illustrate the finer details of our "success," arose, yet my primary concerns fell on deaf ears. Instead of an outright suppression of the fundamental principles of *La Clase Mágica*, a process of selective attention placed the discourse of the 5th Dimension squarely in the center.[10]

I was also struck by the way UC links was being introduced as a response from the ruling to dismantle affirmative action. According to a presenter at the time, UC Links was a way to "provide a model for dealing with issues of diversity in the UC system instead of getting caught up in blue ribbon committees that attempt to look at the problem."[11] The presentation of UC Links as a response to the affirmative action ruling at this meeting set off my internal alarm, but I was not ready to fully grasp the relationship between UC Links and the dismantling of affirmative action until much later. By the time I left UCSD to begin graduate school at Berkeley in the fall of 1996, it was clear to me that whatever UC links was, the fundamental principles leading to *La Clase Mágica*'s success—such as the need for brown bodies at all levels—were not prioritized. I was disillusioned by the fact that many of the minority scholars we did try to recruit into UC links refused on the grounds that their involvement would jeopardize their academic career.

The full impact of my experience with *La Clase Mágica* and UC Links did not take place until I was at Berkeley—the heart of the UC system. It was there, after the dramatic decline in minority admissions resulting from 209 was announced that I began to feel the effects in the flesh. Immediately after headlines announced admissions results, university administrators began a massive campaign to quell the angry voices of rioting students who began system-wide protests. Chancellor Robert Berdahl printed a full page in the Daily Californian stating his disappointment that the entering class was not representative of the diversity of the state and explained what the university was doing about it. The basic logic of the apology issued by Chancellor Berdahl was that although he regretted the results, the real effort to "level the playing field, "must start in first grade.[12] UC President Richard Atkinson joined in stating that, "the only real answers are the long-term answers. . . . We have already begun to apply the tremendous creative energy available within the university to the search for at least some of these answers. . . . Some of our most exciting initiatives involve the Internet and computer technologies."[13] It was at this point, once the effect of 209 was released in percentages, when administrators began to use UC Links as an example of what the university was planning on doing about diversity, that I began to feel like I had inadvertently been complicitious in the dismantling of affirmative action. Who better to develop a model effectively replacing affirmative action than an affirmative action baby herself? It soon became obvious to me that an either/or logic was at work in the rhetoric justifying the dismantling of affirmative action and in this grand institutional drama our *La Clase Mágica* model was used in a process of methodological appropriation, pillage, and plunder. Would I have participated in *La Clase Mágica* for 5 years if I had known of this earlier? Yes, because despite the dismantling of affirmative action the community participants and I benefited greatly.

If I were a cynic before graduate school, I am now equipped with the frames of intelligibility to more fully articulate my cynicism. Given the fact that Latinos are officially the new majority in California, I do believe that those of us who slipped through the back door as the votes for 209 were being counted are the system's primary targets in the maturing effort to justify extant forms of institutional and intellectual racisms.

Project Director: "Being the Only One." Being the only one is a common experience for people of color in academia and in the power elite (Zweigenhaft & Domhoff, 1998). According to the 1992 Special Issue of The Journal of The Association of Mexican American Educators, between the years of 1982 to 1989 "Chicano/Latinos are [were] the most underrepresented of all minority groups in the U.S. professoriate" (Garza, 1992, p. 6). Although there were some gains during this time period, proportionately, the representation of Chicano/Latinos "actually worsened," a pattern that has continued till the present. Nationwide, for example, Hispanics represent only 2.2 % percent of all full-time faculty in higher education in the mid-1990s (Carter & Wilson, 1995). Latina women constitute 1% of the assistant professors. Full and associate rank constitute less than 1%. At UCSD, my home campus, the figures demonstrate an increase in the Chicano/Latino ladder faculty from 3.2% to 4.4% from 1978 to the present, a slight increase in comparison to UCwide figures. However, more than half (20) of the departments at UCSD do not have Hispanic ladder rank faculty (Fujitani et al., 1997). In relation to their proportion in the surrounding population, the representation of Chicano/Latinos at the university is abominably low.

Being the only one in such systems engenders a variety of common sources of anxiety for Chicana/Latina faculty. Some of these stressors are inherent to the phase of the newly initiated; of finding oneself in an uncharted social arena. Others are the direct result of working within a system that on the one hand is in dire need of a dramatic reconstruction and on the other holds steadfast to a hidden curriculum that socializes its newcomers into the norms and expectations of the profession at the same time that it stratifies and reproduces unequal social relations (Margolis & Romero, 1998). There are no formal mechanisms to make the socialization process explicit, making it especially difficult for academics of color, like minority students all up the educational system, to "decode the system" in order to acquire the dominant Discourse needed for successful integration (Stanton-Salazar, 1997). The relatively low numbers of Chicano/Latinos further compromises the ability of those few academics of color to acquire the necessary funds of knowledge within their own social networks of support. These conditions, lamentably, also make it especially difficult for academics of color to contribute to the re-definition of an ideology and curriculum that will adequately reflect the multicultural reality of American society (Auletta & Jones, 1990).

Asserting new lines of thinking in academic circles, Latina academics call for new forms of knowledge and new visions for discourse, content, and structure (Bartlow, Escalante, & Vásquez, 1993). On many campuses across the country, the choice of complementing course readings with local, regional, or third world luminaries, for example, is how academics of color have exercised a new course of action and reflection. This strategy, however, counters conventional notions of knowledge and truth and has lead to heated debate and personal sacrifice. On the one hand, colleagues and students, alike, are not accustomed to the responsibility that accompanies a multicultural curriculum. On the other, to not take an active role in the diversification of the curriculum or ignoring outsiders' perspectives, "artificially restricts and stultifies the scholarly imagination" as Matsuda (1988, p. 3) pointed out.

Without such guide-posts as the "correct answer," the "one truth," and the authority of the teacher to mark their path as Yolanda Alvarez pointed out earlier, students experience anxiety, confusion, and a lack of structure. Becoming comfortable with anxiety, uncertainty, and even fear, as Mechling (1990) suggested, involves a radical departure from the standard norm of compliance, reliance, and anonymity common in most American classrooms. Most students are not ready to give up the security of invisibility in favor of being held accountable for their role in the creation of knowledge. Although most students and faculty, agree that the multicultural approach is open to their opinions, is nonthreatening, and at times enlightening, they, nevertheless, question its credibility, faddishness, and its marginal status. Conventional notions of knowledge, its transmission and acquisition as theoretically and historically based are not easily displaced. In particular, students find difficulty in co-constructing knowledge, of believing that they and others apart from the teacher are valid sources of knowledge.

In my own role as project director, I was also the first Chicana/Latina in the Fifth Dimension universe I helped create. I was the first ladder rank Chicana faculty person hired in my department's 20-year history and one of 39 ladder rank Chicana/Latina faculty in the UC system. Latino academics who had graced LCHC's intellectual community as adjunct faculty had long been gone when I joined the lab in the summer of 1989, first as a postdoctoral fellow and later as an assistant professor in the Department of Communi-cation. By all accounts, I brought a perspective and experience that was not only missing but was readily welcomed in both the department and LCHC. And, although I welcomed the challenge of "being the only one," there was a high price for the privilege in terms of personal and intellectual isolation.

Thus my participation as project director of *La Clase Mágica* and junior faculty member of the Department of Communication at UCSD was fraught with risks. Within an academic quarter of having arrived as a UCSD Chancellor's fellow, I began a journey that would not only guarantee my success as a researcher–implementer but would also compromise the depth of my involvement in the immediate community of my department, the arm of the university charged with the primary appraisal of my development as a scholar. My inexperience and the seductiveness of the new research project, led me down a path others called "professional suicide," but which I considered necessary for the organism I was gestating. Professionally, it was a matter of life and death: If I maintained the intense involvement that the new project required, I would compromise my own scholarship and my visibility in the department. To give my teaching, writing, and social networking the attention they required, threatened the life source of the fledgling project. By my midyear review (fourth year), my forte as a researcher–implementer was clearly evidenced by the successful reshaping of *La Clase Mágica* into a bilingual-bicultural demonstration site. My accomplishments were recognized as "service" and on several occasions I was nominated for the local service award. Yet, without substantive written record, the "analytic scholarship" that the department mandated was not readily forthcoming.

I had taken on a project whose theoretical and organizational framework did not account for the questions I wanted to ask concerning the learning and development of bilingual children from Mexican origin backgrounds. To reframe the Fifth Dimension agenda demanded not only a full understanding of its theoretical base, but it also required a forging of new ways to reconceptualize and study the learning potential of Spanish-speaking learners. On the one hand, the parent project assumed the integral role of language and culture in the making of mind, on the other, its bilingual offspring posed multiplicity as the central role in meditation. Would the children's zone of proximal development, for example, be supported by strategies originating in either of the two main cultures involved? Or, would they represent a separate hybrid culture? Sociohistorical theory offered the basis for new thinking about learning and development but no ready answers for the complexity that *La Clase Mágica* presented.

The ongoing adaptation required a carefully monitored re-vision of the practice and theory under-girding the parent project. Every aspect of the prior foundation had to be analyzed and re-forged with new understandings. Careful attention was required to design the research agenda, an accompanying course curriculum and the organizational theoretical and philosophical foundation of the after-school site. Due to limited resources, I coordinated all of the activities at the university and the community with the help of a small undergraduate staff for the first 3 years. I read all of student fieldnotes and taught the related course all three academic quarters. I attended weekly seminars in the department and at

212

La Clase MágicaLa Clase Mágica

LCHC covering up to 4 to 5 hours weekly, directed my research staff. and helped coordinate the activities of the Bilingual Partnership besides holding office hours and performing committee work for the department. Not only was the intensity and slow development of the project detrimental to "having a social life," it provided little time for written evidence of my growing analytic scholarship. It was not until I physically and emotionally removed myself from the center of the project's management that I had the time for the extended and in-depth reflection that an analytic piece requires.

What Has La Clase Mágica Meant to Me Personally, What Have I Learned? Personally, my involvement with *La Clase Mágica* has had a tremendous impact in many aspects of my life. Although it usurped much of my personal as well as my professional time, it also provided the opportunity to develop intellectually and emotionally in areas that feature prominently in my goal to achieve a meaningful professional and personal life. I grew in leaps and bounds in the areas of research, theory, and practice as a result of my involvement in the project. From a fledgling academic. I became a researcher–implementer. a better teacher, and I would hope a better colleague. The success of *La Clase Mágica* and its influence on the UC Links project gives me a sense of personal confidence in having taken the right path from the very beginning.

I also have learned tremendously from the parents and the children. I took many esoteric concepts such as "the zone of proximal development," "funds of knowledge," "bi–directional relations of exchange." and "scaffolding" to site, but it was the children and the families who really taught us the significance in the real world away from the abstraction of academia. Given the opportunity, both children and their parents rise to the occasion in intellectual development and involvement. Our findings concur with the Latino Eligibility Task Force's conclusion that Latino parents and their children, "place great value in higher education" (University of California, Latino Eligibility Task Force, 1997, p. 14). Further. as individuals and institutions we have the educational expertise and resources to make a significant difference in the schooling experiences of minority students from the time they enter the educational system till they complete graduate school. This achievement cannot be accomplished solely by a lone academic, that it truly "takes a village" as the borrowed phrase proclaims.

Working intimately with the children and their families for such an extended time also brought me full circle to a near-native competence in Spanish and Mexicano culture. Interestingly, after a hiatus of 30 years, it brought me back to my family's faith, one that is 80% of Mexican origin population (Cadena, 1987). Although I consciously sought competence in Spanish and *Mexicano* culture, I had no intention of returning to the Catholic faith. This resolve was especially strengthened each time I walked past the antiabortion signs adorning the doors of the Mission during the first year of the project. The priest, an ardent antiabortionist who had been jailed for obstructing entrance to an abortion clinic, had welcomed *La Clase Mágica* with opened arms but symbolically shut out a choice I actively supported. I should have known, however, how prophetic my own words in my first fieldnote in the database would be: "This project is going to make a Catholic out of me, again." Opening site in front of the altar and spending endless hours with the site coordinator who was also a prayer group leader evoked fond memories of my early involvement in church-related activities and the warmth and comfort of a community-in-faith.

LEARNING THROUGH PARTICIPATION: A COMMUNITY-OF-LEARNERS MODEL

The six voices above constitute the social body of *La Clase Mágica*. In dialogue, the six participants—the electronic entity, a parent, an undergraduate student, a participant child, a research assistant, and the project director—represent what Rogoff (1994) called a community of learners, "playing active but often asymmetrical roles in sociocultural activity" (p. 209). Although each group embodies divergent and group-specific goals and objectives, they are drawn together by "the greater good" for an equitable and culturally relevant approach to education and social action. Their role is not one of receiving or transmitting information but of actively participating in collaborative activity "with purposes connected explicitly with the history and current practices of the community" (Rogoff, 1994, p. 211). Fluidly alternating between experts and novices and in traditionally uneven groups (e.g., children–adults, community members–university representatives, researchers–students), participants create and recreate themselves and their environment through their participation. They locate themselves in the process of "becoming" the object and subject of an activity in-the-making, assuming responsibility and autonomy of the collaborative process as the need arises. Not only do they prepare themselves for further learning, they also set the stage for others who follow.

The dialectic between the development of the participants and that of the project illustrates an alignment of the participants' thinking with the philosophy of the project (Rogoff, 1994). A greater good is accomplished for self and others but so is the goal of achieving sustainability at the participant level. This view targets members of the community rather than institutions as the primary promoters of the perpetuation of the program. In making the cultural activity of *La Clase Mágica* part of their lives, as Lourdes Durán and Yolanda Alvarez point out, the core principles of the project are perpetuated in the immediate and future relationships of the participants. When individuals who have been through the experience of the project interact with those around them in a new way, a ripple affect is set in motion. Thus, each individual member of this community of learners contributes to the learning and development of new generations of participants and relationships.

Importantly, the process of learning through participation adds new meaning to the notion of intervention. Change is not imposed from the outside but is generated through sociocultural activity that makes learning culturally and developmentally appropriate. It comes from within "through a continual process of renewal and change within continuity, as new generations come to play the roles of the newcomers and old-timers in the community, becoming part of the structure" (Rogoff, 1994, p. 220). Together members of the community negotiate the direction of their and the project's development. The object is not replication of a fix set of criteria with set goals but an innovation raising out a set of core principles moving toward optimal growth.

NOTES

[1] Although some of the accounts were previously written for other purposes, each participant was invited to participate. Participants reviewed and consented to the edited versions of their contributions.

[2] The dictionary definition of "encaminar" [to guide, to direct or manage], does not quite capture the connotation of "accompanying someone for part of their journey." "Sending off," while it also lacks the sense of accompaniment is much closer in meaning.

[3] Angie Chabram, "Chicana Studies as Oppositional Ethnography," Cultural Studies 4, no.3 (1990):230.

[4] Hubert Howe Bancroft, "Chapter XVI A Futile Fight With Ignorance," in California Pastoral (San Francisco: The History Company, 1888), 493.

[5] Helen Hunt Jackson, Ramona. Signet Classic edition, 1988:7.

[6] Patricia Penn Hilden, "Readings from the Red Zone: Cultural Studies, History, Anthorpology." Journal citation needed: 1-3.

[7] Yolanda James fieldnote Quarter 21

[8] E-mail to send by Yolanda James to x-mellon 11/14/95

[9] See footnote 8.

[10] Much like the functioning of dominant discourses as essayed by Renato Rosaldo in "Imperial Nostalgia" Representations 26, (Spring 1989): 120.

[11] See footnote 10.

[12] Robert Berdahl, "Message From Chancellor Robert M Berdahl to the Campus Community," Daily Californian, 2 April 1998.

[13] Richard Atkinson, "Admission to the University of California," The San Francisco Chronicle, April 1, 1998.

7

Closing Remarks: The Risk of Challenge

> In our self-reflectivity and in our active participation with the issues
> that confront us, whether be through writing, front-line activism, or
> individual self-development, we also are uncovering the interfaces,
> the very spaces and places where our multiple-surfaced, colored,
> racially gendered bodies intersect and interconnect. (Gloria Anzaldúa,
> 1990, p. xvi)

In the opening passage, Chicana feminist, poet and cultural critic, Gloria
Anzaldúa, suggested an intercultural body that grows out of the a site where
"multiple-surfaced, colored, racially gendered bodies intersect and interconnect.
Her passion and the brilliance of her imagery evoke powerful connections to the
dynamism of *La Clase Mágica*. But, what inspires me to link her voice to mine
as I write the closing remarks of *La Clase Mágica*: Imagining Optimal
Possibilities in a Bilingual Community of Learners is the juxtaposition of the
intercultural body as symbolic of diversity in multicultural America. As my title
suggests, the chapters included in this book deal with an intercultural body
constructed and mediated by the possibilities of social action. It is precisely the
site of interculturalism—which is similarly claimed by Anzaldúa's musings—
where this book locates the challenges and the promises of a multi-system
approach to educational inequity.

Centering our research lens and our social project on an intercultural
body involves facing difficult challenges and taking great risks on pure faith that
the complexity and ambiguity inherent in such enterprise can somehow be
harnessed for the greater good. This is not an easy task given that convention
demands a move towards cultural unity although that unity is often in dispute
(Edwards, 1994). The steady flow of change that blocks a "true" or "complete"
representation of the totality of the *La Clase Mágica*'s nature, especially in the
early stages of development is another significant challenge. The lack of
tangible products and preset lines of action unsettle the most seasoned
multiculturalist. There are no charted waters that can adequately convince
review committees and funding agencies of the magnitude of the project's
impact. It is only the flow of time that can make visible an intercultural body
through its fluidity and continuous transformation. Time after all is the only true

215

measure of development and the only dimension from which individual life choices can be tracked. Time was, after all, the criteria used by the White House Initiative on Educational Excellence for Hispanic Americans for selecting *La Clase Mágica* as one of its. The ability of the project to serve to Latino youth and families in spite of the ebbs and flows of funding, institutional support, and recurrent change in staffing indicated success for the Presidential Commission. It sustainability expressed outcomes that are not easily measured or valued by educational reformers: community uptake, individual empowerment, and most of all, social change.

The writing process was also a great challenge. Forging multiple perspectives, multiple voices, and multiple directions into one unified representation proved a difficult and often frustrating task. First, the project and our conceptualization of it were in continuous flux. Its protean nature variously accorded a macro institutional perspective; a view of the micro dynamics of identity formation; and a glimpse of the finer details of the interrelations among participants, all within a continuous attention to the intricate relationship between the project's tools and its pedagogy. Moments of clarity were intense and short-lived as new understandings were blurred by waves of change. Definition did not hold still as the production and acquisition of culture continued across more than the five facets I present here—the adaptation process, institutional relations, methodologies, language use, and the various participant groups involved. A second difficulty in capturing a fuller account of the project in written form was the positionality from which it was examined. Understanding what the project was depended very much position one viewed it from, not unlike the proverbial blind men holding on to parts of an elephant and thinking it was anything but an elephant. It is only through painstaking care and attention that a coherent account is hammered out. Out of a seemingly uncoordinated and unwieldy effort at cross-system collaboration, grows an alternative vision of what can be or ought to be the social and intellectual goals and actions of learners, teachers, researchers, and institutional agents. At its best, this panoramic highlights critical areas where we as academics, practicioners, and social engineers can and must continue to push for change in spite of exposing ourselves to great challenges and risks.

La Clase Mágica has demanded risks in word and deed from the initial tweaking of the design of the Fifth Dimension to the actual writing of this book. Most risks have born great fruits that have allowed us to imagine optimal possibilities in many areas of the educational enterprise. Yet, as chapter 6 clearly points out, the benefits most of us managed to garner from our involvement in the project came at great personal costs. For anyone who became part of the program for any length of time, the "personal" became intricately woven into the very fabric of every day involvement whether it happened to involve research, practice, or service. And, although all would agree that it was worth the cost, the personal brought about as much pain as it brought satisfaction. One cannot have a vision of a greater day and not suffer the contradiction, the disillusion, and the resignation as Yolanda Venegas proclaims in chapter 6. But, then again, there is no greater joy than listening to the testimonies of long-term participants from children to adults who recognize the positive impact their involvement in *La Clase Mágica* has had on their sense of self, their academic preparation and their constructive approach to the inequities of life and the educational system.

The personal permeates throughout this book because it is here where difference is negotiated, where we as individuals can take our greatest risks. If I were not right smack in the middle of many of the interactions that I use as data, then I was directing all others who were interacting with community participants. Thus, my inquiry and my pedagogy were situated precisely on the personal. Along with every other participant in the system, I was a producer, and reproducer of culture. This level of involvement as Deborah Tannen (1996) pointed out, "introduces the risk—indeed, the certainty—of bias: the lack of objectivity everyone necessarily brings to the interactions" (p. 1152). I forged objectivity and subjectivity into a single perspective of possibilities. This kind of risk, of course, compromised even further the scholarship that is expected at a flagship institution. It held my scholarship in suspect as I concentrated on pushing the boundaries of research, theory, and practice in a community without the exotic essentialism of faraway tribes. At the time, few colleagues understood the merit of exploring new ways to extend and intersect theory and practice beyond conventional notions of what minority languages, cultures, and communities offer social, cognitive, and intellectual development. The risks were high but so were the rewards—ultimately a successful program and tenure for me. Endless, anecdotes recount the rewards a personal involvement such as this held for others as well.

But much more than the personal has to be risked. The advances in information technology, the diversity in the society, and globalization call for massive changes in the way we "do" education. That is, if we want a significant portion of the population to take an active part in sustaining the international viability that the United States presently enjoys (Hayes-Bautista et al., 1988). *La Clase Mágica* leads us part way in defining the types of institutions that must be created and the ways and means by which resources and institutional support can be equitably redistributed to populations with little economic and political muscle. We cannot be satisfied with thinking that one voice is enough. Nor can we be satisfied with counting numbers as the measure of our diversity. We must recommit the university to the risk of challenge within its own walls where challenge "possibly remains the academy's strongest justification and basis for survival" (Lankshear, 1994, p. 162). Importantly, we must also open its commitment to the promise of the new millennium. The new times call for a new vision of society—one that is diverse, technologically advanced, and globally located in the local. The role of the university in this time and age cannot be one of detachment and elitism but must be one of integral involvement in solving the problems of the new society.

One of greatest challenges the university faces in advancing a great society are the policies supporting the boom in the prison industry. At the same time that new kinds of multisystem institutions are being conceived to address social issues brought about by diversity in society, movements guided by ethnocentrism and sheer lack of foresight advocate unilinear, unidimensional approaches. At both the national and state levels, social policy is shaped in part by a commitment to a mythic oneness rooted in long-standing but ill-conceived notions of national identity. For example, in California, the initiative to dismantle affirmative action (Proposition 209) and eliminate resources for noncitizens (Proposition 187) speak more to the preservation of an "American" way of life than to the social and economic costs of supporting people in need. These initiatives falsely assume a society of "equal opportunity and justice for all" in which every individual has equitable access to resources. Rather, these initiatives privilege those who are White, English speaking and well-versed in Western culture. In particular, they single out Spanish-speaking individuals who come from south of the U. S. border in search of the "American dream." These propositions, along with the accompanying English-only movement and efforts to eliminate bilingual education embody truly exclusionary policies, but more dramatically signal an ongoing preference for unilinear and monocultural approaches to social action. Tragically, they also signal an unwise social action initiative whose policy is to "incarcerate rather than educate," as Chunky Sanchez, member of a popular musical group in San Diego. "Los Alacranes del Norte" vocalizes in his songs relating his grass roots activism.

The tremendous growth of the prison system bears out the power of this social policy. Since the late 1980s, this unidimensional system approach to social management has received an overwhelming boost of support from politicians who simultaneously tout collaborative efforts. Without question, the single most insular unidimensional system in society, the prison system, has received massive funding over the last dozen years. From 1985 to 1996, the prison system grew steadily at a rate of 7.9% a year, with a cumulative expansion of 113% for the period (Bureau of Justice Statistics, 1998). California, in particular, had the highest rate of incarceration in the world, spending more than twice as much to incarcerate an inmate as to educate a UC student: $27,898 to $12,005 respectively.

Although prisons represent lucrative economic resources for economically depressed communities (a great number of prisons are located in such areas), they also represent an unwise social investment. To incarcerate rather than to educate has serious implications for the welfare of communities and the competitive edge of the American economy. This is evident in the flourishing prison industry in California (20 prisons have were built in the previous 10 years and only one State University and one University of California campus). This type of investment radically compromises the viability of communities to provide a more integrated approach to social responsibility. Unlike students who graduate from universities, convicts do not face a wide range of positive employment and social opportunities when they are released from prison. Neither are they likely to be able to integrate themselves into the civic or social life of their home communities.[1] The skills convicts acquire during their imprisonment are often ones that perpetuate their life on the fringes of society rather than those that facilitate their re-integration as productive members of the community. The alarmingly high rate of recidivism (74% after 4 years) bears witness to released felons' inability to fit back into their communities where they are released. These figures dispute two current myths: Prisons are a deterrent to crime and prisons serve a rehabilitation function. Instead, prisons create hard core criminals who paradoxically have a higher retention rate and advancement in this institution than most educational systems in the country.

Prisons constitute a social investment that functions as a powerful lever for maintaining the status quo. The overrepresentation of minorities in prisons and the tendency to locate prison facilities in remote areas is testimony to a marked intolerance to diversity in American society. Blacks and Latinos total 59% (43.5% and 14.7%, respectively) of the general state and federal prison population nationwide.[2] The percentages of inmates on death row are similarly dramatically skewed. Nowhere in the country outside of Black colleges are the rates of these two minority groups represented so prominently in secondary institutions.[3] The growth of the prison industry obscures the possibilities that preventive or interventionist measures can achieve if given the same kind of fiscal and institutional support. Common sense compels us to think that social investment should seek a highly integrated, highly skilled constituency that is able to contribute to the well being of society. However, reality points to an investment in unwise social alienation, disenfranchisement, and poverty.

This boom signals an imprudent policy in social investment and tremendous waste in human resources. Although stated in a context suggesting that crime news is not a deterrent to offenders, the following statement by a former prison director clearly articulates the need for educational reform. He stated that the majority of the inmate population is not:

> the intelligent, the cunning, and the glamour offenders portrayed in
> the television and pictured in the cinema. Rather, they are the poor,
> the stupid, the inept. (quoted in Lotz, 1991, p. 5)

This statement also overtly signals the need for educational and social policies that have better outcomes than incarceration. The fact that inmates are "the poor, the stupid, and the inept," and I may add, non-White, points more to a lack of access to educational resources and institutional support than to a propensity of these individuals to crime. Low IQ scores, high school grades in combination with low literacy rates may predict adult criminality, but they also suggest that offenders will most likely not be reading print media. These characteristics clearly disclose a poor educational experience and a lack of cultural knowledge that speaks to the need for divestment of funds from incarceration and an investment in education.

Hayes-Batista et al.'s (1988) description of the worst case scenario is clearly supported by the growth in the prison industry. These researchers' point out that social polices ignore the need for a heavy investment in the education of increasingly large numbers of minorities. The choice is clear. Allow a large part of our future's workforce to be undereducated and be susceptible to crime. Or, take the risk in providing greater opportunities for individuals from all walks of life to develop their optimal potential and contribute to the well being and international viability of the nation. The experience of directing and studying the development of *La Clase Mágica* leads me to choose the latter.

The choice is also clear for the university. Take an active and decisive role in advancing relevant and inclusive education. Conventional education in a Global Age is impracticable. The energies invested on improving test scores, for example, are lost to a measure that reflects little of what individuals can actually do in a highly technological and integrated world. The emphasis on one language and one culture of knowledge jeopardizes the linguistic resources of language minority students and at worst handicaps monolingual speakers in a multicultural world. Insistence on monolingualism also limits the possibility of individuals to move easily from one cultural context to the next, a necessity that increasingly characterizes the Global Age. Furthermore, the common rigid adherence to a scope and sequence curriculum more likely than not limits the learning potential of advanced students and frustrates those who require more time and attention. Regrettably, in many classrooms across California, the potential of technology for powerful learning encounters has not been achieved. In many others, the potential is virtually nonexistent.

A great society in the new Global Age demands a dynamic, high-quality education that is beyond what John Dewey describes as the education of elders. It calls for an education of the future; a multilingual and multicultural education that is mediated by the latest information technology. Education must reinforce advanced knowledge of multiple languages as well as versatility in maneuvering through multiple cultural norms. Importantly, education must move away from focusing on pathologies and instead focus on possibilities and the potentialities of every learner. It must lead us to carve out new visions of self and the institutions that serve our society. Anzaldúa and others working on the borders between disciplines, identities, and realities give us the tools to construct this new vision alive with difference and ambiguity as well as with the obstacles and risks that lay ahead. Importantly, pioneers, like our own *El Maga* and many of the participants of *La Clase Mágica* illustrate that considerable risk taking is the only way to chart new directions in unfamiliar or inflexible social and psychological arenas.

The evolving nature of *La Clase Mágica* makes the descriptions and analyses that I have presented opportunities for imagining optimal possibilities to address the exigencies of the new day. In place of definitive conclusions and detailed prescriptions, the many angles from which I have presented *La Clase Mágica* offer researchers, practitioners, and policymakers much-needed guidance, insight, and, perhaps, inspiration for rethinking the goals and objectives as well as the content of curriculum and instruction. These perspectives suggest many areas for research, practice, and service, the threefold mission of the University of California. It also implores the university to make diversity its fourth mission. Importantly, they also suggest ways in which local children, parents, and institutional agents can take an active and integral role in creating their own learning opportunities. By extension, educators and policymakers, too, can find useful the systems approach for pursuing parent and community involvement in the educational enterprise.

One of the most logical next-steps for further implementation and research is the transplantation of the basic principles of *La Clase Mágica* /Fifth Dimension model to the formal context of schooling. How, for example, would *El Maga, el laberinto Mágico* [the magical Maze], the *Amigos/as* and many of its other components translate to the context of the classroom? Inquiry into the survival, transformation, or disappearance of many of the system's artifacts and guiding principles would offer fertile ground for exploring ways to examine the force of educational systems and the viability of innovation. It also would provide an opportunity to study transference not as a package of knowledge and skills but as a process of negotiation (Engeström, 1996). A case in point, is a comparative study of the social and academic performance of the amiguitos/as and Wizard Assistants at *La Clase Mágica* and school? Would the cultural relevance of *La Clase Mágica* have a differential effect on the academic performance and social integration of its participants in school activities? Will children who have been socialized into actively directing their own learning and development function successfully in a context where decisions, in effect, are made for them? And, relevant to the overall aims of *La Clase Mágica*, will participation ultimately effect college-going rates and retention over regular program offerings?

Many of these questions will be answered by the ongoing research at *La Clase Mágica* proper as well as the research initiatives of the newly formed university–community partnerships that comprise the UC Links Consortium sponsored by the University of California. Each new extension and new project while setting its own agenda for research, practice, and service and developing individually according to the local conditions will in some form extend the principles of the original Fifth Dimension/*La Clase Mágica* model. Some will build on the earlier research. adding new insights to the existent body of knowledge. Others will develop new and divergent threads of research that have yet to be explored (e.g. areas focusing on critical pedagogy, organizational theory, and activity theory). The system-wide agenda will also be able to build on the systems model perspective that I cover in chapter 3. The diversity in the projects' target age group, research foci, and relevant fields of interests make it possible to examine the local systems model from a global perspective. In other words, we will be able to learn how the notion of life-span approach to social action is conceived and practiced across distances and different populations.

NOTES

[1] Felons are not allowed to vote and most are shunned in middle-class neighborhoods. Many minority activists suggest that the increase in prison funding is a willful attempt to suppress minority voting power.

[2] See the Internet Website of the Bureau of Justice Statistics, U. S. Department of Justice, at http://www.soci.american.edu/justice/corrstat.html for further details.

[3] Interestingly, historically Black colleges, however. have trailed below regular colleges in the rate of increase in minority representation.

REFERENCES

American Association of University Women. (1991). *Shortchanging girls, short- changing America: A call to action.* Washington, DC: Initiative for Educational Equity.

Anderson, N. C. (1993). *An improbable venture: A history of the University of California, San Diego.* La Jolla, CA: The UCSD Press.

Andre, T., & Melton, S. (1992). *Separate stories of shared spaces.* Unpublished manuscript, University of California, San Diego, Laboratory of Comparative Human Cognition, La Jolla.

Anzaldúa, G. C. (1987). *Borderlands/La frontera: The new mestiza.* San Francisco, CA: Spinsters/Aunt Lute Foundation.

Anzaldúa, G. C. (1990). Introduction. In *Making face, making soul: Haciendo caras, creative and critical perspectives by women of color.* San Francisco: Aunt Lute Foundation.

Appel, R., & Muysken, P. (1987). *Bilingualism and language contact.* Baltimore, MD: Edward Arnold.

Assembly Committee on Higher Education. (1993). *Master plan for higher education in focus* (Draft report). Marguerite Archie-Hudson, Chair. Assembly California Legislature.

Auletta, G. S., & Jones, T. (1990). Reconstituting the inner circle. *American Behavioral Scientist,* 34(2),137-152.

Bartlow, D. R., Escalante, V. T., & Vásquez, O. A. (1993). Exploring new frontiers: Women of color in academia. In Pamela J. Creedon (Ed.), *Women in mass communication,* (2nd ed., pp. 264-275). Newbury Park, CA: Sage.

Barton, D. (1994). *Literacy: An introduction to the ecology of written language.* Cambridge, MA: Blackwell.

Bernal, M. E., Saenz, D. S., & Knight, G. P. (1991). Ethnic identity and adaptation of Mexican-American youths in school settings. *Hispanic Journal of Behavioral Sciences,* 13(2), 135-154.

Bourdieu, P. (1977). Cultural reproduction and social reproduction. In J. Karabel & A. H. Halsey (Eds.), *Power and ideology in education* (pp. 487-511). New York: Oxford University Press.

Brown, A. L. (1992). Design experiments: Theoretical and methodological challenges in creating complex interventions in classroom settings. *The Journal of the Learning Sciences,* 2(2), 141-178.

Bruner, J. S. (1986). *Actual Minds, possible worlds.* Cambridge, Mass: Harvard University Press.

Bruner, J. S. (1990). *Acts of Meaning.* Cambridge, Mass: Harvard University Press.

Buriel, R. (1993). Acculturation, respect for cultural differences, and biculturalism among three generations of Mexican American and Euro American school children. *Journal of Genetic Psychology,* 154(4), 531-544.

Buriel, R., & Cardoza, D. (1988). Sociocultural correlates of achievement among three generations of Mexican American high school seniors. *American Educational Research Journal,* 25, 177-192.

Bureau of Justice Statistics, U.S. (1998). Department of Justice [Internet Website] http://htm.www.soci.american.edu/justice/corrstat.html.

Cadena, G. R. (1987). *Chicanos and the Catholic Church: Liberation theology as form of empowerment.* Unpublished doctoral dissertation, University of California, Riverside.

223

California Education Performance Report. (1994). *The first annual report to the governor, legislature, and California citizens in response to Assembly Bill 1808* (Chapter 741, statues of 1991). Sacramento, CA: California Post-Secondary Education Commission.

California Basic Education Data Systems. (2000). California Department of Education (chap1).

Carlson, D. (1997). Gayness, multicultural education, and community. In M. Seller & L. Weis (Eds.), *Beyond black and white: New faces and voices in U.S. schools* (pp.233-256). Albany: SUNY Press.

Carter, D. J., & Wilson, R. (1995). *Minorities in higher education: 1994*. Thirteenth annual status report, city published: Office of Minorities in Higher Education of the American Council on Education.

Center for Educational Research and Innovation. (1982). *The university and the community: The problems of changing relationships*. The Organization for Economic Co-operation and Development: Paris.

Chavez, L. (1991). *Out of the barrio: Toward new politics of Hispanic assimilation*. New York: Basic Books.

Chicano/Latino Concilio. (1995). *Response to the University of California Latino Eligibility Task Force Recommendations*. Unpublished paper,University of California, San Diego.

Cognan, J. J., & Derricott, R. (Eds.). (1998). *Citizenship for the 21st century: An international perspective on education*. London, England: Kogan Page.

Cole, M. (1986). *Creating sustainable new forms of educational activity in after-school settings* (Final report). Spencer Foundation. La Jolla, CA: Laboratory of Comparative Human Cognition, University of California, San Diego.

Cole, M. (1990, May). *Cultural psychology: Some general principles and a concrete example*. Paper presented at the Second InternationalCongress of Activity Theory, Lahti, Finland.

Cole, M. (1991). *Capitalizing on diversity: A proposal for a distributive literacy consortium* (Research Proposal 91-5215 submitted to the Andrew Mellon Foundation). La Jolla, University of California, San Diego.

Cole, M. (1996). *Cultural Psychology: Once a future discipline*. Cambridge, MA: Harvard University Press.

Cole, M., & Cole, S. (1993). *The development of children (2nd ed.)*. New York: Scientific American Books.

Cole, M., & Nicolopoulou, A. (1991). *Creating sustainable new forms of educational activity in after-school settings* (Final Report to the Spencer Foundation). Laboratory of Comparative Human Cognition, University of California, San Diego.

Colomb, G. G., & Simutis, J. A. (1996). Group dynamics in an e-mail forum. In S. C. Herring (Ed.), *Computer-mediated communication: Linguistic, social and cross-cultural perspectives* (pp. 81–106). Amsterdam and Philadelphia: John Benjamins.

Corson, D. J. (1986). Language, gender, and education: A critical review of linking social justice and power. *Gender and Education*, 4, 229-254.

Crawford, J. (1992). *Hold your tongue: Bilingualism and the politics of "English only."* Redding, MA: Addison-Wesley.

Cummins, J., & Sayers, D. (1995). *Brave new schools: Challenging cultural illiteracy through global learning networks*. New York: St. Martin's, Press.

De Avila, E. A. (1981). Relative language proficiency types: A comparison of prevalence, achievement level, and socio-economic status. Virginia: National Clearinghouse for Education.

Delgado-Gaitan, C. (1990). *Literacy for empowerment: The role of parents in children's education*. New York: Falmer Press.

Delgado-Gaitan, C. (1994). Socialization in a Mexican American community. In P. Greenfield & R. R. Cocking (Eds.), *Cross-cultural roots of minority child development* (pp. 55-85). Hillsdale, NJ: Lawrence Erlbaum Associates.

Delgado-Gaitan, C. (1996). *Protean literacy: Extending discourse on empowerment*. Washington, DC: Falmer Press.

Dewey, J. (1938). *Experience & education*. New York: Collier Books.

Durán, R. P. (1995, September). *Cultural accommodation and family literacy among English language learners*. CHAIR, Family Literacy Research Symposium, U.S. Department of Education, Washington DC.

Edwards, P. A. (1987). *Educating black children: America's challenge*. Washington DC: Howard University, Bureau of Educational Research, School of Education.

Engeström, Y. (1996). Developmental Work Research as Educational Research: Looking ten years back into the zone of proximal development. *Nordisk Pedagogik*, 16(3):131-143.

Erikson, E. H. (1963). *Childhood and society* (2nd ed.). New York: Norton. Ferdman, B. M. (1990). Literacy and cultural identity. *Harvard Educational Review*, 60(2), 181-204.

Fine, M. (1991). *Framing dropouts: Notes on the politics of urban public high school*. Albany: SUNY Press.

Fishman, J. A. (1985). *The rise and fall of the ethnic revival: Perspectives on language and ethnicity*. New York: Mouton.

Flores, J. (1984). "Que assimilated, brother, yo soy assimilao": The structuring of Puerto Rican identity in the U.S. *The Journal of Ethnic Studies*, 13(3), 1-17.

Foot, K. (1996). *Telecommunications policy in Russia*. Unpublished manuscript, University of California, San Diego.

Foot, K. (1999). *Writing conflicts: An activity theory analysis of the development of the network of ethnological monitoring and early warning*. Unpublished doctoral dissertation, University of California, San Diego, La Jolla.

Franke, D., & Janikas, K.. (1992). *Ollie-popping over the walls of Eden Gardens. And the walls come tumbling down: New perspectives on learning*. Unpublished manuscript, University of California, San Diego. Communication in the Community Seminar, La Jolla.

Friere, P. (1981). *Pedagogy of the oppressed*. New York: Continuum.

Fujitani, T., Cruz-Takash, P., Evans, I. T., Gabbai, F. B., Gough, D. A., Harvey, D. F., Hirsch, H. N., Mitchell, S. D., & Ramanathan, V. (March 12, 1997). *Letter by the Members of the Academic Senate Committee on Affirmative Action and Academic Subcommittee*, University of California, San Diego, Chancellor's Affirmative Action Advisory Committee to the Academic Senate Key Academic Administrators.

Gallego, M. (1995, Summer). Community based school reform: Service learning lessons from "La Clase Mágica." *The Journal. Sylvania*, OH: Michigan-Ohio Association of Teacher Educators.

Gallego, M., & Cole, M. (2000). Classroom culture and culture in the classroom. In V. Richardson (Ed.), The handbook of research on teaching (4th ed.). pp. 961-997. Washington DC: American Education Research Association.

Garza, H. (1992). Dilemmas of Chicano and Latino professors in U.S. universities. *The Journal of the Association of Mexican American Educators, Inc.*, 1. 6-22.

Gee, J. P. (1990). *Social linguistics and literacies: Ideology in discources*. New York: Falmer Press.

Gibeau, M. (1997). *Vision of a safety continuum for crisis response to incidents of violence*. San Jose, CA: East Side Union High School District.

Gleason, P. (1983). Identifying identity: A semantic history. *Journal of American History*, 69(4), 910-931.

González, N. E. (1995). The funds of knowledge for teaching project. *Practicing Anthropology*, 17(3), 3-6.

Greenfield, P. M. (1994). Independence and interdependence as developmental scripts: Implications for theory, research, and practice. In P. Greenfield & R. R. Cocking (Eds.), *Cross-cultural roots of minority child development* (pp. 1-40). Hillsdale, NJ: Lawrence Erlbaum Associates.

Griffin, P., & Cole, M. (1984). Current activity for the future: The Zoped. In B. Rogoff & J.V. Wertsch (Eds.), *New directions for child development*, (pp. 45-63). San Francisco: Jossey Bass.

Gutierrez, K., Baquedano-López, P., & Tejeda, C. (1999). Rethinking diversity: Hybridity and hybrid language practices in the third space. *Mind, Culture, and Activity*, 6(4), 286-303.

Gutierrez, K., Rymes, B., & Larson, J.. (1995). Script, counterscript, and underlife in the classroom: James Brown versus Brown v. Board of Education. *Harvard Educational Review*, 65(3), 445-471.

Hakuta, K. (1986). *Mirror of language: The debate of bilingualism.* New York: Basic Books.

Hayes-Bautista, D. E., Schink, Werner O., & Chapa, J. (1988). *The burden of support: Young Latinos in an aging society.* Stanford, CA: Stanford University Press.

Heath, S. B. (1983). *Ways with words: Language, life and work in communities and classrooms.* Cambridge, England: Cambridge University Press.

Heath, S. B. & McLaughlin, M. W. (1993). *Identity and inner-city youth: Beyond ethnicity and gender.* New York: Teachers College Press.

Heath, S. B., Alvarez, L. P., Vásquez, O. A. (August, 1987). *"Stanford Interactive Reading and Writing Project."* Final Report, San Francisco Foundation.

Heller, M. (1987). The role of language in the formation of ethnic identity. In J. S. Phinney & M. J. Rotheram (Eds.), *Children's ethnic socialization: Pluralism and development* (pp. 180-200). Newbury Park, CA: Sage.

Henry, T. (1993). *La Clase Mágica: A sociocultural approach to multicultural education.* (Staff Report) La Jolla: University of California, San Diego, Laboratory of Comparative Human Cognition.

Holland, D., & Cole, M. (1995). Between discourse and schema: Reformulating a cultural-historical approach to culture and mind. *Anthropology and Education Quarterly*, 26(4), 475-489.

Hurtado, A., Figueroa, R., & Garcia, E. E. (1996). *Strategic intervention in education: Expanding the Latino/Latina pipeline.* Oakland: Regents of the University of California.

Hurtado, A., & Gonzalez, R. (1994, April). *Anchor study: The high school survey preliminary findings.* Paper presented at the meeting of the Latino Eligibility Task Force, Berkeley, CA.

Jackson, J. E. (1990). "I am a fieldnote": Fieldnotes as a symbol of professional identity. In R. Sanjek (Ed.), *Fieldnotes: The makings of anthropology* (pp. 3-33). Ithaca, NY: Cornell University Press.

Kalantzis, M., Cope, B., & Slade, D. (1989). *Minority languages and dominant culture: Issues of education, assessment and social equity.* New York: Falmer Press.

Keefe, S. E., & Padilla, A. M. (1987). *Chicano ethnicity.* Albuquerque: University of New Mexico.

Kerr, Clark (1961). *Proposed Academic Plan for the University of California.* Report submitted to the Board of Regents.

King, C., Kelly, C. Tregre, L. & Edwards, J. (1992, May). *Children's writing in the fifth dimension.* Paper presented at The International Reading Association Annual Convention, Orlando, FL.

King, C., & McNamee, G.. (1994, April). *The development of children's voice in written language in their home community and in far away places.* Paper presented at the American Educational Research Association Meeting, New Orleans, LA.

Krashen, S., & Biber, D.. (1988). *On course: Bilingual education's success in California.* Sacramento: California Association for Bilingual Education.

Laboratory of Comparative Human Cognition (1982, July). A model system for the study of learning difficulties. *The Quarterly Newsletter of the Laboratory of Comparative Human Cognition*, 4(3), 39-65.

Lamont, M., & Lareau, A. (1988). Cultural capital, allusions, gaps and glissandos in recent theoretical development. *Social Theory*. 6(2), 153-168.

Langer, J. A. (1987). A sociocognitive perspective on literacy. In J. A. Langer (Ed.), *Language, literacy, and culture: Issues of society and schooling* (pp. 1-38). Norwood, NJ: Ablex.

Lankshear, C. (1994). Afterward. In M. Escobar, A. L. Fernández, G. Guevara-Niebla, with P. Freire (Eds.), P. *Freire on higher education: A Dialogue at the National University of Mexico.* Albany: SUNY Press.

La Ponce, J. A. (1987). *Bilingualism and identity: Language and their territories.* Toronto: University of Toronto Press.

Lareau, A. (1989). *Home advantage: Social class and parental intervention in elementary education.* New York: Falmer Press.

Leont'ev, A. N. (1978). *Activity, consciousness & personality.* Englewood Cliffs, NJ: Prentice Hall.

Litowitz, B. E. (1990, October). Just say no: Responsibility and resistance. *The Quarterly Newsletter of the Laboratory of Comparative Human Cognition,* 12(4), pp. 135-141.

Lotz, R. E. (1991). *Crime and the American press.* New York: Praeger.

Luke, A. (1999). Cultural Globization. Paper presented at the Annual Conference of National Conference of Australian Literacy Educators and Australian Association of Teachers of English on " Global Citizenship: Languages and Literacies. Adelaide, Australia, July, 6-10.

Luria, A. R. (1979). Vygotsky. In M. Cole and S. Cole (Eds.), *The making of mind* (pp. 38-57). Cambridge, MA: Harvard University Press.

Margolis, E., & Romero, M. (1998). "The department is very male, very white, very old, and very conservative": The functioning of the hidden curriculum in graduate sociology departments. *Harvard Educational Review,* 68(1), 1-32.

Matsuda, M. (1988). Affirmative action and legal knowledge: Planting seeds in plowed-up ground. *Harvard's Women's Law Journal,* 11, 1-17.

Matusov, E. (1996). Intersubjectivity without agreement. *Mind, culture, and activity,* 3(1), 25-45.

McDermott, R. (1998). Achieving school failure, 1972-1997. In G. J. Spindler (Ed.), *Educational and cultural processes.* Prospect Heights, IL: Waveland Press.

McGill, W. J. (1982). *The Year of the Monkey: Revolt on Campus, 1968-69.* New York: McGraw-Hill.

McKay, S. L., & Wong, C. S. L. (1988). *Language diversity: Problem or resource?* Boston: Heinle & Heinle.

McLaughlin, D. (1989). The sociolinguistics of Navajo literacy. *Anthropology and Education Quarterly,* 20(4), 275-291.

McLaren, P., & Sleeter, C. E. (1995). *Multicultural education, critical pedagogy, and the politics of difference.* Albany: SUNY Press.

McNamee, G. D.. (1993, April). *Written language development of school-aged children in an African American community.* Paper presented at the Annual Meeting of the American Educational Research Association Meetings, Atlanta, GA.

Mead, M. (1939). *From the south seas: Studies of adolescence and sex in primitive societies.* New York: William Morrow.

Mechling, Jay. (1990). Theory and the other: Or is this session the text?. *American Behavioral Scientist,* 34(2), 153-165.

Mehan, H. (1991). *Sociological foundations supporting the study of cultural diversity.* (Research No. R117G10022). Santa Cruz, CA:National Center for Research on Cultural Diversity and Second Language Learning.

Mehan, H. (1992a). *Sociological foundations supporting the study of cultural diversity* (Report No. 1). Santa Cruz, CA: National Center for Research on Cultural Diversity and Second Language Learning.

Mehan, H. (1992b). Understanding inequality in schools: The contribution of interpretive. *Sociology of Education,* 65(1), 1-20.

Mehan, H., Villanueva, I., Hubbard, L., & Lintz, A. (1996). *Constructing school success: The consequences of untracking low-achieving students.* Cambridge, England: Cambridge University Press.

Menchaca, M. (1997). *The Mexican outsiders: a community history of marginalization and discrimination in America.* Austin: University of Texas Press.

Moll, L. C. (1992). Bilingual studies and community analysis: Some recent trends. *Educational Researcher, 21*(2), 20-24.

Moll, Luis C., Anderson, A., & Díaz, E., (1985, May). *Third college & CERRC: A university-community system for promoting academic excellence.* Paper presented at the University of California Linguistic Minority Conference, Lake Tahoe, CA.

Moll, L. C., & Díaz, E.. (1987). Change as the goal of educational research. *Anthropology and Education Quarterly, 18*(4), 300-311.

Moll, L. C., & Gonzalez, N. (1994). Lessons from research with language minority students. *Journal of Reading Behavior, 26*(4), 439-456.

Moll, L. C., & Greenberg, J. (1990). Creating zones of possibilities: Combining social contexts for instruction. In L. C. Moll (Ed.), *Vygotsky and education* (pp. 319-348). Cambridge, MA: Cambridge University Press.

Moll, L. C., Velez-Ibañez, C. G., Greenberg, J., Whitmore, K., Dworin, J., Saavedra, E.. & Andrade, M. (1990). *Community knowledge and classroom practice: Combining resources for literacy instruction.* Tucson: University of Arizona, College of Education and Bureau of Applied Research in Anthropology.

Morris, G. (1995). *Head of the class: An oral history of African-American achievement in higher education and beyond.* Twayne Publishers: New York.

Nicolopoulou, A., & Cole, M. (1993). Generation and transmission of shared knowledge in the culture of collaborative learning: The fifth dimension, its play-world, and its institutional contexts. In E. A. Forman, N. Minick, & C. Addison Stone (Eds.), *Contexts for learning: Sociocultural dynamics in children's development* (pp. 283-314). New York: Oxford University Press.

Nocon, H. (1997). *Altars and computers: Learning in the borderlands.* Unpublished manuscript, University of California, San Diego, La Jolla.

Oakes, J., Gamoran, A., & Page, R. N. (1992). Curriculum differentiation: opportunities, outcomes, and meanings. In P. Jackson (Ed.), *Handbook of research on curriculum* (pp. 570-608). New York: Macmillan.

Ochs, E. (1993). Constructing social identity: A language socialization perspective. *Research on Language and Social Interaction, 26*(3), 287-306.

O'Dwyer, E. (1994). *Jake: Uncovering misconceptions of ability.* Unpublished manuscript, University of California, San Diego, Department of Communication and Psychology, La Jolla.

Padilla, A. M., Lindholm, K. J., Chen, A., Durán, R., Hakuta, K., Wallace, L., & Tucker, R. G. (1991). The English-only movement: Myths, reality, and implications for psychology. *American Psychologist, 46*(2), 120-130.

Padilla, A. M., & Durán, R. (1995). The psychological dimension in understanding immigrant students. In R. G. Rumbaut & W. A. Cornelius (Eds.), *California's immigrant children: Theory, research, and implications for educational policy* (pp. 131-160). La Jolla: University of California, San Diego, Center for U.S.-Mexican Studies.

Paredes, A. (1977). On ethnographic work among minority groups: A folklorist perspective. *New Scholar, 4,* 1-32.

Pease-Alvarez, L., Hakuta, K., & Bayley, R.. (1998). Spanish proficiency and language use in a California Mexicano community. *Southwest Journal of Linguistics, 15*(1-2),137-152.

Penuel, W. R., & Wertsch, J. V. (Spring, 1995). Vygotsky and identity formation: A sociocultural approach. *Educational Psychologist, 30*(2), 83-93.

Percy, W. A. (1975). *The message in the bottle: How queer man is, how queer language is, and what one has to do with the other.* New York: Farrar, Straus & Giroux.

Phillips, A. (1993). *Democracy and Difference.* University Park, Pennsylvania: Pennsylvania State University Press.

Porter, R. P. (1990). *Forked tongue: The politics of bilingual education.* New York: Basic Books.

Quirante, J. S. (1996). *The culture of La Clase Mágica as a positive educational experience for young women.* Unpublished manuscript, University of California, San Diego, Department of Communication, Faculty Mentor Program, La Jolla.

Reed, I. (Ed.). (1998). MultiAmerica: Essays on cultural wars and cultural peace. New York: Penguin Books.

Reyes, M. D. (1992). Challenging venerable assumptions: Literacy instruction for linguistically different students. *Harvard Educational Review, 62*(4), 427-446.

Rodriguez, R. (1983). *Hunger of memory: The education of Richard Rodriguez, an autobiography.* New York: Bantam Books.

Rogoff, B. (1994). Developing understanding of the idea of communities of learners. *Mind, Culture, and Activity: An International Journal, 1*(4), 209-229.

Rogoff, B. (1995). Observing sociocultural activity on three planes: Participatory appropriation, guided participation, apprenticeship. In J. V. Wertsch, P. Del Río, & A. Alvarez (Eds.), *Sociocultural Studies of mind* (pp. 139-164). Cambridge, England: Cambridge University Press.

Romo, H. (1984). The Mexican origin population's differing perception of their children's schooling. *Social Science Quarterly, 65*(2), 635-650.

Rosaldo, R. (1986). Ilongot hunting as story and experience. In V. Turner & E. Bruner (Eds.), *The anthropology of experience* (pp. 97-138). Urbana: University of Illinois Press.

Rosaldo, R. (1989). *Culture and truth: The remaking of social analysis.* Boston: Beacon Press.

Rotheram, M. J., & Phinney, J. S. (1987). Definitions and perspectives in the study of children's ethnic socialization. In J. S. Phinney & M. J. Rotheram (Eds.), *Children's ethnic socialization: Pluralism and development* (pp. 180-200). Newbury Park, CA: Sage.

Ruiz, R. (1987). Introduction. In W. A. Van Horne & T. V. Tonnesen (Eds.), *Ethnicity and language.* Madison: The University of Wisconsin, System Institute on Race and Ethnicity.

Schustack, M. W., Strauss, R., & Worden, P. (1997). Learning about technology in a non-instructional environment. *Journal of Educational Computing Research, 16*(4), 337-351.

Scollon, R., & Scollon, S. B. K. (1981). *Narrative, literacy, and face in interethnic communication.* Norwood, NJ: Ablex.

Sellers, M., & Weis, L. (1997). *Beyond black and white: New faces and voices in U.S. schools.* Albany: SUNY Press.

Shieffelin, B. B., & Ochs, E. (1986). Language socialization. *The Annual Review of Anthropology, 15,* 163-191.

Skutnabb-Kangas, T., & Cummins, J. (Eds.). (1988). *Minority education: From shame to struggle.* Philadelphia: Multilingual Matters.

Sleeter, C. E. (Ed.). (1991). Empowerment through Multicultural Education. Albany: SUNY Press.

Sleeter, C. E. & McLaren,P. L. (1995). *Multicultural education, critical pedagogy, and the politics of difference.* Albany: SUNY Press.

Spradley, J. P. (1980). *Participant Observation.* New York: Holt, Rinehart, and Winston.

Stanton-Salazar, R. D. (1990). *The role of social and informational networks in the formation of educational and occupational expectations among Mexican-origin high school students.* Unpublished doctoral dissertation, Stanford University, Stanford, CA.

Stanton-Salazar, R. D. (1997). A social framework for understanding the socialization of racial minority children and youths. *Harvard Educational Review, 67*(1), 1-40.

Stanton-Salazar, R. D., & Dornbusch, S. M. (1995). Social capital and the social reproduction of inequality: Informal networks among Mexican-origin high school students. *Sociology of Education, 68*(2), 116-135.

Stanton-Salazar, R. D., Vásquez, O. A., & Mehan, H. (1995). *Engineering success through institutional support.* University of California, Berkeley, The Latino Eligibility Project.

Stowitschek, J. J. (2000). *Observing children's engagement to enhance best practice: A total quality outreach model.* (http://depts.washington.edu/tqoweb/#bestpr), Seattle: University of Washington.

Stromberg, P. G. (1990). Ideological language in the transformation of identity. *American Anthropologist, 92*(1), 42-56.

Stuhr, P., Krug, D., & Scott, A. P. (1995). Partial tales of three translators: An essay. *Studies in Art Education. 37*(1), 29-46.

Swartz, D. (1977). Pierre Bourdieu: The cultural transmission of social inequality. *Harvard Educational Review, 47*(4), 545-555.

Tannen, D. (October, 1996). The inevitability of the personal. In *Forum, PMLA*, 3(5), 1146-1169.

The National Center for Educational Statistics. *(http://nces.ed.gov./pbus/9602.html)*, Comendium: Historically Black Colleges and Universities: 1977-1994.

Thorne, B. (1993). Boys and girls together but mostly apart. In B. Thorne (Ed.), *Gender play: Girls and boys in school* (pp. 29-48). New Brunswick, NJ: Rutgers University Press.

Tinto, V. (1987). *Leaving college: Re-thinking the causes and cures of student attrition.* Chicago: The University of Chicago Press.

University of California, Task Force on Black Student Eligibility. (1992). *Making the future different: Report of the task force on Black student eligibility.* Berkeley, CA: Office of the President.

University of California, Campus Planning Office. (1992). *Pocket Statistics.* La Jolla, CA: Campus Planning Office, University of California, San Diego.

University of California, *Chancellor's Advisory Committee Report on Affirmative Action and diversity.* (1997). La Jolla, CA: University of California, San Diego.

University of California, Latino Eligibility Task Force. (1997). Latino student eligibility and participation in the University of California: YA BASTA. Berkeley,CA: Office of the President.

University of California, *President's Task Force on Chicanos and the University of California.* (1975). Berkeley, CA: University of California.

U.S. Department of Health and Human Resources. (1992). *Head Start Program Performance Standards* (45-CFR1304). (DHHS Publication No. (ACF) 92-31131). Washington, DC: Administration for Children and Families.

Valenzuela, A. (1999). *Subtractive schooling: U.S.-Mexican youth and the politics of caring.* Albany: SUNY Press.

Vásquez, O. A. (1989). *Connecting oral language strategies to literacy: An ethnographic study among four Mexican immigrant families.* Unpublished doctoral dissertation, Stanford University, Stanford, CA.

Vásquez, O. A. (1992). Reading the world in a multicultural setting: A Mexicano perspective. In D. Murray (Ed.). *Diversity as a resource: A redefinition of cultural literacy* (pp. 113-134). TESOL.

Vásquez, O. A. (1993). A look at language as resource: Lessons from La Clase Mágica. In. U. Casanova, & B. Arias (Eds.). *Bilingual Education: Politics, Research, and Practice, 17*(2), 199-224. Chicago, IL: National Society for the Study of Education.

Vásquez, O. A. (1994). The magic of La Clase Mágica: Enhancing the learning potential of bilingual children. *The Australian Journal of Language and Literacy, 17*(2), 120-128.

Vásquez, O. A. (1995). "Porque soy Mexicano": Language and identity in an afterschool setting. Invited talk, Fall seminar series at the Center for U.S.-Mexico Institute, University of California, San Diego.

Vásquez, O. A. (1996). *A model system of institutional linkages: Transforming the educational pipeline.* In The University of California Latino Eligibility Study. University of California, Santa Cruz.

Vásquez, O. A. (1999). Coming of Age in Post Modern America. *Human Development, 42*(2), 109-112.

Vásquez, O. A., Durán, R. (2000). La Clase Mágica and El Club Proteo: Multiple literacies in new community institutions. In M. Gallego & S. Hollingsworth (Eds.), *What Counts as lit.er.a.cy: Challenging a single standard: Multiple perspectives on literacy.* New York: Teachers College Press.

Vásquez, O. A., Pease-Alvarez, L., & Shannon, S. M. (1994). Pushing boundaries: Language and culture in a Mexicano community. Cambridge, England: Cambridge University Press.

Veltman, C. (1988). *The future of the Spanish language in the United States.* Washington, DC: Hispanic Development Project.

Vygotsky, L. S. (1978). *Mind in society: The development of higher psychological processes.* Cambridge, MA: Harvard University Press.

Wiersema, B. (1984). They called the valley Eden: The Mexican pioneers discovered that the garden wasn't a bad place. It was paradise. And it was their home. *San Diego Union Tribune,* May, 17, front page.

Wilbur, F. P., & Lambert, L. M. (1991). *Linking America's schools and colleges: Guide to partnerships and national directory.* Washington, DC: American Association for Higher Education.

Wilcox, K. (1982). [A review of the book Ethnography as a methodology and its application to the study of schooling]. In G. & L. Spindler (Eds.), *Doing the ethnography of schooling: Educational anthropology in action* (pp. 456-488). New York: Holt, Rinehart & Winston.

Wilgoren, J. (1999). Early education tied to adult achievement: High-quality day care improves kids' learning, lives, study finds. *The San Diego Union-Tribune,* October 22, front page.

Wong-Fillmore, L. (1991). When learning a second language means losing the first. *Early Childhood Quarterly. 6*(3), 323-346.

Yin, R. K. (1994). *Case study research: Design and methods (2nd ed.).* Thousand Oaks, CA: Sage.

Zweigenhaft, R. L., & Domhoff, G. W. (1998). *Diversity in the power elite: Have women and minorities reached the top?* New Haven, CT: Yale University Press.

AUTHOR INDEX

SUBJECT INDEX

A

Acting locally, thinking globally, 13, 57
Adaptation process, 13, 39-46
    of materials,
Adult-child interaction, 48, 160-162
Affirmative Action, 4, 68, 188, 205-209, 218
Artifacts
    cultural, 157
    system of, 7-8, 17-19, 105-109
Amigos/as (undergraduate assistants), 193-196
    role of, 101, 114, 160-162
Andrew Mellon Foundation, 133, 141, 136

B

Background experiences, 19-21, 34, 80, 165
    cultural resources, 132
    prior history, 14, 17, 111, see also
    Funds of knowledge
Bi-directional relations of exchange, 5, 13, 35
Bilingual-Bicultural innovation, 49-50
Bilingualism, 148, 161-162

C

Change
    deliberate and continual, 52-60
Collaboration
    across systems, 2, 5-7, 19, 23, 80, 216
Collapsing the paradox, 14, 84-85, 114-118
Community
    involvement, 6-8, 196-198
    of learners, 2, 12, 15, 34-35, 215
Comprehensible input
Computer-Based fantasy world, 46-47
Continuity of experience, 115
Cultural relevance, 10, 12, 47-49, 62, 115
Culturally relevant approach, 13, 43, 48, 63,
    84, 93, 99
Culture of collaborative learning, 47-48, 94, 136

D

Development
    child, 58, 84-85, 93-94, 99, 139
    cognitive, 7, 37, 46-50, 54, 135
    individual, 8, 15, 19
Distributive literacy, 85-87
Dungeons and Dragons, 38

E

Educational pipeline, 8, 14, 24, 44, 61-63,
    96-97, 100
Eligibility, 13, 20-22, 25-27
    as social practice, 24
    Black Eligibility Task Force, 4-5
    Latino Eligibility Task Force, 44,
    137
El Maga, 157-160
    role of, 14, 48, 183-185
Ethnographic field methods, 14, 119-123
Evaluation
    outside evaluators, 133-135
    challenges, 104-108

F

Fieldnotes
    excerpts, 54, 59
    format, 121-123
    undergraduate, 13, 92, 95
Funds of knowledge, 101, 132
    journey log, 109, 117, 134-136
    Langue Assessment Scales
    (LAS), 124-127

W

X

Z